Thomas Middleton, Renaissance Dramatist

Titles in the Series
Christopher Marlowe, Renaissance Dramatist
Lisa Hopkins
Ben Jonson, Renaissance Dramatist
Sean McEvoy
Thomas Middleton, Renaissance Dramatist
Michelle O'Callaghan

Forthcoming
John Webster, Renaissance Dramatist
John Coleman

Thomas Middleton, Renaissance Dramatist

Michelle O'Callaghan

Edinburgh University Press

© Michelle O'Callaghan, 2009

Edinburgh University Press Ltd
22 George Square, Edinburgh

Typeset in 11.5/13 Monotype Ehrhardt
by Servis Filmsetting Ltd, Stockport, Cheshire and
printed and bound in Great Britain by
CPI Antony Rowe, Chippenham and Eastbourne

A CIP record for this book is available from the British Library

ISBN 978 0 7486 2780 6 (hardback)
ISBN 978 0 7486 2781 3 (paperback)

Contents

Acknowledgements

I would like to thank Mark Hutchings, Paul Salzman, Adam Smyth and Tiffany Stern for offering suggestions, useful advice, passing on references, and talking through ideas. Particular thanks are due to the series editor, Sean McEvoy, for his careful reading of the manuscript, and to the editorial staff at Edinburgh University Press: Jackie Jones, Mairead McElligott and Padmini Ray Murray. I am grateful for the advice and assistance provided by Madeleine Cox and the staff at the Shakespeare Centre Library and Archive, Stratford. Finally, I would like to thank my family, Mathew, Grace and Joseph, for their patience, and to remember Leo.

Note on the text

The source-text for all references to Middleton's plays is *Thomas Middleton: The Collected Works*, edited by Gary Taylor and John Lavagnino (Oxford: Clarendon Press, 2007). Act, scene and line numbers will follow quotations from this edition in parenthesis in the text of the essay. Editors of individual plays and authors of introductory essays in this edition are cited under Middleton 2007 and not in individual entries.

Chronology

Many of the dates for plays given here are for the approximate year of the first performance. In many cases there is some dispute about when early modern plays first appeared. Readers are directed to the introductions of individual editions of plays.

	Plays and playwrights	Theatre and politics
1564	Shakespeare born Marlowe born	
1570		Queen Elizabeth excommunicated by Pope Pius V
1572	Jonson born	Bartholomew's Eve Massacre in France
1576		James Burbage opens The Theatre
1578	Webster born (?)	
1580	Middleton born	Last performance of miracle plays at Coventry
1587	Kyd *The Spanish Tragedy* Marlowe *Tamburlaine*	Mary Queen of Scots executed Rose Theatre opens
1588	Marlowe *Dr Faustus*	Defeat of Spanish Armada
1589	Marlowe *The Jew of Malta*	
1592	Marlowe *Edward II* Marlowe *Massacre at Paris* Shakespeare *Richard III*	Azores expedition

	Plays and playwrights	Theatre and politics
1593	Marlowe killed Shakespeare *The Taming of the Shrew*	
1594	Shakespeare *Titus Andronicus*	First of four bad harvests
1595	Shakespeare *Richard II*	Spanish raids on Cornwall O'Neill's revolt in Ireland
1597	Jonson *The Case is Altered* Shakespeare *The Merchant of Venice*	Private Blackfriars Theatre constructed
1599	Shakespeare *Julius Caesar*	Satires proscribed and burnt Globe Theatre opens
1600	Marston *Antonio's Revenge* Shakespeare *Hamlet*	Fortune Theatre opens East India Company founded Children of the Chapel at the Blackfriars Theatre
1601	Dekker *Satiromastix* Jonson *Poetaster* Shakespeare *Twelfth Night*	Essex's rebellion and execution Defeat of joint Irish/Spanish army in Ireland
1603	Jonson *Sejanus* Marston *The Malcontent*	Death of Elizabeth; accession of James I Lord Chamberlain's Men become the King's Men
1604	Chapman *Bussy D'Ambois* Shakespeare *Measure for Measure* Shakespeare *Othello*	
1605	Middleton *A Mad World, My Masters* Shakespeare *King Lear*	Gunpowder Plot

	Plays and playwrights	Theatre and politics
1606	Jonson *Volpone* Middleton *Michaelmas Term* Middleton *The Revenger's Tragedy* Shakespeare *Macbeth*	
1607	Shakespeare *Antony and Cleopatra*	
1608		King's Men lease the Blackfriars Theatre
1610	Beaumont and Fletcher *The Maid's Tragedy* Jonson *The Alchemist*	
1611	Dekker and Middleton *The Roaring Girl* Jonson *Catiline* Shakespeare *The Winter's Tale* Shakespeare *The Tempest*	Authorised Version of the Bible published
1612	Webster *The White Devil*	
1613	Middleton *Chaste Maid in Cheapside*	Overbury scandal begins Globe Theatre burns down
1614	Jonson *Bartholomew Fair* Webster *The Duchess of Malfi*	
1615	Middleton and Rowley *A Fair Quarrel*	
1616	Jonson *The Devil is an Ass* Middleton *The Witch* Shakespeare dies	Jonson Folio published
1617	Webster *The Devil's Lawcase*	Jonson made Poet Laureate
1618		Thirty Years War begins

	Plays and playwrights	Theatre and politics
1621	Middleton *Women Beware Women*	
1622	Middleton and Rowley *The Changeling*	
1623		Prince Charles's unsuccessful visit to Spain to marry the Infanta Shakespeare First Folio published
1624	Middleton *A Game at Chess*	
1625		James I dies; accession of Charles I
1626	Jonson *The Staple of News*	
1627	Middleton dies	Failure of La Rochelle expedition
1628		Petition of Right
1629		Buckingham assassinated Beginning of Charles I's personal rule
1630	Ford *'Tis Pity She's a Whore*	
1632	Webster dies (?) Jonson *The Magnetic Lady*	
1637	Jonson dies	

Introduction

'I'faith, 'tis true too; I am an uncertain man' (*The Revenger's Tragedy*, I, ii,133)

Spurio, the bastard son of the Duke in *The Revenger's Tragedy*, realises that the one truth he can be certain of is that the identity of his father, and hence his own identity, is uncertain. Middleton's plays are characterised by such witty ironies. Social identities are destabilised, and made contingent on shifting relations of wealth and power. The nature of Middleton's critical identity has proved just as uncertain. Rising to the challenge posed by T. S. Eliot's arguments for Middleton's 'impersonality', for most of the twentieth century, critics searched for Middleton-the-man in his plays, 'hunt[ing] for his missing "personality" and "point of view"' (Chakravorty 1996: 2). In the closing decades of the last century, critics and directors discovered in Middleton a modern, even postmodern, sensibility that speaks to the preoccupations of our age with sex, money and power. The 'permissive' society of the 1960s had already found its reflection in *The Revenger's Tragedy*, and revived this play and Middleton's other dark tragedies, *The Changeling* and *Women Beware Women*, which had been regarded as unplayable for centuries. More recently, Alex Cox celebrated an anarcho-punk Middleton in his film version of *The Revenger's Tragedy*, while Melly Still's 2008 production for the National Theatre presented us with a playwright who is able to capture, with disturbing clarity, the twisted workings of a culture of excess in which anything goes – incest, rape, and murder.

The Revenger's Tragedy is an instructive play to introduce a study of Middleton because it problematises the relationship between the man and his work. For many years, *The Revenger's Tragedy* was regarded as the work of Cyril Tourneur. Gary Taylor and John Lavagnino's 2007 edition of Middleton's *Collected Works* includes *The Revenger's Tragedy* together with other plays Middleton had a hand in, working alongside other playwrights as co-writer or reviser. Any study of Middleton's great plays – *The Roaring Girl* and *The Changeling* – is necessarily a study of his creative partnership with his fellow playwrights, in these cases, Dekker and Rowley. This reappraisal of Middleton engages with recent work on collaboration both to consider how we might reconceptualise authorship in the light of these studies and as part of a wider reading of his plays within the working environment and practices of the early modern theatre.

This study will suggest that one answer to the question of whether there is a distinctive style that we can identify with Middleton might be found in his contemporaries' admiration for his witty muse. The concept of wit brings together the theatrical, stylistic and thematic aspects of his plays. Middleton's plays are distinguished by an 'esthetics of tricks', to borrow a phrase from Michel de Certeau, that has stylistic, social and political resonances (1988: 26). He is a technically masterful improviser, evident in his complex multiple plots and inventive use of staging. His plays favour ludic forms – burlesque, parody, travesty and other low forms of carnivalesque – in which order and convention are tricked by artful play. The figure of the trickster is frequently employed in a critique of humanist certainties that can veer towards scepticism, forcing attention to the ethical rift between words and actions.

The way that I describe the tactical role of wit in Middleton's plays, and early modern culture more broadly, has clear affinities with postmodern critical interest in the states of 'ethical undecidability' produced by Middleton's word and stage play (Middleton 2007: I, 1,635). Yet I also want to emphasise the violence and misogyny inherent in the aesthetics of tricks in Middleton's plays to which feminist critics, in particular, have drawn attention. One source of this misogyny is Calvinism, which, as John Stachniewski and others have shown, cannot be ignored in Middleton's word play. The contingency of identity in Middleton's plays may make him available as our postmodern contemporary, and yet it also draws attention to his seventeenth-century Calvinism which declared man uncertain when blind to God's grace. Does one way of theorising states of uncertainty necessarily cancel out the other, or is there a productive critical tension between the two? By reviewing the ways in which Middleton has been staged, read, theorised and revised, from early modern to contemporary productions and across a range of critical approaches, this study provides avenues into exploring Middleton's plays and the distinctive questions that they pose.

CHAPTER I

Life

Thomas Middleton is the foremost Jacobean dramatist alongside Ben Jonson and William Shakespeare. His dramatic career spans the reign of James I. He was one of the dramatists who produced devices for James's coronation pageant, and one of his earliest plays, *The Phoenix*, was possibly first performed before the new king in early 1604 (Middleton 2007: II, 346). His last known play, *A Game at Chess*, was performed in August 1624 at the end of James's reign – the king died in March 1625. Middleton's career provides an index to the theatre of his time: he wrote solo and collaboratively, for private and public playhouses, and for the city and the court; and he experimented with, and helped to shape, a range of dramatic genres that came into vogue in this period: city comedy, tragicomedy, romance and revenge tragedy. Middleton was also a thoroughly London playwright: he was born in London and made his career in that city. What is known about the details of his life tells us much about the society of which he was part – its class structures, educational opportunities, the role of property, the growth of the city and, of course, the place of the theatre.

FAMILY LIFE: BIRTHS, DEATHS AND MARRIAGES

Thomas Middleton was 'a gentleman born'. But what did this mean in Elizabethan England? His father, William Middleton, was a gentleman with a coat of arms. He was also a well-to-do citizen, a member of one of the lesser London guilds, the Honourable Company of Tilers and Bricklayers (Eccles 1957: 517–18). Around 75 per cent of adult men in the City of London belonged to trade guilds or livery companies. These were the citizens or 'freemen' who governed the City, and regulated its economic, religious and civic life. The upper echelons of the guilds, the aldermen, were wealthy and powerful men of rank (Archer 1991: 18–19, 100, 114). William may have been a gentleman of blood, in other words, descended from landed gentry. It was not uncommon for sons of gentlemen to enter the guilds given the opportunities to move through the ranks and join the City elite. Yet there were other ways of becoming a gentleman in the period. Many argued gentility had its origins in 'gentle deeds' rather than simply birth. A citizen could therefore rise through his industry and by holding office to earn the right to a coat of arms and so become a gentleman. In either case, social standing was highly fluid in this period; the wealth and status secured by one generation could easily be lost in the next.

William married Anne Snow in 1574. Thomas, their first son, was born six years later – he was baptised on 18 April 1580. A daughter, Avis, was born in 1582, other children died in infancy (Eccles 1931: 431). William died in January 1586, when Thomas was just six years old. He left his children shares of an estate that included substantial holdings of land and property in London. The City of London had a duty to aid the widows and orphans of its citizens. The City's Court of Orphans ensured that Thomas and Avis would be provided for, and undertook to provide a legacy of £25 each when they came of age (Eccles 1957: 516–17; Archer 1991: 119–21).

Anne, now forty-eight, was left a propertied City widow. She was soon courted by Thomas Harvey, a gentleman grocer, and they married later that year. Harvey was an adventurer. He had recently returned to London after a disastrous year as chief factor in Sir Walter Raleigh's failed colony at Roanoke in North America, and was destitute, 'poore and unable to pay his Creditors'. He probably saw Anne as a solution to his money troubles. Certainly the marriage was not happy. They quarrelled bitterly over money; there were countless lawsuits as Harvey tried to access William's estate; there were even accusations of poisoning, and at one time they spoke of divorce. In property disputes, women and minors were particularly vulnerable to predations of relatives and associates. Avis had married Allan Waterer, a clothworker, in 1598 when she was sixteen, and was soon embroiled in lawsuits with her mother as her husband also fought for control of the Middleton inheritance. By June 1600, Thomas Middleton had sold all his shares in his father's property to his brother-in-law, Waterer (Eccles 1957: 519–33; Phialas 1955: 187–92).

From the age of seventeen, Middleton had been helping his mother with lawsuits over his father's property and presumably was well-versed in domestic and legal double-dealing. The late sixteenth century witnessed a dramatic increase in litigation. We can understand the legal disputes that often drive the plots of his city plays not simply as autobiographical material making its way into the drama, but as one of the stories of the new metropolis of which Middleton had direct experience. In plays such as *Trick to Catch the Old One* and *Michaelmas Term*, patrimony is disrupted; the son's inheritance is precarious, and difficult to secure from predatory relatives, business associates or servants.

Middleton's marriage to Mary or Magdalen Marbeck around 1603 brought with it connections that in many ways typify the complex social dynamics of post-Reformation England. Mary's family had risen through humanist occupations rather than through the trade and craft guilds. Her grandfather, John Marbeck, was musician to Henry VIII and a Calvinist theologian, who published the earliest concordance to the English bible – he narrowly escaped burning at the stake under Mary I.[1] Her uncle, Dr Roger Marbeck, became provost of Oriel College, Oxford and physician to Elizabeth I. Edward, her father, was one of the Six Clerks in Chancery (Eccles 1931: 440–1). Her brother, however, was an actor with the Admiral's Men and her new husband, although a university-educated gentleman, earned his living by writing for the stage – Mary and Thomas probably met through this theatre connection. Such movement up and down the social scale across generations – from court musician to official in the Court of Chancery to actor on the public stage – is a feature of early modern social mobility.

UNIVERSITY

Like other young men of his class, Middleton went from grammar school to university, matriculating at Queen's College, Oxford in April 1598. The grammar school was one of the engines of the sixteenth-century 'educational revolution' (Stone 1964). The social group that benefited from increased educational opportunities was the middling classes. Students attending grammar school were taught to write, translate and speak in Latin – Greek was introduced in the final year – and they studied rhetoric, classical history and poetry. Middleton was a precocious youth, publishing his first work, *Wisdom of Solomon Paraphrased*, in 1597, when he was just seventeen. The next year he went up to Oxford. Three years earlier the dramatist John Marston, the son of a well-to-do lawyer, had graduated BA from Brasenose College, Oxford; he finished his education at the Inns of Court, where students studied law and rhetoric as well as the arts of gentlemanly behaviour, such as music and versifying. Middleton's future collaborator, John Webster, the son of a senior member of the Merchant Taylors' Company, attended the highly-regarded Merchant Taylors' School before entering one of the Inns of Court in 1598.

University life could provide a pathway into the professional theatre. Acting in plays was an element of training in rhetoric at grammar schools and universities. It ensured students had the opportunity, in the words of William Gager, the Latin dramatist and fellow of Christ Church College, Oxford, 'to try their voices and confirm their memories, and to frame their speech and conform it to convenient action' (Elliot 1984–97: IV). Thomas Heywood's *Apology for Actors* (1612) made the same argument, although for a different reason. By identifying acting with the skills of the orator, and by aligning the professional theatre with the university, Heywood sought to give the acting profession cultural authority:

In the time of my residence in *Cambridge*, I have seen Tragedies, Comedies, Histories, Pastorals and Shows, publicly acted, in which Graduates of good place and reputation, have been specially parted: this is held necessary for the

> emboldening of their Junior scholars, to arm them with audacity, against they come to be employed in any public exercise, as in the reading of Dialectic, Rhetoric, Ethic, Mathematic, the Physic, or Metaphysic Lectures. (cited in Gurr 1992: 96)

During his first two years at Oxford, Middleton would have had the opportunity to observe, and perhaps perform in, the plays which were acted during the Christmas revels.

Training in rhetoric and logic at the universities, Heywood enthused, makes the 'bashful Grammarian' into

> a bold Sophister, to argue *pro et contra*, to compose his Syllogisms, Categoric, or Hypothetic (simple or compound) to reason and frame a sufficient argument to prove his questions, or to defend any *axioma*, to distinguish of any Dilemma and be able to moderate in any Argumentation whatsoever. (cited in Gurr 1992: 96)

Middleton wore his own learning lightly, and was more than capable of parodying the new university man. Tim, the son of the goldsmith, Master Yellowhammer, in *Chaste Maid in Cheapside*, is sent to Cambridge University to acquire the signs of gentility. He has read logic, but as his tutor wryly observes he is an idiot. Tim is a parody of Heywood's 'bold Sophister': as he unwittingly puns he is able 'To prove a fool by logic' (IV, i, 38). At the end of the play, his mother urges him to marry the Welsh gentlewoman and prove 'A whore an honest woman' (V, iv, 102). Just as Tim will love his new wife 'for her wit', regardless of her morals, the play similarly displays a taste for paradox and sophistry.

The poetry Middleton published during this period was typical of the fashionable genres favoured by the young university and Inns of Court wits of the 1590s. *Microcynicon: Six Snarling Satires* (1599) was his contribution to the vogue for satire in the late 1590s. Yet whereas Marston's *The Scourge of Villanie* (1598) and Everard Guilpin's (1598) *Skialetheia* personified vices in such a way as to invite the reader to identify actual figures at court, Middleton's satire was less risky and more generalised and conventional. His *The Ghost of Lucrece*, published a year later, is an Ovidian female-voiced complaint that once again responded to the taste for Ovid cultivated at the universities and Inns of Court.

Middleton left Oxford without a degree sometime between June 1600 and February 1601. He had made considerable efforts in the summer of 1600 to stay in Oxford, selling his inheritance so he could buy food, clothes and 'other necessaries' to maintain himself. It is difficult to determine just why he left (Eccles 1957: 524–6). One of the paths open to him as a university man was patronage. The influential patron could use his connections and wealth to support the careers of worthy and useful men. Middleton's dedication of *The Ghost of Lucrece* to William, 2nd Baron Compton, in 1600 had not borne fruit, and he may have despaired of gaining preferment. With his mother harassed by lawsuits, his inheritance gone and few other prospects, it is possible he decided to cut his losses and return to London to lend his mother assistance. And he could look forward to his £25 legacy from the City when he turned twenty-one in 1601, which would help him to find his feet in London.

EARLY MODERN THEATRE: 'DAILY ACCOMPANYING THE PLAYERS'

By February 1601, Middleton was 'in London daily accompanying the players' (Eccles 1957: 530). With at least three published works to his name, he sought his living in the precarious world of print and the stage. Middleton is said to have penned a self-portrait in his character of the university scholar turned poet:

> in the very pride and glory of all my labours, I was unfruitfully led to the lickerish study of poetry, that sweet honey-poison that swells a supple scholar with unprofitable sweetness and delicious false conceits, until he bursts into extremities and become a poetical almsman, or at the most, one of the Poor Knights of Poetry. (*Father Hubburd's Tales*, Middleton 2007: I, 1,146–51)

For all its pitfalls, London was an exciting place at that time. Middleton had been caught up in this world even as a student. His

Microcynicon had fallen victim to censorship and was burnt by the hangman in June 1599 under the censorship imposed by the so-called Bishop's Ban. The authorities feared sharp satires and epigrams were fuelling public disorder and bringing the court into disrepute (Clegg 1997: 215). This was the year the star of the charismatic and impetuous Robert Devereux, 2nd Earl of Essex, began crashing to earth. Middleton was an early admirer; he had addressed his first publication, *The Wisdom of Solomon Paraphrased*, to Essex in 1597. Once the triumphant and popular royal favourite, in 1600 Essex lost all his offices and was briefly imprisoned for disobeying Queen Elizabeth. Determined to recover his influence by force, he gathered his followers in January 1601 and led a rebellion to take control of the City. Essex was sentenced to death in February. Since Middleton was in London at this time, he could well have been among the crowds that witnessed the execution.

The players were engaged in their own civil war in 1601. The so-called 'War of the Theatres' or 'That terrible *Poetomachia*' in the words of one of its combatants, Thomas Dekker, was raging on stage. Ben Jonson had satirised Marston and Dekker in his *Poetaster* (1601) and Dekker hit back with his *Satiromastix* (1601). Middleton must have made the acquaintance of Dekker soon after returning to London in early 1601, given they were writing plays together by May 1602. This 'war' was not simply a personal squabble that erupted on stage; it was also a culture war, a debate about nature of the theatre – and it was also caught up in the turbulent politics of the times. Those in power feared being libelled on stage. The Privy Council complained in 1601:

> that certain players that use to recite their plays at the Curtain in Moorfields do represent upon the stage in their interludes the persons of gentlemen of good desert and quality that are yet alive under obscure manner, but yet in sort as all the hearers may take notice both of the matter and the persons that are meant thereby. (cited in Steggle 1998: 18–19)

The early modern theatre thus played its own part in contemporary politics. Middleton would get into serious trouble in 1624 when his own play, *A Game at Chess*, impersonated persons of quality, namely the Spanish ambassador, on the public stage.

Middleton's father had a share in four acres of gardens and tenements adjoining the Curtain playhouse in Moorfield, in the suburb of Shoreditch, and Thomas collected the rents for his mother from the age of seventeen (Eccles 1957: 525–6). The Curtain, one of the earliest purpose-built theatres, had opened in 1577. It was an open amphitheatre, like its near neighbour, the Theatre, built by James Burbage, the theatre manager, the previous year. The amphitheatres were located in the suburbs, outside the jurisdiction of the City authorities. Hall playhouses, which were opening in the City near St Paul's Cathedral and in Blackfriars around this time, were similarly outside the City's jurisdiction, although within its walls, since they were located in a self-governing, former monastic precinct. The amphitheatres had a larger capacity than the halls, and theatre-goers paid less for their tickets. Amphitheatres were typically round or polygonal structures, with three tiers of galleries, covered by thatch or tile roofing, around the yard and stage. Admission to the yard was a penny, to the galleries two pennies, and to sit in the higher galleries was another penny, while the 'lords rooms' near the stage cost 6d. This was the minimum charge for entering the galleries in indoor hall playhouses (Gurr 1987: 14–26). The auditorium of a hall playhouse was very different from that of an amphitheatre. There was a pit around the stage, and two, possibly three ranges of galleries. It was an extra shilling to sit in the pit, and a further shilling to sit on the stage – this was a favourite pastime of gallants who wanted to display their finery or advertise their disdain at the quality of acting or the play. To hire a box that flanked the stage was half-a-crown. Differences in location, seating arrangements, ticket prices and clientele were social differences that distinguished the open cheaper 'public' amphitheatres from the exclusive, more expensive 'private' playhouses (Gurr 1992: 14–18, 156–64).

Middleton received his first payment for writing a play, the lost tragedy *Caesar's Fall*, for the Admiral's Men in May 1602. His co-writers were Dekker, Michael Drayton, Anthony Munday and John Webster and they shared payment of £8 – collaboration was at the heart of early modern theatrical practice. The Admiral's Men, along with the Chamberlain's Men, had dominated the London stage since the mid-1590s. Playing companies were typically run by managers who paid for costumes and preparing the playhouse, commissioned plays, and sometimes drew up contracts with players and playwrights to guarantee their exclusive service. Managers and players received a proportion of the takings; playwrights might be paid up front for the delivery of a play or given a day's takings or be employed on contract. The Admiral's Men was run by Philip Henslowe and the Chamberlain's Men by James Burbage – his two sons took over the company following his death in 1597 (Gurr 1992: 41–5). The accession of James I in 1603 marked a new phase of royal patronage. He took over the patronage of the Chamberlain's Men, now the King's Men. Other leading companies were placed under the patronage of members of the royal family – Middleton wrote for not only for the King's Men, but also for Prince Henry's Men, Lady Elizabeth's Men, and Prince Charles' Men.

Middleton wrote plays for performance in the public amphitheatres, such as Henslowe's Fortune built to the west of the Theatre and Curtain in 1600, and for the 'private' hall playhouses. From 1603 to 1606, he worked for the Children of Paul's, an all-boy company playing indoors at a playhouse in the churchyard of St Paul's Cathedral, producing satiric comedies that took London as their subject. Middleton was also writing tragedies for the King's Men – he collaborated with Shakespeare on *Timon of Athens* and is thought to have written *The Revenger's Tragedy* (1606) around this time. His versatility testifies to the variety of theatrical experiences available in Jacobean London. 'Middleton always remained a free agent,' as Gary Taylor reminds us in his essay in the *Oxford Dictionary of National Biography*, 'working for at least seven acting companies; his plays exploited the varied artistic opportunities offered by different casts, theatres, and audiences.'

In the 1610s and 1620s, Middleton produced his most celebrated plays: *The Roaring Girl* (1611), with Dekker; *A Chaste Maid in Cheapside* (1613); *Women Beware Women* (c. 1621) and *The Changeling* (1622), with William Rowley. His plays were performed at the public theatres and at court; he wrote the *Masque of Heroes* for Inner Temple, and his masque, co-written with Rowley, *The World Tossed at Tennis*, was performed at court and on the public stage. In 1624, Middleton wrote *A Game at Chess*, which was both a spectacular success and effectively brought his career as a writer for the theatre to an end. This controversial political play capitalised on popular hostility to Spain, and played to packed houses for nine days before it was closed down by the authorities. Middleton was pursued by the Privy Council and may even have spent some time in prison. It is possible there were restrictions against him writing for stage, since no plays have been credibly attributed to Middleton after this date – he died just two years later. The dramatic career of this quintessentially Jacobean dramatist guides us through Jacobean theatre practices and theatrical fashions as well as the social changes, scandals and political conflicts that shaped the times.

LONDON

Middleton stands alongside Jonson and Dekker as one of the leading dramatists of early modern London. His pamphlets and plays depict London's taverns and shops, its streets and parks, its houses and prisons. These places are populated with characters drawn from across the social spectrum – beggars, cutpurses, prostitutes, servants, shopkeepers, merchants and their wives, gallants and noblemen. London grew into a bustling metropolis over the course of the sixteenth and seventeenth centuries. Its population increased dramatically as people migrated from the country to the city. One of the moralising stories Middleton's *Mad World, My Masters* tells is that of the naive country girl lured to the city and into prostitution. Popular cony-catching or rogue pamphlets, penned by Robert Greene and Dekker, portray a city governed by an alternative order of criminal fellowships. Middleton's own pamphlets (*The Meeting of Gallants at an Ordinary*, *The Black Book* and *Father Hubburd's Tales*), written when plague closed the theatres over 1603–4, are in this vein and rehearse themes and characters to appear in a few years in his satiric London comedies. They depict the city as a type of hell, a place populated by creatures that prey on the unwary – lawyers and punks, 'his devouring cheater and his glorious cockatrice', who gull prodigal gentlemen out of their inheritance (*The Nightingale and the Ant*, Middleton 2007: I, 570–1).

Yet there are other views of London to be found in Middleton's repertoire. London was the centre of trade, government and the law. Its economic growth was cause for civic pride, and celebrated by the mercantile class that had benefited from it with magnificent civic pageantry. Between 1613 and 1626, Middleton produced elaborate civic pageants and entertainments for the City of London and its wealthy merchants. The hostility of the City of London to the public theatres is well-known. Yet, it was not necessarily anti-theatrical in principle; hence the great expense guilds went to in the production of elaborate mayoral shows. The problem with public theatres from the City's point of view was that playhouses undermined good order. The civic authorities wanted sanctions imposed to ensure their members, particularly apprentices, were at work and not idly watching plays. The hostility to secular stage plays also had a religious dimension. As the governing elite were predominantly godly Protestants, in very stark terms, this meant they preferred preaching to playing. We should remember, however, that Protestantism encompassed a range of religious viewpoints, not all hostile to poetry or plays (Heinemann 1982: 18–36). There were non-conformists or puritans who believed the Reformation had not gone far enough and who attacked all image-making as papist idolatry. And there were Protestants, particularly those influenced by humanist ideas, who believed that the arts – music, poetry and drama – had a moral and spiritual role to play. Hence, John Marbeck was a Calvinist theologian *and* a court musician.

The City governors were developing their own interests in theatricality as a means of conveying powerful images of social order and civic harmony. From the mid-sixteenth century, the Lord Mayor's Show, held to celebrate the annual inauguration of the Lord Mayor of London in October, became a permanent feature of the festive calendar. Guilds competed to produce the most magnificent show. The Lord Mayor's Show mirrored the royal entry into London and was similarly designed to dramatise the civic authority of the City of London in spectacular fashion. As the new mayor returned from his inauguration at Westminster to Guildhall, his guild staged a series of allegorical tableaux along the route. These pageants became increasingly elaborate, and reached their dramatic peak under James I (Bergeron 2003: 126–7).

Middleton produced seven mayoral shows and helped to transform the civic pageant into a highly sophisticated allegorical and theatrical medium. His final years as a loyal servant of the City, however, were tied to London's own fortunes, and so dogged by political instability, economic recession and plague. The fallout from *A Game at Chess* probably meant that Middleton was not considered for the 1624 mayoral show, and the plague that swept through London in 1625 resulted in the cancellation of the pageant for that year. The City of London's coronation pageant for Charles I and his new bride, Henrietta Maria, was also cancelled by the new king. Middleton was not paid for the devices he designed along with his long-standing collaborator on civic pageants, Gerard Christmas. Nor did he receive payment for his final show for the Drapers, *The Triumphs of Health and Prosperity* (1626). The Drapers were in severe financial difficulties and, although they claimed the devices were badly executed, it is likely funds were low (Bergeron 2003: 246–7). Middleton's own health and prosperity were probably at low ebb in 1626 – he died the following year and was buried on 4 July 1627. His widow, Mary, petitioned the City for relief, and received a gift of twenty nobles.

AFTERLIVES

Middleton's plays continued to influence the next generation of dramatists in the later 1620s and 1630s. Philip Massinger, James Shirley and Richard Brome, among others, returned to the earlier Jacobean city comedies, including those of Middleton, for their own comic plays set in the fashionable West End of London (Sanders 1999: 43, 58). When the theatres re-opened at the Restoration in 1660, after the closure by Parliament in 1642 with the onset of civil war, Middleton's plays also returned to the stage. Pepys saw a performance of *The Changeling* in 1661, and the play was in performance until 1668. After the Restoration, his plays disappear from the stage – his tragedies were not revived on the professional stage until the 1960s when there was a marked resurgence of interest in performing Middleton.

Part of the difficulty with establishing Middleton's reputation from the later seventeenth century onwards is that unlike his more famous contemporaries, Shakespeare and Jonson, he was not canonised early on through the publication of his collected works – this had to wait until Alexander Dyce's 1840 edition (Middleton 2007: I, 50–2). The absence of a corpus of works is accompanied by a critical view of Middleton as strangely disembodied. It was put forward most cogently by T. S. Eliot, who wrote: 'Of all the Elizabethan dramatists Middleton seems the most impersonal, the most indifferent to personal fame or perpetuity, the readiest, except Rowley, to accept collaboration.' For Eliot, Middleton's disturbing lack of personality, in other words, a clearly identifiable author-function, is a consequence of his willingness to collaborate and, relatedly, the difficulty of identifying a canon of his plays. Instead, Middleton is 'merely the name which associates six or seven great plays' (Eliot 1990: 133; Hutchings and Bromham 2008: 36).

Middleton's 'impersonality' can be understood in terms of the working practices of the early modern theatre. Plays were owned by the theatre companies rather than the playwright. Part of the reason why Shakespeare's plays could be gathered together in one volume, the first Folio, published posthumously in 1623, was because his plays were owned by the one company, the King's Men, in which Shakespeare himself was a shareholder. If Shakespeare's situation was unusual, then Ben Jonson's was even more so. Jonson took back control of his play-texts from the theatre companies by publishing them in 1616 as his *Works* and thus asserted his individual rights of ownership (Brooks 2000: 144, 153). Middleton does not appear to have had this type of investment in his play-texts. Many were published as quartos in his lifetime, but they were not gathered together as his collected works. Unlike Jonson, he did not attempt to secure his status as the sole progenitor of his plays through the mechanisms of print. Middleton scholarship in the twentieth century has grappled with the problem of establishing a reliable canon of his plays, a coherent body of work that can be authoritatively identified as 'Middleton'.

Recent work on collaboration has questioned editorial practices that seek to canonise individual playwrights. Douglas Brooks argues that this type of project necessarily goes hand-in-hand with what he describes as 'Man-and-Works criticism'. Editorial practice is frequently driven by assumption that it is possible to chart 'the author's personal and artistic development . . . from revision to revision', and relies on a model of authorship that privileges authorial intention (Brooks 2000: 8–9). Does it impair Middleton scholarship and the popularity of his plays in the classroom and on stage if we cannot discern the outlines of his personality delineated in the body of his works? One consequence of prioritising a collaborative model of authorship is a heightened awareness of Middleton's collaboration with other dramatists. While Gary Taylor and John Lavagnino's 2007 edition of Middleton's *Collected Works* includes Middleton's collaborative plays written with Dekker, Rowley and others, more controversially it also incorporates a number of plays previously attributed solely to Shakespeare – *Timon of Athens*, *Macbeth* and *Measure for Measure*. Taylor, along with John Jowett, argues for the status of *Timon* as a collaborative play with Shakespeare; in the case of *Macbeth*, Middleton added a song from his play *The Witch* and had a hand in other parts of Shakespeare's play; and he revised *Measure for Measure* for a revival around 1621 (Middleton 2007: I, 1,543).

The 2007 edition of Middleton's *Collected Works* is innovative in that the inclusion of the plays of such an iconic author as Shakespeare foregrounds the collaborative nature of authorship in the early modern theatre. However, this does not mean that the edition rejects a notion of the 'author'. On the contrary, Taylor argues that the early modern period recognised 'individual authorial agency'. In any case, the function of an edition is to assign the 'name of the author' to his collected works (Middleton 2007: II, 38, 40). One effect of these editorial practices is an instructive tension between collaborative and individualised models of authorship. This study of Middleton will draw attention to collaboration and its implications for the study of Middleton's plays, yet it will also attempt to discern various elements of a dramatic style or styles that we might assign to 'Thomas Middleton'. There have been other Middletons – the moralised Middleton of the mid-twentieth century, the oppositional parliamentary puritan of Margot Heinemann, and Jonathan Dollimore's radical subversive. Throughout the book, I will return to an epigram published in *Wit's Recreations*, just over a decade after his death, which writes of 'Facetious *Middleton*' and his 'witty Muse' (1640: sig. B7v), to assess what this characterisation of 'Middleton's' personal style might mean to the analysis of his plays.

NOTE

1. Calvinism takes its name from the French Protestant reformer, John Calvin, whose writings and theological beliefs strongly influenced English reformers. The key aspects of Calvinism are its view of man as morally and spiritually fallen and thus totally dependent on God's grace for salvation; and its theory of election which argues that God has chosen to save some individuals, the Elect, and to damn others, the unregenerate, hence salvation is entirely down to God's will.

CHAPTER 2

City Comedies: *Mad World, My Masters, Michaelmas Term* and *A Trick to Catch the Old One*

Middleton's early career as a dramatist was shaped by his part-nership with the company of boy actors, the Children of Paul's. From around 1604 to 1608, when the company ceased public performances, Middleton wrote at least five plays for the boy players: *The Phoenix, Mad World, My Masters, Michaelmas Term, Your Five Gallants* and *Trick to Catch the Old One*. These plays were performed at an indoor theatre situated inside the churchyard of St Paul's Cathedral and surrounded by the fashionable West End of London. The plays he wrote for the company, to take Middleton's own metaphor, were similarly cut to the latest 'fashion of playmak-ing' (('Epistle', *The Roaring Girl*) 2007: I, 1). *The Phoenix* is a dis-guised-ruler play, and was performed before King James soon after he came to London in 1604. This chapter will concentrated on three of Middleton's wittily sardonic London comedies – *Mad World, My Masters, Michaelmas Term* and *Trick to Catch the Old One* – in order to explore his early experimentation with a particular the-atrical form, city comedy, and his developing reputation for a distinctive witty style, which meant that he was remembered by his near contemporaries as 'Facetious Middleton'.

While a number of critics have disputed the stability of 'city comedy' as a generic label, it remains a useful term for examin-ing the vogue for satiric comedies set in London in the late six-teenth and early seventeenth centuries. Middleton, along with Ben Jonson, is identified as the leading exponent of the form. Plots of city comedies are typically based on Roman New Comedy – the young lovers, often with the aid of a trickster-figure, overcome the obstacles posed by the *senex*, the 'old one' (Howard 2007: 19). *Michaelmas Term* and *Trick to Catch the Old One* set gentleman gallants against avaricious merchants in a battle of wits in which the gentleman is both reformed and triumphs. *Mad World, My Masters* takes a different tack – the gallant has not been dispossessed by a wily merchant but through the aristocratic prodigality of his own grandfather, and has formed an alliance with rogues and vagabonds, the dispossessed criminal classes. The play is a variant on the comedy of humours, recently brought to the stage by Jonson. The distinctive feature of these plays in comparison with the higher mode of tragedy is that 'they pitch their social [and literary] register lower'. They are enlivened by a scurrilous, bawdy humour and 'mark a moment in early modern culture' when London in all its social diversity became a distinctive presence on the stage (Howard 2007: 19).

WRITING FOR THE CHILDREN OF PAUL'S: INDOOR THEATRES AND THE TRANSVESTITE BOY ACTOR

Middleton's early comedies were written for a company of boy actors. A number of boy companies flourished in the late sixteenth and early seventeenth centuries: the Children of Paul's, who performed at a theatre in the cathedral churchyard; the Children of the Chapel who performed at Blackfriars Theatre (they became the Children of the Queen's Revels in 1603); and the Children of the King's Revels, who were briefly resident at Whitefriars Theatre for nine months over 1607–8. The Children of Paul's were primarily a 'professional liturgical ensemble', a company of choristers who sang in the cathedral choir and attended Paul's grammar school; the Children of the Chapel similarly drew their company from the choristers of the Chapel Royal (Bowers 2000: 71). Early plays performed by the Children of Paul's took advantage of the boys' skills as choristers. Middleton was skilled in music composition: one of his first publications, *Wisdom of Solomon* (1597), incorporated various forms of song. He may have composed the songs incorporated in his plays for the Children of Paul's, such as Audrey's song in *A Trick* and other songs in *Mad World* and *Your Five Gallants* (Middleton 2007: II, 119–59). Acting, as we have seen, was part of the grammar school curriculum because it enabled students to practise oratorical skills by training the memory and polishing the pronunciation and delivery of speeches. Students performed plays at school, both in Latin and English, and were also called upon to provide the entertainments at court for the Christmas festivities as well as for foreign dignitaries. By 1575, the Paul's boys were no longer just performing at court, but were also putting on plays before the public in a playhouse in the churchyard of St Paul's Cathedral (Gair 1982: 76, 44).

By the time Middleton came to write for the Children of Paul's in the early years of James's reign, the company had already had a number of successful partnerships with key Renaissance playwrights: John Lyly in the 1580s and John Marston in the late 1590s and early 1600s. These partnerships played a decisive role in shaping theatrical fashions and the history of early modern theatre. Why were these boy companies so significant? The famous disparaging reference by Hamlet to 'little eyases', a line delivered on the stage of the Globe, has been taken as evidence for a profound rivalry between the adult and children's companies. Alfred Harbage argued for 'rival traditions' in the early modern theatre, and set in motion a moralising contrast between the wholesome and populist Shakespearean drama performed in the public amphitheatres and the decadent coterie drama played before aristocratic audiences at the private indoor theatres. The assumptions underlying this view of rival traditions have been questioned, as well as the strict division between public and private theatres – playwrights wrote for both venues, and the plays sometimes made the transition from indoor to outdoor theatres (Munro 2005: 13–14). That said, the satiric city comedies Middleton wrote for Paul's Boys constitute a distinct stage in the dramatist's career and, as such, the particular culture of the boy's companies and the theatres they performed in provide a valuable framework for analysing these plays.

The boy's companies continue to be associated with more subversive, avant-garde theatre. Dramatists writing for the children's companies were 'self-consciously innovative' and led theatrical fashions; as Lucy Munro points out, the combined repertoire of the children's companies includes 'every significant' early seventeenth-century dramatic mode, from railing satiric comedies to bloody revenge tragedies. The children's companies had a reputation for pushing the boundaries. Thomas Heywood complained in his *Apology for Actors* (1608) about the licence taken by dramatists writing for the boy players: 'The liberty, which some arrogate to themselves, committing their bitterness, and liberal invectives against all estates, to the mouths of Children, supposing their juniority to be a privilege for any railing, be it never so violent' (cited in Munro 2005: 14). The Children of the Queen's Revels were guilty of just such 'liberal invectives': they put on a series of plays in 1605 and 1606 that satirised members of the royal court and hit very sensitive political nerves; because of these transgressions they lost the patronage of Queen Anne. This was the lively theatrical environment in which Middleton began his career as a dramatist. To what extent can we attribute the distinctive features, even the edginess of Middleton's early satiric comedies to this experimental and innovative atmosphere?

Whereas the adult companies before 1608 played in the public amphitheatres located in the suburbs, the boy's companies performed in indoor 'private' theatres in newly fashionable areas of London. Little is known of the exact dimensions of the indoor playhouses. Unlike the amphitheatres, they were not purpose-built structures, but adapted from pre-existing halls or large communal spaces. It is assumed that the stage space was similar to that of amphitheatres given that plays were transferred relatively easily between indoor and outdoor theatres. Other aspects, such as organisation of seating, were dependent on pre-existing structures. Seating was around the stage and in the galleries – gallants who wanted to display their new cloaks or new suits could sit on stools on stage (Gurr 1992: 155–60). That said, theatre historians have suggested that the Paul's playhouse might have been so small that the stage space could not accommodate stools and the theatre itself may have been able to hold 'no more than a few dozen persons' (Bowers 2000: 81). To an extent, historians can only speculate about the dimensions of the Paul's playhouse since there is no decisive evidence for its location. Most recently, Roger Bowers has argued that the company of boy choristers performed in the communal hall of their residence, the Almonry House. We need to ask ourselves whether the size of the theatre and its audience makes a difference to the way that we understand and interpret Middleton's comedies written for the Children of Paul's. If we see these plays as coterie plays, performed for a small, select audience in an intimate setting, what kind of reading does this open up, or close down?

The assumption is often made that the location of the indoor hall theatres and the higher ticket prices they charged meant that their audiences were primarily drawn from the gentry, who lived in the parishes around St Paul's, and Inns of Court men, the young law students who resided at nearby Lincoln's Inn, Middle and Inner Temples and Gray's Inn. However, if we look closely at this area, a different picture emerges. The theatre in which the Children of Paul's performed was in the busy and crowded churchyard of St Paul's Cathedral, surrounded by shops that had sprouted up not only in the churchyard, but also in the cathedral itself. Services were held in the choir area of the cathedral, which meant that the main, middle aisle of St Paul's was free for trade. Reavley Gair has described the cathedral as 'an Elizabethan version of an indoor shopping mall' (1982: 31). It was filled with people transacting business: lawyers had their own pillars where they met clients; a glazier was in the chapel at the far end of the south aisle; trunkmakers rented the lower cloisters around the Chapter House; in the side chapels were joiners, carpenters, bookbinders, mercers and hosiers.

The theatre was part of the thoroughfare of Paul's. While merchants, shopkeepers and tradesmen went about their business in the churchyard, others came to shop or to pass through on their way to other areas, or to go to the theatre. Parishes around the cathedral grew rapidly in the late sixteenth and early seventeenth centuries, their population doubling in size. The area in and around St Paul's was therefore not simply a gentry enclave, but socially diverse and heavily populated. This means that audiences at Paul's playhouse were probably socially mixed rather than drawn primarily from the elite, and may have included shopkeepers along with lawyers, merchants and tradesmen as well as gentry; in other words, the range of individuals who lived, worked and spent their leisure time in and around St Paul's (Gair 1982: 69–74). Ben Jonson pictured a 'shops

Foreman' in the audience at a performance of John Fletcher's *The Faithful Shepherdess* at the Blackfriars Theatre (Gurr 1987: 223).

Middleton's *Michaelmas Term*, probably written and performed in 1605 or early 1606, draws the immediate environs of Paul's playhouse into the plot of the play. The first scene, following the Induction, is set in the middle aisle of St Paul's Cathedral, known as Paul's Walk. Those attending Paul's Theatre would pass through the middle aisle, and possibly stop to observe the 'Paul's walkers' or to converse with acquaintances or buy goods. Characters in the play read the notices on the great west door otherwise known as the '*siquis*' door after the '*siquisses*' or notices, typically advertisements for employment, that were displayed on the door and pillars. The scene opens with two prodigal gentlemen, Rearage and Salewood, exchanging greetings: 'Exceedingly well met in town; comes your father up this Term?' (I, ii, 2–3). By the early seventeenth century, there was a distinct London season that followed the terms of the law year. Hence the title of the play: 'Michaelmas term' was the autumn term, when the London season began and the gentry came up to London to pursue legal cases in the law courts; transact business; shop and socialise; visit acquaintances; frequent plays, taverns and gaming houses; and promenade in Paul's Walk. Rearage's use of the word 'town' to denote London was new; it was first coined in its modern sense as a synonym for fashionable society around this time.

Paul's Walk was the place where the young gentleman, newly arrived from the country, was first inducted in the fashionable ways of the town. One way a gentleman could advertise that he was a gallant – a fashionable man about town – was through the company that he kept. Easy, the green young country gentleman from Essex, is now at liberty to visit London since his father's death. His acquaintance Cockstone advertises the human ware on display in Paul's Walk: 'Here's gallants of all sizes, of all lasts;/Here you may fit your foot, make choice of those/Whom your affection may rejoice in' (I, ii, 48–50). The metaphor Cockstone uses in this speech is grounded in the particular nature of Paul's Walk; the play on walking and shoes ('lasts' are shoe moulds (*OED* 2b)), available in the nearby shops in the churchyard, invites the audience to imagine the gallants promenading like goods on sale. Choosing a companion is like choosing a pair of shoes; the suggestion is that in the town the gallant will change his friends as often as he changes his clothes. Social relations are commodified in this place.

In his plays written for the Children of Paul's, Middleton takes advantage of other features of Paul's playhouse for his satire on the appetite of the gentry for new goods. *Mad World, My Masters* is a study of prodigality in its many forms. Sir Bounteous Progress takes the traditional value of hospitality, one of the defining virtues of the country gentleman, to extremes by keeping a house that is far too open. He is trusting to the point of folly and is therefore unable to distinguish between worthy and unworthy guests. In order to encourage a guest to take advantage of his hospitality, he lays out his household goods and lavish furnishings to full view: 'cloth o'gold chamber' (II, i, 33–4), 'a great gilt candlestick, and a pair of silver snuffers', and 'a pair of fair organs' (II, i, 38–9). The portable organ or regals was 'a novel instrument at Paul's' (Gair 1982: 154). Middleton builds his satire on the conspicuous consumption of the gentry around this instrument, which are 'double gilt', as Progress boasts to Lord Owemuch (his grandson, Dick Follywit, in disguise), 'some hundred and fifty pounds will fit your lordship with such another pair' (II, i, 119–22). The scene ends with an organ recital, providing an opportunity for the musicians at Paul's to showcase their talents and advertise the playhouse's novel attractions to the theatre-goers.

The boy actor has attracted a great deal of critical interest. Critics have tended to use this figure to theorise early modern period discourses of gender and sexuality. Much has been written on Shakespeare's punning on the figure of the transvestite boy actor in his comedies, such as *Twelfth Night*. When the playing company consists solely of boy actors these issues are thrown into sharp relief. Boy actors were imagined pederastically as erotic objects promising manifold delights (Munro 2005: 48). The young gallant was advised in Middleton's satiric pamphlet, *Father Hubburd's Tales* (1604), 'to call in at the Blackfriars where he should see a nest of Boys, able to ravish a man' (Middleton 2007: I, 502–3). The boy actor enabled dramatists and actors to play with the slippage between 'male' and 'female' for erotic and comic effect, typically by punning on the homoerotic attractions and sexual availability of the boy's body, 'turn[ing] a boy actor literally into a visual pun'. The audiences who enjoyed the homoerotic jokes, Mary Bly argues, constituted a 'self-aware homoerotic community', bound together by their 'sympathetic awareness' of a shared 'homoerotic desire' (2000: 6–7).

We can see such homoerotic punning at work throughout the comedies Middleton wrote for the Children of Paul's. Theodore Leinwand argues that 'beggary', which *Michaelmas Term* turns into a pun in the Induction, is a *double entendre* for buggery that knowingly invites the audience to collude in and enjoy the sodomitical joke (1994: 54–5). The play constantly asks the audience to understand male homosocial relations, such as friendship, in homoerotic terms.[1] Quomodo instructs his creature, Shortyard, to don the guise of the gallant, Master Blastfield, and tempt Easy to his fall: 'Drink drunk with him, creep into bed to him, kiss him and undo him, my sweet spirit' (I, ii, 129–31). John Rainolde's *Th'Overthrow of Stage-Plays* (1599) warned that 'beautiful boys by kissing do sting and power secretly in a kind of poison, the poison of incontinency'. The financial bond they enter as friends is sexualised by Shortyard/Blastfield through a pun that links the open purse and their intimacy as bedfellows: 'our purses are brothers; we desire but equal fortunes; in a word, we're man and wife; they can but lie together, and so do we' (II, iii, 171–4). When Easy is abandoned by his 'sweet bedfellow' (II, iii, 151) we are made aware of the extent of the 'sting' as 'Easy is "sick" with "a great desire" for "his bedfellow"' (III, v, 47–51; Leinwand 1994: 57–8).

Much of this erotic punning plays on the mechanics of the costume which takes us once more to the transvestite boy actor and the practices of the early modern stage where the women's parts were taken by boy actors. The transformation of the Country Wench into a city whore in *Michaelmas Term* is achieved through the semantic power of clothes; the Country Wench must take off and forget her 'wholesome weeds . . .,/ And welcome silks, where lies disease and wants' (I, iii, 55–6). This 'alteration' of the Country Wench through apparel leaves 'her' open to sodomitical punning that plays on the eroticised body of the boy actor beneath the costume: the tirewoman arranges the hair of the boy actor/Country Wench so that it is worn 'like a mock-face behind; 'tis such an Italian world, many men know not before from behind' (III, i, 20–

1). Similarly, in *Mad World, My Masters*, when Follywit disguises himself as the Courtesan in order to dupe his grandfather, the actor becomes the object of homoerotic punning. His confederate, Mawworm, makes a joke about sodomising Follywit that plays on the cross-dressed body: 'I'll give thee thy due behind thy back' (III, iii, 125–6). As Leinwand points out, 'anal sex crosses gender boundaries insofar as all are left spread open' (1994: 56). The joke also participates in contemporary condemnation of the current fashion for women wearing the male doublet, which implies they therefore assume the prerogatives of men: ''Tis an Amazonian time – you shall have women shortly tread their husbands' (III, iii, 118–20). As we shall see in the discussion of *The Roaring Girl* in the following chapter, these jests speak to a notion of gender in which gender identity is performed, rather than inherent in the body (see below, pp. 49–54).

If boy actors provided ready-made figures for liminality in terms of gender and sexuality, they could also perform a similar function in terms of generational issues. One of the themes of *Mad World, My Masters*, for example, is the transition from youth to adulthood which is dramatised in the play through the mechanisms of primogeniture and inheritance. Follywit, the heir to Sir Bounteous Progress, has been left in penury, while his grandfather lavishes his hospitality on strangers and on his mistress. The young man therefore plots to take his inheritance from under Progress's nose. With grandson pitted against grandfather, the generation gap is dramatically widened. This allows Middleton to portray a situation which emphasises the sterility of the older generation, who squander their own patrimony, beggaring their heirs rather than generating wealth for future generations. Follywit rails against his grandfather's venery: 'Oh fie, in your crinkling days, grandsire, keep a courtesan to hinder your grandchild! 'Tis against nature, i'faith, and I hope you'll be weary on't' (IV, iii, 48–51).

The company of boy actors at the fashionable indoor Paul's Theatre exerted an influence over Middleton's plays written for this company, from the inclusion of song to puns exploiting the liminality of the boy actor. One way of understanding this interrelationship is to recognise the profoundly collaborative nature of the early modern theatre. Middleton's city comedies were commissioned for the Children of Paul's, written with an eye to their particular theatrical conditions, and revised by the company in performance. These plays were therefore not simply the finished product of an individual author, but produced through a complex dialogue between dramatist, playing company, and audience.

CITY COMEDY: THE CULTURE OF CREDIT AND HOMOSOCIALITY

The term 'credit' recurs throughout these city comedies. Master Easy in *Michaelmas Term* says guilelessly, 'It seems you're well known, Master Blastfield, and your credit very spacious here i'th'city' (II, i, 101–2). The young gentleman, Witgood, in *Trick to Catch the Old One*, is accosted by his creditors and begs their silence about his debts since, 'I am to raise a little money in the city toward the setting forth of myself, for mine own credit and your comfort' (III, I, 30–2). Follywit, a version of the prodigal son who has fallen into bad company in the city, says of his companions in *Mad World, My Masters* 'how can they keep their countenance that have lost their credits?' (I, i, 33–4). Credit is being used in two interrelated ways across these plays. The first meaning arises from the Latin *credo* which means to trust, including to entrust something to someone; and to believe, to place confidence in someone. Thus, 'credit' is used in all these passages primarily as another word for 'reputation', which in turn refers to the individual's trustworthiness. It is an individual's credit that encourages others to have confidence in them, and to entrust them with information, objects or even money. This brings us to the second meaning of credit, which is an economic one and arises out of the social power derived from having a reputation for trustworthiness: to lend on credit is to trust an individual with goods or money on the faith of future payment (*OED*, 3a). Witgood needs to be seen as a man of credit, in possession of a trustworthy reputation, if he is to have the power 'to raise a little money in the city': without one he cannot have the other.

The historical process that city comedies have been said to dramatise as a genre is the transition from a feudal marketplace to the market economy of early capitalism (Wells 1981: 37–60). Recent work by the historian Craig Muldrew has decisively challenged this historical trajectory and his findings have important implications for the study of city plays. Early modern society, he argues, was not a capitalist society, nor was its economy primarily monetary. Rather, its economic transactions operated within a culture of credit based on the 'currency of reputation' – a 'highly mobile and circulating language of judgement' about the creditworthiness of individuals and households (Muldrew 1998: 2–3). The obligations of a credit economy structured early modern society:

> People were constantly involved in tangled webs of economic and social dependency which linked their households to others within communities and beyond, through the numerous reciprocal bonds of trust in all of the millions of bargains they transacted. Although society was divided by hierarchical gradations of status, wealth and patriarchy, it was still bound together by contractually negotiated credit relationships made all over the social scale and this introduced some limited degree of equality to social exchanges. (Muldrew 1998: 97)

Given its all-pervasiveness, we should not be surprised that this economy of obligation structures the plots and plotting of *Michaelmas Term* and *Trick to Catch the Old One*. In *Michaelmas Term*, the 'currency of reputation' has been devalued within the city to the extent that the systems of credit can be perverted and short-circuited. The processes of judgement no longer have a firm basis in the ability to fulfil obligations, whether social or economic. The transformation of Andrew Gruel into Andrew Lethe, whose name refers to the waters of oblivion, signifies this process of cultural forgetfulness of the reciprocal bonds of trust which should bind the community. Lethe cannot remember and therefore does not 'know' acquaintances, thereby preventing the possibility of lasting bonds of trust and fellowship forming. In a society where it is now a commonplace that 'Esteem is made of such dizzy metal' (I, ii, 180), as Lethe notes sententiously, it is possible to attract gifts from 'friends' and so 'keep a house with nothing' (I, ii, 217). The play imagines a culture in which credit is over-extended; reputations have no firm basis in creditworthiness, either in the moral and financial sense.

Land does hold the possibility of securing credit and providing security for social and economic transactions. However, as the elite spent more time in London, the anxiety arose that the gentry were squandering their estates, the very basis of their social identity, and selling their lands in the country to buy a lifestyle in the city. These anxieties are evident in the names of the two city gallants, Rearage (in arrears or debt) and Salewood (sold woods on his estate); the potential fate of Easy's estate is similarly spelt out in the name Shortyard takes when gulling this gentleman – Blastfield. This beggaring of the country to feed city appetites is figured in the distortion and corruption of the bonds of obligation and trust that bind communities and should ensure the proper circulation of goods and capital between the country and the city.

Act II, scene i plays out this dynamic. The contrast between the simple virtues of the country and the sophisticated corruptions of the city goes back to classical writers. Middleton reworks this commonplace for his times by foregrounding the economic dimension of the relations between the country and the city. Easy laments that he has spent 'all my rent till next quarter' (II, i, 79), while at the end of this scene, Rearage and Salewood are delighted by the news that their country tenants have arrived, presumably bringing rents to fund their city spending. The scene is set in a private room in a London tavern, a social space identified with city recreation and conspicuous consumption. Here the gallants – Rearage, Salewood, Easy and Shortyard (disguised as Master Blastfield) – play at dice. In order to gain Easy's confidence, Shortyard pretends to be a close friend of Easy's Essex neighbour, Master Alsup, and thus is 'bound in my love to him [Alsup] to see you furnished' (II, i, 17–18). This is a notorious cony-catching trick practised by the petty thieves of the London underworld, and fictionalised in pamphlets, such as Robert Greene's *The Art of Cony Catching*. The trick works by mobilising the reciprocal bonds of trust and obligation that are integral to the early modern culture of credit, but in a relatively anonymous city environment in which these bonds have become attenuated. Once Shortyard has secured Easy's trust, then he binds his prey tighter by extending credit, while at the same time renegotiating the terms of the 'currency of reputation', to ensure that Easy over-extends himself financially. When Easy loses heavily and wants to stop gaming, Shortyard furnishes him with funds in order to maintain his credit in the city: '[Y]ou shall not give out so meanly of yourself in my company for a million. Make such privy to your disgrace? You're a gentleman of fair fortunes; keep me your reputation' (II, i, 39–42). The 'care of your reputation here in town' (II, i, 44–5) does not involve care for one's substance – in other words, one's morality, capital, or estate – but rather maintaining the appearance of having means through conspicuous consumption, whether it is gaming, entertaining or the latest fashions.

Once Easy has bought into Shortyard's new city 'currency of reputation', he can be drawn into forming a 'bad' credit relationship with the draper, Quomodo. Gentlemen were advised to befriend merchants for reasons of good finance, 'both in exchanging, returning, and borrowing of money, and in keeping credit, if money be not present' (Brathwaite 1617: 18). For this relationship between gentleman and merchant to be mutually beneficial, trust must be secured. But Easy is too easy and falls victim to Quomodo's commodity scam. Quomodo and Easy play out the stereotypes of the avaricious merchant and prodigal aristocrat to the point of parody. It is fascinating to observe the way this gulling plot unfolds through, and exploits the expansive chains of obligation that structure the credit economy. Quomodo complains that Easy, by failing to meet the terms of their contract, has made 'me wound my credit, fail in my commodities, bring my state into suspicion. For the breaking of your day to me has broken my day to others' (III, iv, 137–40). The problem for Easy is that his credit and friends are in the country, in Essex. Shortyard, now disguised as a Sergeant come to arrest Easy for breaking his bond, quickly disabuses Easy of the belief that his Essex neighbour, Master Alsup, can aid him 'in London, where now your business lies; honesty from Essex will be a great while a-coming, sir' (III, iii, 50–2). Easy, seeking out 'friends i'th'city' (III, iv, 184) to bail him, enters into a further bond with alderman's deputies (alias Shortyard and Falselight). It prompts a darkly comic scene in which Easy binds himself to the contract because of the 'aldermen's' fears that he will prove true to the type of the prodigal gentlemen, thus cleverly shifting the risk from Easy to themselves: 'Come, we'll make a desperate voyage once again; we'll try his honesty, and take his single bond, of body, goods, and lands' (III, iv, 239–41).

It is possible to read Quomodo's appropriation of Easy's lands in terms of the triumph of merchant values of thrift (and cunning) over gentry profligacy (and folly). The canny merchant vows to ensure his son's patrimony in contrast to the prodigal gentry represented by Easy: 'And for the thrifty and covetous hopes I have in my son and heir, Sim Quomodo, that he will never trust his land in wax and parchment, as many gentlemen have done before him' (IV, i, 43–7). Yet Quomodo's dream of what he will do with Easy's land contradicts this mercantile ideal of thrifty productivity. Instead, he fantasises a life of leisure and festivity:

> A fine journey in the Whitsun holidays, i'faith, to ride down with a number of citizens, and their wives . . . I and little Thomasine i'th'middle, our son and heir, Sim Quomodo, in a peach-colour taffeta jacket, some horse-length or long yard before us. There will be a fine show on's, I can tell you, where we citizens will laugh and lie down, get all our wives with child against a bank, and get up again. (IV, i, 77–85)

Since land for Quomodo represents aristocratic ease, once he possesses it he begins to turn into Easy and take his place in the plot – the trickster becomes the gull. This reversal culminates in the signing of the contract (Middleton 2000: 23, 44; Leonidas 2007: 1–4). Just as Easy signed the original contract for 'fashion's sake', rather than with a sound business head, so too Quomodo signs away his rights to his household for a 'jest' (V, iii, 72). Within the patriarchal logic of the play, the 'death' of fathers renders the estate vulnerable (Chakravorty 1996: 49–50). With Quomodo's mock-death, Shortyard is free to prey on Sim and deprive him of his patrimony. Easy, in turn, is transformed through his marriage to the wily citizen's wife. It is, in fact, Thomasine's agency that restores his estate. Yet, the marriage is brief, since Thomasine must return to her husband, and thus does not offer a new, reformed model of community or the possibility of social renewal. One of the difficulties in making judgements about Middleton's satiric city comedies is that there are no obvious heroes, all are flawed.

Trick to Catch the Old One, in some ways, is a more straightforward play. The main protagonist Theodorus Witgood, as his name suggests, is a more positive character than his counterparts in *Michaelmas Term* and *Mad World*, Richard Easy and Dick Follywit (Gill 1983: 27). Witgood is at a different stage of plotting and characterisation from Easy. Whereas the audience witnesses Easy's folly and fall, Witgood begins the play already fallen: he is reputed the 'common rioter' (I, i, 111) who has consumed his patrimony through dissolute behaviour and mortgaged his lands to his uncle, Pecunious Lucre. The 'trick' to catch the old one is Witgood's plot to recover his estate and his wit, rather than folly, drives the play (Chakravorty 1996: 57–8). Lucre is a comparable figure to Quomodo in that, along with his rival, Walkadine Hoard, he represents the avaricious merchant. Both characters are the traditional New Comedy blocking figures – 'the old one'. The sterility identified with this role is represented in economic terms: as Eric Leonidas notes, Lucre and Quomodo are 'unproductively acquisitive' (2007: 7). In this way they are related to the usurer, represented in *Trick* by the colourful self-made man, Harry Dampit. Usury in the early modern period was understood as a form of economic cannibalism. Money and goods are not productively kept in circulation for the benefit of the community, but hoarded by the individual (Sullivan 2002: 45–7). Lucre's usurious nature is symbolised by his willingness to prey on his kin, as Hoard exclaims, somewhat hypocritically:

Thou that canst defeat thy own nephew, Lucre, lap his lands into bonds and take the extremity of thy kindred's forfeitures because he's a rioter, a waste-thrift, a brothel-master, and so forth – what may a stranger expect from thee but *vulnera dilacerata*, as the poet says, dilacerate dealing? (I, iii, 26–31)

The credit economy is communal rather than individualist in orientation and relies on the circulation of credit to bind individuals, households and communities through reciprocal bonds of trust. Witgood's skilful manipulation of the currency of reputation in order to restore his credit and his estate is relatively sociable when compared to the scheming of his usurious anti-types, Lucre, Hoard and Dampit. The circulation of money and goods ideally is generative and secures the wider interests of the community. Sir

Bounteous Progress in *Mad World, My Masters* may keep an open house and embody the principle of hospitality, however, since he prefers to entertain strangers indiscriminately rather than prudently extending his network of credit, the bonds of kinship and community have become parasitic and corrupted:

> [T]his cousin and that cousin puts in for a dish of meat – a man knows not till he make a feast how many varlets he feeds. Acquaintances swarm in every corner, like flies at Bartholomewtide that come up with the drovers. 'Sfoot, I think they smell my kitchen seven mile about. (V, i, 4–9)

Witgood cannot achieve his ends alone, and enters into a partnership with his Courtesan.[2] The play appears to stage Witgood's initial violent rejection of the Courtesan, only to reverse it and to emphasise that he is bound to his fellow prodigal by social and moral obligations: 'I do thee wrong/To make thee sin, and then to chide thee for't' (I, i, 41–2). Their partnership is comparable to the brief marriage of Easy and Thomasine, the good-natured and lusty citizen wife, which also plays a key role in the reformed prodigal's restoration to his estate. In *Trick*, in particular, this strategic and affectionate partnership between Witgood and the Courtesan displaces the traditional love relationship between the gentleman and the chaste maid in romantic comedy. As his 'aunt' (slang for prostitute) does indeed become his aunt at the end of the play, thus the restoration of networks of credit is mirrored in the witty extension and reconfiguration of kinship relations.

It should be pointed out that, although female characters like the Courtesan and Thomasine do have a limited agency in these plays, the culture of credit is a homosocial formation. Women function as objects of exchange between men to be transacted within this system. Witgood is able to raise credit by using the promise of marriage to the wealthy widow as security. When Hoard contemplates the benefits of his marriage, he does so through the trope of the woman's body as landscape:

> Not only a wife large in possessions, but spacious in content. She's rich, she's young, she's fair, she's wise. When I wake, I

think of her lands – that revives me. When I go to bed, I dream
of her beauty, and that's enough for me. She's worth four
hundred a year in her very smock, if a man knew how to use
it. (IV, iv, 5–11)

The irony is that the wife, as an economic and sexual object, is in
the same structural position within this economy as the prostitute.

The homosocial culture of credit and obligation provides the
idiom of and structures the plotting of these satirical London plays.
Its values are attenuated or perverted by the negative and fragmen-
tary forces of an accumulative individualism. Yet, while the materialist ethos of this mode of individualism is represented as a negative
social force, these plays celebrate the virtuosity, energy and wit of
the trickster.

LIVING BY WIT: THE PRODIGAL AND TRICKSTER

Over a decade after his death, Middleton continued to be admired
for his wit: 'Facetious Middleton, thy witty muse,/Hath pleasèd all
that books or men peruse' (*Wit's Recreations* (1640: sig. B7v)). Wit
had a range of meanings in the early modern period. It denoted both
a quality of mind and a mode of expression, in particular, a clever,
skilful way with words. To be possessed of wit was to have rhetorical and social power. In his *Art of Rhetoric* (1553), Thomas Wilson
wrote of the power of the wit: 'Now then who is he, at whom all men
wonder, and stand in amaze, at the view of his wit and whose doings
are best esteemed and who[m] do we most reverence, and [account]
half a God among men' (quoted in Biester 1997: 10). The power,
inventiveness and ingenuity of wit in Middleton's plays is integral
to the process of plotting in the sense of both the dramatist's skill
and the 'tricks' devised by the witty protagonists in the plays.
Game-playing and plotting requires a quick wit which in turn
relies on an ability to improvise and change tactics. Witgood, in particular, is very adept at taking advantage of rapidly changing
events. The trickster figure is a tactical improviser in that he is frequently depicted as having to make it up as he goes along, typically
because of the absence of social structures or in order to disable

their operation (de Certeau 1988: 18). The trickster's creative, improvisatory skills are also those to which the dramatist lays claim. It is therefore highly appropriate that when Follywit plays his final trick, robbing his grandfather and giving his pursuers the slip, he does so by staging a comedy, a play-within-a-play called *The Slip* (Chakravorty 1996: 55). This metatheatrical moment sets up a witty equation between the trickster and the playwright.

The 'trick', as *The Slip* foregrounds, is part of the structure of the traditional comic plot. It is a device that characterises the New Comedy plot in which a trick must be devised by the protagonist in order to overcome the patriarchal blocking figure. As we have seen in *Michaelmas Term* and *Trick to Catch the Old One*, Middleton translates the New Comedy plot into the materialist and mercantile terms of the city. His blocking figures are avaricious merchants rather than paternal figures, per se, and the protagonist is a prodigal gentleman who has squandered his credit and lost his patrimony to the city. In the case of *Mad World, My Masters*, this scenario is played out in the subplot, where it is given a sexual rather than an economic rendition, which plays on the city commonplace, voiced by Quomodo in *Michaelmas Term*, that gentlemen are 'busy 'bout our wives, we 'bout their lands' (I, ii, 112). The prodigal figure, Penitent Brothel, desires the citizen wife, Mistress Harebrain, and uses the wit of the courtesan, Frank Gullman, to gain access to her. In the main plot, the young prodigal gentleman, Dick Follywit, sets out to trick his grandfather, Sir Bounteous Progress, who acts as a type of blocking figure, in that he keeps his heir in penury while lavishing great expense on entertaining the nobility. Follywit plays a trickster version of the prodigal son when, disguised as Lord Owemuch, he is unwittingly entertained by his grandfather with an elaborate banquet, 'the fatted calf'. Middleton improvises on the conventional prodigal plot. Sir Bounteous Progress is a festive character, identified with traditional rural and aristocratic customs of hospitality and charity. The problem is that he embodies these values in an extreme form, resulting in the paradox that his bounty is unproductive and sterile. Like Easy's prodigal consumption of his lands to play the gallant in the city, Progress's excessive and indiscriminate hospitality beggars his heir.

Wit marked out its possessor as a man of education and quality, and was a signifier for social and intellectual capital. Andrew Lethe's lack of real substance as a social actor in *Michaelmas Term* is signified by his lack of rhetorical skill. He tries for a piece of wit, but cannot rhyme and others must supply his deficiencies (I, ii, 194–205). Follywit is admired for his ingenious wit. When Sir Bounteous prefers his grandson to Lord Owemuch's service, his main recommendation is his 'wit': 'He's carried many things cleanly' (II, i, 148–9). The stage joke, which confirms Follywit's ingenuity, is that Lord Owemuch is Follywit in disguise. That said, Follywit's tricks are of a different order from those of Witgood, as their names suggest. Whereas Witgood's trick has a communal impulse, Follywit's tricks are plain anti-social. Middleton borrows motifs from the type of humours comedy that Jonson popularised on stage with his *Every Man In His Humour* and *Every Man Out of His Humour*. Hence, the humour that Master Harebrain must be tricked out of is jealousy, Penitent Brothel's is lust, and Sir Bounteous's is indiscriminate hospitality. Penitent Brothel's soliloquy on folly, delivered just after Follywit has appeared on stage with his fellow pranksters, relates how Follywit is so enamoured of his own wit, it has become his humour:

> Here's a mad-brain o'th'first, whose pranks scorn to have precedents, to be second to any . . . a fellow whose only glory is to be prime of the company, to be sure of which he maintains all the rest. He's the carrion, and they the kites that gorge upon him. (I, i, 92–9)

Brought low by his parasitical companions, Ancient Hoboy and particularly Lieutenant Mawworm (whose name denotes an intestinal worm), Follywit is the victim rather than master of his own pranks (Chakravorty 1996: 52–3).

The tricks Follywit plays on his grandfather possess a certain viciousness. The play clearly presents his pranks as criminal in nature and intent. His companions are disbanded or disgraced soldiers, no longer bound by military codes of honour, and instead have taken their violence to the streets to become types of 'roaring boys'. As we shall see in relation to *The Roaring Girl*, this renegade

military subculture was closely associated with the criminal underworld in early modern pamphlets (see below, p. 57). Follywit
becomes a desperate thief who will hazard all not simply to trick but
to defraud his grandfather:

> We now arrive at the most ticklish point, to rob and take our
> ease, to be thieves and lie by't. Look to't, lads, it concerns
> every man's gullet. I'll not have the jest spoiled, that's certain,
> though it hazard a windpipe. I'll either go like a lord as I came,
> or be hanged like a thief as I am, and that's my resolution. (II,
> iv, 97–102)

Follywit shows no fondness or pity for his grandfather when he
binds him. Rather the grandson nastily mocks the impotence of the
old man: '[N]othing comes stiff from an old man but money; and
he may well stand upon that, when he has nothing else to stand
upon' (II, iv, 69–71). Later, disguised as a bound Lord Owemuch
pretending to call for the aid of servants, Follywit mocks his
grandfather with derogatory names denoting sexual deficiency –
Singlestone and Simcod. Bounteous's refusal to answer to these
jibes carries a note of pathos: 'I am not brought so low, though I be
old' (II, vi, 32–3). The traditional conflict between younger and
older generations that structures the New Comedy plot becomes a
battle over virility. Yet Sir Bounteous is not Lucre, and regularly
speaks of his fondness for his grandson. The trick is played out with
such dark cruelty by Follywit, it takes the audience into an uncomfortable comic field.

The play introduces issues that will take centre stage in
Middleton and William Rowley's *A New Way to Please You, or The
Old Law*, first performed around 1618, and recently revived in a
wonderfully wicked production by the RSC in 2005. The 'old law'
is a decree that all men over the age of eighty and women over sixty
must be executed as they have served their usefulness and must give
way to the younger generation. Simonides joys in the impending
execution of his parents: '[H]ere's a spring for young plants to
flourish!' (I, i, 72). Although it is a trick devised by the Duke to rein-
force the patriarchal order at the level of family and state, the
humour of this 'wild play', as Charles Lamb described it

(Middleton and Rowley 2005: xix), is so black and anarchic that it unsettles the tragicomic ending, when the 'dead' parents are restored. The 2005 RSC production emphasised the black and anarchic humour of the play and intensified the generational conflict by depicting Simonides and his friends as part of a hedonistic and amoral youth culture more interested in clubbing and immediate gratification than the responsibilities identified with the older generation. The programme notes included a photograph of skinheads body-slamming – an image that associates 'today's youth' with anarchic and violent energies. On the facing page were thought-pieces from the *Guardian* writers Alexander Chancellor and Annalisa Barbieri on the contemporary meanings of 'old age', thereby mediating the way the audience viewed the play through these images and issues.

As we have seen, the wit of women characters is fundamental to the success of tricks in Middleton's city comedies. Middleton's female wits are very different from Shakespeare's witty heroines, such as Rosalind in *As You Like It* or Beatrice in *Much Ado About Nothing*. Middleton's most effective wits are the courtesans – the Courtesan in *Trick* and Frank Gullman in *Mad World*.[3] Frank Gullman's name suggests a paradox, that of the honest or frank whore, who is none too honest. Frank Gullman is Follywit's counterpart, although she lacks his folly. Penitent Brothel says of her: 'The wit of man wanes and decreases soon,/But women's wit is ever at full moon' (III, ii, 175–6). One could argue that, in this example, female wit is conceived negatively since it is her trick that opens the citizen wife to adultery – a 'trick' that is repeated by Livia in *Women Beware Women*. Thus it would seem the female wit is a sexually unruly woman who is identified with lechery. The recurrent analogy between sex and death tends to find its point of reference in Frank Gullman and is realised in the moralising logic of her trickster plot, which ends when Penitent Brothel is visited by a succubus in the likeness of Mistress Harebrain. Thus cured of his humour, he gives vent to a nasty piece of misogyny: 'To dote on weakness, slime, corruption, woman?' (IV, i, 18). A useful comparison can be made with the Country Wench in *Michaelmas Term*. Just as the Country Wench is transformed by her costume into a gentlewoman, Frank Gullman employs her superior acting ability to play the part of modest and 'sweet virgin' (III, i, 28). Her final trick is to gull Follywit into marriage by adeptly performing the role of 'a perfect maid' (IV, vi, 77) – this is the trick that finally catches Follywit. It too could be seen to mirror the punishment of Andrew Lethe in *Michaelmas Term*, who is forced to marry his whore. It is also a trick that rebounds on Frank: marriage would have made her 'honest' (IV, vi, 149), but she finds that she has married a thief. However, as her mother points out, 'Comfort thyself. Thou art beforehand with him, daughter' (V, ii, 269–70). The marriage of Frank Gullman and Follywit is very different from that of Lethe and the Country Wench in that it is positively conceived within the comic ending of *Mad World* and is a witty improvisation on the New Comedy plot. The obstacle that the blocking figure, Sir Bounteous, represents to the union of the lovers is financial and erotic, but in the sense that the beloved was his mistress. The closing speeches travesty the concept of marriage as a homosocial exchange between men by jesting that the woman being transacted has been sexually possessed by the grandfather before being passed on to the grandson. Sir Bounteous jokes beneficently: 'The best is, sirrah, you pledge none but me./And since I drink the top, take her and hark,/I spice the bottom with a thousand mark.' To which Follywit good-naturedly replies: 'By my troth, she is as good a cup of nectar as any bachelor needs to sip at./Tut, give me gold, it makes amends for vice./Maids without coin are caudles without spice' (V, ii, 306–12).

Since the union of Frank Gullman and Follywit is coupled with the reconciliation of grandfather and grandson, the comic ending indicates the way that unruly social and erotic desires can be balanced with the need for communal stability. Leonidas makes a similar point about the ending of *Trick*, which celebrates the reformation of the two prodigals, Witgood and the Courtesan (2007: 27). The Courtesan is arguably a more comfortable version of the female wit for patriarchal society than Frank Gullman. Whereas Frank operates independently and has a subplot devoted to her wit, the Courtesan operates in unison with Witgood, who describes her as his 'best invention' (I, i, 44) both his creature or agent and his wife in wit, in that together they will conceive and breed a trick: 'What trick is not an embryo first' (I, i, 57). The Courtesan claims her part in this metaphor: 'Though you beget, 'tis I must help to breed. . .

I'd fain conceive it' (I, i, 60–1). Middleton is here punning on the derivation of *ingenium* (wit) from *geno*, meaning 'to beget' and 'bring forth', thus denoting the male poet's powers of conception. By contrast, Frank Gullman is mistress of her own inventions. Her superior acting and plotting skills, particularly her ability to improvise, are aligned with the 'facetious wit' of the poet dramatist.

The female wits of Middleton's city comedies look forward to his later tragicomedy, *No Wit, No Help Like a Woman's*. Yet this figure also finds its negative expression in Livia in *Women Beware Women*. She uses her wit in a similar fashion to Frank Gulman, who trains Mistress Harebrain in the arts of adultery, and facilitates her liaison with Penitent Brothel. So, too, Livia is instrumental in the corruption of Bianca and acts as a bawd to her niece, smoothing the way for her incestuous affair with her brother. Genre does make a difference in the treatment of this figure – in the comedies, female wit, on the whole, is aligned with the movement towards marriage, whereas in the tragedies it has a corrosive effect on familial and social structures. Moll in Middleton and Dekker's *The Roaring Girl* is similarly a version of the female trickster, with the added dimension of cross-dressing. While Moll, like other comic female wits, facilitates the romantic marriage, her transvestism is part of a wider destabilising of the patriarchal imperatives that govern conservative gender discourses and insist on and uphold the authority of husbands, fathers, and manly men.

NOTES

1. Homosocial 'describes social bonds between persons of the same sex'. In its masculine form, it is most often applied to forms of male bonding, such as friendship, and to describe 'the structure of men's relations with other men'. Patriarchy is understood as a male homosocial formation since its structures enable men to promote the interests of men. See Eve Kosofsky Sedgwick, *Between Men: English Literature and Male Homosocial Desire* (New York: Columbia University Press, 1985), pp. 1–3.
2. Valerie Wayne's edition for *The Collected Works* gives this character the name 'Jane' on the basis of her assumed name, 'Jane

Meddler', although as she points out, 'We never learn her "real" name.' Wayne gives her a 'familiar proper name' as part of a feminist strategy to individualise the character, 'so that the subject positions of the character are associated with a name rather than a misleading occupational or sexual category' (Middleton 2007: I, 375–6). I have retained 'Courtesan' as it foregrounds the misogyny of the play's discourses and the contradictory construction of her character.

3. Peter Saccio's edition of *Mad World* for the *Collected Works* uses the title 'The Courtesan' for 'Frank Gullman'. I am following the practice of earlier editions in using 'Frank Gullman' to distinguish this character from the Courtesan in *A Trick*.

CHAPTER 3

Authorship, Collaboration and the London Theatre: Middleton and Dekker, *The Roaring Girl*

The Roaring Girl is the culmination of a successful partnership between Middleton and Thomas Dekker. The play, performed by Prince Henry's Men at the Fortune Theatre in 1611, introduced a London celebrity, the larger-than-life character of Moll Cutpurse, to the public stage. 'Mad Moll' dominates this city comedy. She links the conventional New Comedy plot, in which the two upper-class lovers, Sebastian Wengrave and Mary Fitzallard, overcome the opposition of his hard-hearted father, and the multi-faceted city comedy which sets in play the various plots and counter-plots of gallants, citizens and their wives. In the last decades of the twentieth century, feminist critics turned their attention to Moll because of the questions this figure raised about women and gender, and the relationship between gender and performance. The play continues to attract critical attention, from those interested in early theatre production and collaboration to those studying the staging of London, in all its early modern complexity.

AUTHORSHIP AND COLLABORATION: THE PARTNERSHIP OF DEKKER AND MIDDLETON

Dekker and Middleton had much in common. Both were distinctly London writers, who wrote city comedies, civic pageants and sharp urban pamphlets. Middleton's name first appears in the surviving records of early modern drama alongside Dekker's in 1602 as part of a team of writers assigned to write a play, *Caesar's Fall*, now lost. Two years later, Middleton wrote another play with Dekker, *The Honest Whore, Part 1* (1604). When theatres closed due to the terrible plague raging through London in 1603, the two wrote pamphlets together: *News from Gravesend* (1604) and *The Meeting of Gallants at an Ordinary* (1604). Dekker and Middleton were chosen, alongside Ben Jonson and others, to contribute to the civic entertainments for the long-awaited triumphant entry of the new king, James I, into the City of London, which had been delayed by plague.

Honest Whore, Part 1 was part of Philip Henslowe's repertoire for Prince Henry's Men at the Fortune. In early March 1604, Henslowe advanced Dekker and Middleton £5 to complete 'their play called the patient man and the honest whore'. Seven years later, Middleton and Dekker co-wrote *The Roaring Girl*, again for Henslowe and Prince Henry's Men at the Fortune. Since both partnerships were for the same company, it is likely that Henslowe played a part in arranging the collaboration. Collaboration was firmly embedded in the institutional practices of the early modern theatre. Even so, since Middleton and Dekker chose to work together outside the theatre, writing at least two pamphlets collaboratively, it suggests that their partnership was something more than a fact of their working environment, and that they found working together both congenial and stimulating. Mark Hutchings and Tony Bromham point to their 'compatibility', both in terms of their staunch Protestant politics and their fascination with London: 'More than any of their contemporaries, they took London as their subject, reflecting but more importantly *refracting* London, showing it in its many guises, good and ill' (Hutchings and Bromham 2008: 40).

The majority of Renaissance dramatists co-wrote plays at some stage in their career – Shakespeare, Jonson, Dekker, Middleton, Webster, Ford, the list goes on. Collaboration challenges many assumptions about the nature of authorship. The word 'author' derives from the Latin *auctor*, meaning an originator. The author is understood to be the sole producer of original works and therefore is a privileged source of authority in determining the text's meaning and its provenance. This notion of authorship has become enshrined in editorial practices. It is conventional editorial practice to try to identify the authoritative text of a play by plotting a history of textual transmission in order to ascertain which edition is closest to the author's own manuscript of the play-text, and thus can be said to be closest to the author's original intent. Critics of this type of editorial practice argue that it is based on a modern rather than early modern concept of authorship (Brooks 2000: 8–9, 153–4). Michel Foucault, in his influential essay, 'What is an Author?', argued that an ideology of authorship which privileges the individual as the singular creative source of the text only became dominant in the eighteenth century (1979: 141–60). The early modern author did not 'own' his work in the same way as a modern author. In the case of literary texts, the author may have owned the manuscript of his work, but he had no legal rights over it. Once it was sold to the publisher or stationer, and entered in the Stationers' Register, the copyright was held by the stationer and not the author. This does not mean that authors did not have a sense that their intellectual labour belonged to them – they did, and they frequently complained their work was stolen by unscrupulous publishers. However, it was not a right that had a legal or institutional basis (Rose 1993: 9–25). In the case of dramatic texts, once the manuscript of the play was passed over to the theatre companies it was owned by the company rather than the playwright. It is an open question as to what kind of role the writer played in shaping the text for the stage, and then for publication. As we have seen in the case of Shakespeare and Jonson, this probably varied according to the individual circumstances of the author (see above, p. 16; Hutchings and Bromham 2008: 28–30).

A number of theatre historians over the past decade have argued that collaboration was the dominant model of textual production within the early modern theatre, and that 'authorship' itself was a communal, collaborative practice (Masten 1997: 375–6). Many now argue that the production of plays cannot be encompassed within the single author model, but is a thoroughly collaborative process. As the play-text makes the transition from the stage to the printed page, it moves through a series of collaborations:

between playwrights, between playwrights and playing companies, between playwrights and actors, between playing
companies and scribes, between playing companies and
censors, between playing companies and publishers, between
publishers and printers, between printers and compositors.
(Brooks 2000: 1)

The play is therefore to be understood not as the expression of the
individual author's original idea, or his personality or views. Rather,
it is part of the transactions of the early modern stage. The value of
this approach is that it draws our attention to the organisation,
structures and practices of the early modern playhouse.

There is little evidence for the precise nature of collaboration in
the playhouse and the evidence that exists 'suggests a variety of
methods existed'. One criticism of earlier assumptions about
collaborative practices, which take their cue from G. E. Bentley
(*The Profession of the Dramatist in Shakespeare's Time* (Princeton:
Princeton University Press, 1971)), is that it continues to prioritise
the individual author by arguing that collaboration usually took the
form of dramatists writing different scenes. The critical goal is
therefore to separate out and distinguish the work of the individual
dramatists (Nochimson 2001: 42–6). Against such a ' "disintegra-
tionist" approach to the text', Hutchings and Bromham put
forward a model drawn from accommodation theory to argue that
'the process of collaborative composition, the marrying-together of
components, characters and stage business, would suggest plausi-
bly that writers reworked not only their "own" text to fit in with
others', but also revised that of others' (2008: 35; see also Cathcart
2000: para 11). Plays are exemplary dialogic texts at a number of
levels: they are multi-voiced in structure, in performance, and in
production.[1] In the case of *The Roaring Girl*, the hands of both
dramatists can be found in the majority of scenes. It suggests a close
working relationship perhaps along the lines of Robert Daborne's
account of collaborating with Philip Massinger and Nathan Field,
which involved 'a great deal of Time in conference about [the] plot',
and may have also involved exchanging ideas and influencing each
other in terms of subject-matter and even 'choice of expression'
(Nochimson 2002: 51; Cathcart 2000: para. 11).

Where does this leave the individual author? Gordon McMullan, while advocating a collaborative model, retains a notion of 'the distinctiveness of the individual as an *orchestrator* of voices' (1994: 155). One of the skills of a collaborative performance is to tune your voice to another's, so that it does not sound an overly dissonant note within the whole, and yet nonetheless remains distinctive. Heather Anne Hirschfeld similarly reconciles a notion of individual style within a collaborative model of authorship by arguing that dramatists in the period were self-consciously developing recognisable personal styles and were increasingly identified with particular dramatic styles (2004: 23–7). The most obvious example in *The Roaring Girl* is the canting scene in scene x that draws extensively on Dekker's rogue pamphlets. It is possible that those in the audience familiar with his pamphlets would recognise Dekker's voice in this scene. Collaboration was a partnership that required writers to engage with and negotiate each others' style. In *The Roaring Girl*, the variant dramatic styles may be harmonised, yet there is still space for Dekker to showcase his individual style in scene x, which suggests that collaboration could incorporate competition. Collaboration was a particularised activity, and different writing partnerships had their own dynamics. In Chapter 7, we will take up these questions again in the discussion of the creative partnership of Middleton and William Rowley.

PERFORMANCE AND GENDER: MARY FRITH ON THE LONDON STAGE

The Roaring Girl is arguably the product of collaboration not only between Dekker and Middleton, but between the two dramatists and the London celebrity, Mary Frith. *The Constitutory of London Correction Book* recorded that Frith appeared at the Fortune Theatre 'in mans apparel and in her boots and with a sword by her side' and 'sat there upon the stage in the public view of all the people there present in mans apparel and played upon her lute and sang a song' (Middleton and Dekker 1997: xvii–xviii). It is very possible that at one or more performances of *The Roaring Girl* at the Fortune, she sang accompanying herself on the lute in scene viii, the point in the play when Moll performs two songs on the viol; or perhaps Frith gave an impromptu performance at the end of the play. In any case, the Epilogue advertises to its audience that 'The Roaring Girl herself, some few days hence,/Shall on this stage give larger recompense' (viii, 35–6). The play declares itself reliant on the performances of the 'real life' roaring girl, Mary Frith, both on and off the stage at the Fortune. 'Moll Cutpurse', as Coppélia Kahn points out, 'is a nexus of interchanges between the living woman and the fictional character, the performed and the real' (Middleton 2007: I, 721). The reason Frith achieved such notoriety was her transgressive performance of gender; the fact that she dressed 'in man's apparel . . . with a sword by her side', and both acted like a man, while insisting that she was a woman: 'she told the company there present [at the Fortune] that she thought many of them were of the opinion that she was a man, but if any of them would come to her lodging they should find that she is a woman' (Middleton and Dekker 1997: xvii–xviii).

Moll is an atypical character in early modern comedy – the cross-dressed heroine had become a stock-type in Shakespeare's romantic comedies, yet unlike this figure Moll does not abandon her male dress and take a husband at the end of the play. She is a trickster-figure, yet her performances are not overtly theatricalised, and instead are grounded in the social structures of early modern London. T. S. Eliot famously wrote that watching Moll in *The Roaring Girl*, the viewers 'suddenly realize that we are, and have been for some time without knowing it, observing a real and unique human being' (cited in Forman 2001: 1,541). This 'reality effect' relies, in part, on Moll's dependence on a notorious real-life figure, Mary Frith, already known to many of the audience. The play's sense of its own popularity and marketability, evident in the Epilogue, derives from the way it has imported the 'currency' of this London character onto the stage. Much energy is devoted to identifying Moll as a local celebrity. When she is first introduced, it is in terms of her notoriety. Sebastian Wengrave tells his beloved, Mary Fitzallard, of this London celebrity:

> There's a wench
> Called Moll, Mad Moll, or Merry Moll, a creature
> So strange in quality, a whole city takes
> Note of her name and person. (i, 101–4)

Moll is a dramatically rich, overdetermined character. 'Because so much has been loaded into the fictional Moll – the energy and instability of contemporary London with its new fashions, circulating commodities, and fascination with a new form of criminal underworld,' Valerie Forman writes, 'she appears to be larger than life and therefore "real", unnaturally natural' (2001: 1,540–1).

Such is the stage appeal of Moll that when Barry Kyle revived the play for the RSC in 1983 he altered the order and structure of scenes in order to concentrate on Moll, played by Helen Mirren (Comensoli 1987: 249). The production sought to capitalise on Mirren's star quality, and Mirren's performance was impressive for its sheer physical energy. Her first actions on stage are to take an apple to give to a beggar, and then kiss the citizen wives. While one reviewer quibbled that she played the part 'with the swaggering heartiness of a pantomime Robin Hood' (quoted in Middleton and Dekker 1997: xxvi), Mirren's performance did try to capture the larger-than-life quality of Middleton and Dekker's Moll. Although one theatre reviewer mocked the production as driven by the 'militant and loud' demands of 'Woman's Lib', both Kyle and Mirren were clear that for them Moll was an exception, 'a real one-off', in the words of Kyle, and 'not a conceptual feminist' (McLuskie 1989: 1–3). In contrast, contemporary criticism of the play has focused on how to interpret Moll's character from a feminist perspective, in particular, the extent to which her performances as a cross-dressed woman are contained within or subvert the structures of early modern gender ideologies. For Stephen Orgel, *The Roaring Girl* asks questions not simply about gender stereotypes but about the performative nature of gender, 'what constitutes acting like a man or a woman?' (Orgel 1992: 13).

One of the models available for investigating this question is that of the transvestite boy actor (see above, pp. 25–7). It is not only Moll who cross-dresses. In scene viii, the love object, Mary Fitzallard, dresses as a page, presumably to allow this young gentlewoman to move unaccompanied through the streets of London. Yet there is more to this use of apparel than simply disguise. An explicit association is established between the two cross-dressed 'Molls'. Moll says:

> I pitied her for name's sake, that a Moll
> Should be so crossed in love, when there's so many
> That owes nine lays apiece, and not so little.
> My tailor fitted her: how like you his work? (viii, 66–9)

By drawing the audience's attention to the body beneath the costume, this scene is playing around with the 'specifically theatrical context of cross-dressed boy/women' (Orgel 1992: 20–2). Given that the two Molls were both played by boy actors, what is supposed to be tantalising – the idea of the woman's body or the theatrical fact of the transvestite boy's body? In this scene, Mary Fitzallard has much in common with Shakespeare's eroticised boy-women. Hence, the play quite consciously stages a same-sex erotic embrace when it has the male protagonist and the crossed-dressed boy-woman kiss. Sebastian responds to Moll's 'How strange this shows, one man to kiss another', with 'I'd kiss such men to choose, Moll;/Methinks a woman's lip tastes well in a doublet' (viii, 45–7). The kiss is the moment when the 'homoerotic reality of the material conditions of stage production' are brought into alignment with 'the expressed desires of particular male characters' (Howard 1992: 174–5). The kiss is simultaneously 'strange' and totally desirable. It produces an erotic fantasy for the male audience which insists on the sexual pleasure to be derived from kissing boys *and* from the sexual fluidity of the love object, the easy slippage between women and boys. Thomas Laqueur's seminal work on early modern theories of the body has profoundly influenced studies of the transvestite boy actor. As Jean Howard notes, 'Galenic biological models depicting both boys and women as unfinished men may have enabled adult males – to some yet undefined extent – to treat boys and women as interchangeable sexual objects' (1992: 171).[2] Boys and youths were different from men in social terms, and more like women, in that they occupied subordinate positions within the household. The boy's smooth cheek and lip, often a site of eroticism in literature and drama of the period, was a tangible sign that they were not men, given that facial hair distinguishes men from boys (Munro 2005: 41, 48–9). In this context, it is important that Mary is dressed as a young page, a boy servant, therefore not a man and, in class terms, both subservient and available to his master.

Moll's cross-dressing is a variant on this dramatic trope. Unlike Mary, who is dressed as a young page, Moll is given greater sartorial scope and appears on stage wearing male *and* female clothing – a man's doublet and a riding skirt – and adopts the behaviour of an *adult* male. The play still wants the audience to consider the sexual nature of Moll's body. This is particularly noticeable in scene iv, which provocatively plays with the idea of the body underneath the clothing. It is an explicitly voyeuristic scene staged for the benefit of Sir Alexander, who thinks he is hiding undetected, that fetishises the hermaphroditic body. The tailor fitting Moll for a pair of 'great Dutch slop[s]' is given lines that attribute to Moll not simply a penis, but an erect penis: 'It shall stand round and full, I warrant you', 'I know my fault now; t'other was somewhat stiff between the legs' (iv, 93, 95–6). Sir Alexander's response to the scene – 'I have brought up my son to marry a Dutch slop and a French doublet: a codpiece daughter' (iv, 98–100) – may identify clothing as determining gender identity, yet it continues to fantasise about the nature the body underneath. Male clothes should denote that she is a man anatomically, 'a monster with two trinkets' (iv, 83), and yet she is still a woman. The recurrent play on apparel and body parts, as Marjorie Garber argues, 'discloses a dangerous, carnivalized fantasia of dislocation, in which the fetishization of commodities is the cover for the fetishization of body parts' (1991: 223–5). What Sir Alexander and, by extension, the audience, find so enticing and disturbing is Moll's very indeterminacy, her monstrous man-womanishness. As Follywit said in *A Mad World*, ''Tis an Amazonian time' (III, iii, 118–19), anticipating the pamphlets that appeared in the 1620s, for example *Hic Mulier; or, The Man Woman* (1620), which condemned women adopting male apparel, such as the French doublet, because it signified their usurpation of male prerogatives and female insubordination in general (Middleton 2007: I, 722–3).

Arguably it is Moll's adoption of the identity of an adult male rather than a young boy that defines her cross-dressing as radically transgressive because it signifies an aggressive self-assertion that was not available to boys or women. At points in the play, Moll's 'mannish' claims to autonomy are foregrounded in order to place her outside the heterosexual economy:

> I have no humour to marry. I love to lie o' both sides o'th'bed myself; and again o'th'other side, a wife, you know, ought to be obedient, but I fear me I am too headstrong to obey, therefore I ne'er go about it . . . I have the head now of myself, and am man enough for a woman; marriage is but a chopping and changing, where a maiden loses one head, and has a worse i'th'place. (iv, 37–41, 43–7)

Moll rejects marriage because she understands it primarily and negatively in terms of female subordination to men. Her claim to socioeconomic autonomy is eroticised by the suggestion that Moll swings both ways sexually, as she chooses. The theme of sexual autonomy returns in the viol-playing scene, which is driven by a sexual *double entendre* on playing this 'instrument' (viii, 87). With the viol played between the legs, the performance can suggest either heterosexual or auto-erotic sex, or both. It is argued that Moll plays upon this instrument to express her ownership of her erotic desire against a community that seeks to appropriate it and label her a 'whore' (viii, 123). For Jean Howard this scene 'acknowledges, insists upon, female erotic desire, while making clear the cultural imperatives that operate to shape, channel, and control that eroticism' (1992: 184).

The radicalism of Moll's assertion of self-possession – social, economic and sexual – is limited by the play's insistence on her exceptional status. Moll accepts that women 'ought to be obedient', that they should submit themselves to their husbands, even if it is for the 'worse' – just not her. This apparent gender conservatism raises the question of how far the disruptiveness of Moll extends. As has been frequently noted, the play offers a highly romanticised version of Moll as the 'roaring girl', Mary Frith, that simultaneously advertises the charges of 'immodest and lascivious' behaviour made against Frith (Middleton and Dekker 1997: xviii), and refutes these charges in its idealising characterisation of its 'chaste' roaring girl. Moll may reject marriage for herself, but her role within the romantic plot is to facilitate the idealised marriage between the two young lovers, Sebastian and Mary (Orgel 1992: 24). Her role as the type of trickster in the New Comedy plot who aids the lovers against the 'old one' is invoked by Sebastian:

'Twixt lovers' hearts she's a fit instrument,
And has the art to help them to their own.
By her advice, for in that craft she's wise,
My love and I may meet, spite of all spies. (iv, 205–8)

Moll may champion the reputation of women against the lecherous
and venal Laxton, even to the extent of taking the man's part and
fighting a duel in defence of women's honour in scene v. Yet she
often takes the man's part in other, less celebratory ways, and talks
like a man, among men, arguing in misogynist tones that women are
only virtuous because men are 'shallow lechers' and that she is 'of
that certain belief there are more queans [prostitutes] in this town
of their own making than of any man's provoking' (iii, 330, 333–5).

In keeping with her role as the champion of the romantic marriage, Moll censures the citizen-wives in this scene for their false
chastity. It is the citizen-wives who are the unruly, incontinent
women in the play (Howard 1992: 182). Mistress Gallipot is a negative type of the lusty citizen-wife, who is sexually and financially
open to the predations of the venal gallant, Laxton. Her unruly
nature is expressed through her open mouth, her shrewishness,
which turns her husband into less than a man, evident in the way she
infantilises him in a tirade: 'What a pruing keep you! I think the baby
would have a teat, it kyes so. Pray be not so fond of me, leave your city
humours. I'm vexed at you to see how like a calf you come bleating
after me' (vi, 2–5). The resolution of the citizen-gallant plot is not
the punishment of the predatory gallants, but of the unruly citizen-
wife, Mistress Gallipot, who is put firmly back into her place.
Gallipot warns his wife, with a veiled threat, to 'brag no more/Of
holding out: who most brags is most whore' (ix, 353–4), and invites
the gallants to dine with him and his fellow citizens. Homosociality
triumphs as gender is prioritised over class, and citizens and gallants
unite against their unruly women (see above, pp. 34–5, 41 n. 1).

That said, Moll's presence on stage, instead of focusing on the
problem with women, often turns the audience's attention to the
problem with men. Femininity and masculinity, like other forms of
social identity, rely on performance, on adopting and acting out the
proper codes of behaviour and appearance; the problem in *The
Roaring Girl* is that the men are often under-performing. Laxton's

name is a pun on lack-stone as in lacks testicles, thereby identifying him as less than man. His failed seduction of Moll, which culminates in his defeat through her manly prowess with her sword, is less a reflection on her hermaphroditic qualities than his inability to play the part of a gentleman. Moll does not symbolically castrate Laxton in this scene, since he is already a sign of lack. Similarly, as we have seen, Gallipot's over-fondness for his wife has made him less than a man and unable to perform the role of the husband within the marriage effectively. In this case, gender instability is part of a wider satire on the city: 'These marriages of sexual lack seem to indict the merchant-class man for impotency and the merchant-class woman for insatiability' (Howard 1992: 176–7). Other male characters, Jack Dapper and Sir Beauteous Ganymede, represent a new urbane masculinity that is effeminised by its over-investment in the new fashions and the emerging culture of consumption. If *The Roaring Girl*, like other city plays, dramatises the changing commercial face of London, one effect of these profound social and economic transformations was to place traditional forms of masculinity in question.

The Roaring Girl 'seems to invite' a debate over the extent of Moll's subversiveness. The transgressive and cross-dressed Moll dominates the stage, yet her actions across both plots support often conservative domestic and social ideologies. 'Reading all these critics together . . . with their convincing evidence for both sides', as Valerie Forman concludes, 'suggests that the question of whether or not Moll is subversive is not a particularly useful one, precisely because Moll is not a coherent character who is the source of action'. Rather than attribute a psychological and ideological coherence to her character, Moll instead should be viewed as 'a locus of cultural fantasies, an embodiment of the culture's contradictions' (Forman 2001: 1,542). Howard similarly reads Moll's character as a function of the ideological contradictions that energised early modern society (1992: 183). Both arguments reject a concept of gender identity as biologically given and inherent in the body, and instead theorise gender in terms of performance. Rather than a set of fixed categories, gender is understood, in the words of Stephen Orgel, as a 'socially constructed, historically variable set of practices and ideologies' (1992: 24–5).

THE STAGE AND THE PRINT MARKET: THE ROARING GIRL AND PAMPHLET LITERATURE

Early modern pamphlets inhabited the same terrain as stage plays. Pamphlets were sold by vendors at plays, and may even have been read out aloud by theatre-goers as they waited for the play to commence. Reading a text aloud in company is a mode of performance, and it alerts us to the way texts were not only performed but written with an idea of performance in mind (Stern 2007: 138–42). Middleton's *The Black Book* (1604), which describes the perambulation of Lucifer through the London underworld, self-consciously theatricalises his journey to offer the reader of his pamphlet a similar experience to that of the theatre-goer: Lucifer vaults 'Above the stage rails of this earthen Globe' and 'must turn actor, and join companies/To share my comic sleek-eyed villanies' (61–3). Pamphlet writing was also an alternative career for dramatists, if less lucrative than writing for the stage. Middleton and Dekker quickly turned their hand to writing pamphlets when the theatres were closed due to plague in 1603, co-writing *Newes from Gravesend: Sent to Nobody* and *The Meeting of Gallants at an Ordinary; or, the Walks in Pauls*, both published in 1604.

Pamphlets and city plays enjoy a particular proximity in that they are both emerging genres of the early modern city. Dekker and Middleton's London pamphlets share a satiric idiom with their city plays. *Newes from Gravesend* is a response to the 1603 plague, which killed more than a sixth of the population of London. Plague intensified the conventional analogy between physical diseases and the social decay of the city, and provided the metaphoric ground for satirising the moral corruption of the city governors, both the citizenry and aristocracy (Middleton 2007: I, 183). While plague pamphlets mapped the city through the social pathology of disease, other pamphlets were marketed as guides to London, mapping its unknown places for the unwary urban traveller. Middleton's epistle to the reader before *The Black Book* promises to 'discover vices and unmask the world's shadowed villanies . . . and [lay] bare the infectious bulks of craft, coz'nage and panderism' (10–11, 24–5). This moralising 'discovery' of the London underworld offers the reader illicit and criminal pleasures from the safety of the moral high ground.

Middleton's *The Black Book* has affinities with the popular cony-catching or rogue pamphlets of the late sixteenth and early seventeenth centuries in that both promise to discover and anatomise the so-called London underworld for the entertainment and supposed edification of the reader. Dekker penned a number of these pamphlets: *The Seven Deadly Sins of London* (1606), *The Bellman of London* (1608) and *English Villanies Discovered by Lanthorn and Candlelight* (1608). The canting scene in scene x of *The Roaring Girl* draws on cant words and canting dictionaries from Dekker's own pamphlets, *The Bellman of London* and *Lanthorn and Candlelight*, as well as those by other writers, such as Greene's well-known *Notable Discovery of Cozenage*. An important feature of scene x is Moll's adoption of the role of guide and interpreter of this 'underworld' for her gentry audience – Davy Dapper, Sir Beauteous Ganymede and Lord Noland. As the 'discoverer' of this world, she occupies a similar position to the pamphlet-writer; and like the pamphlet-writer, she simultaneously claims privileged knowledge of it and distances herself from it. The canting scene, as Peter Womack notes, is a complex theatricalisation of the production and consumption of this type of pamphlet literature: 'The rogues are the characters in the pamphlets, the gentlemen are the readers, and Moll herself is the narrator, who speaks both languages and can interpret between them' (2006: 206).

Mary Frith was the subject of her own rogue pamphlet. *The Life and Death of Mrs. Mary Frith commonly called Mal Cutpurse* was published in 1662, within three years of her death. This pamphlet describes Moll's relationship to the criminal world of thieves, pickpockets and highwaymen as that of 'a perfect *Ambodexter*' who 'lived in a kind of mean betwixt open, professed dishonesty, and fair and civil deportment, being an *Hermaphrodite* in Manners as well as in Habit' (Todd and Spearing 1994: 7). This 1662 biography does not necessarily provide privileged access to the 'real' Moll. That said, it does provide insight into the way this figure was characterised and her reputation shaped in the seventeenth century. In both *The Roaring Girl* and the 1662 pamphlet, Moll assumes an eccentric respectability – she is both familiar with the criminal workings of the underworld, and 'an interpreter of that world to the middle-class world' (McManus 2006: 200). Moll's in-betweenness, her status as 'a perfect *Ambodexter*' is clarified through the presence of early modern criminal types on the stage. Moll is both associated with and distinguished from Ralph Trapdoor, a discharged soldier, whose vagrancy is identified with criminality in a similar way to Follywit's company of rogues (see above, pp. 37–8). Trapdoor is hired by Sir Alexander to trap Moll into revealing her 'true' criminal nature. Sir Alexander sets out expensive, luxury items – a 'German watch', a 'gold chain' – to 'lie/Full in the view of her thief-whorish eye' (viii, 7, 12, 16–17). Whereas Trapdoor is receptive to the bait, 'I see't so plain/That I could steal't myself' (viii, 18–19), Moll detects the temptation, 'Here were a brave booty for an evening thief' (viii, 137) and wryly 'discovers' the moral for the audience: 'if men's secret youthful faults should judge 'em,/'Twould be the general'st execution/That e'er was seen in England!' (viii, 137, 141–3).

Moll is more at home with her gentleman friends, Jack Dapper, Sir Beauteous Ganymede and Lord Noland. As their names indicate, they do not represent the aggressive, unruly masculinity of the roaring boy, but rather embody the new urban cultures of fashion and consumption. In scene x, Moll 'discovers' and neatly packages the London underworld as a safe fantasy world for this new class of consumers. A journey is proposed to Pimlico, a London tavern at Hogsden, in the words of Dapper, 'a boon voyage to that nappy land of spice cakes' (x, 57–8). Mundane detail is transformed into the stuff of festive fantasy – 'that nappy land of spice cakes' alludes to the foaming ale sold in the inn, usually consumed with spice cakes, and metaphorically opens out to encompass the mythic 'Land of Cockaigne', the land of milk and honey. This festive world is, in part, a response to the anxiety that London, which had expanded rapidly in size and population, was being transformed from a knowable community of neighbours into a dark nightmarish world, an 'alien realm honeycombed with shadowy sub-communities' (Twyning 1998: 63). The London underworld was frequently represented in texts of the period as another, foreign country contained within the city. The biography of Mary Frith writes of how she became an inhabitant of this other world within London to escape transportation to Virginia:

I listed my self of another Colony or Plantation (but neither sow nor reap) of the *Divers* or *File-clyers* [pick-pockets]. A cunning Nation being a kind of Land *Pirates*, trading altogether in other men's *Bottoms*, for no other Merchandizes than *Bullion* and ready Coin, and keep most of the great Fairs and Marts of the world. (Todd and Spearing 1994: 20)

Through the recurrent voyage motif in scene x – Lord Noland says, 'I could find it in my heart to sail to the World's End with such company' (x, 59–60) – the London underworld is marketed as entertainment, and the audience is encouraged to view themselves as tourists within their own city (McManus 2006: 219–20).

If rogues were imagined as an alien sub-culture within the city, then it follows that they speak a different, foreign language. Cant, the distinctive dialect of vagabonds in rogue literature, is a counterfeit language. The description of cant as 'pedlar's French' (x, 184), as McManus notes, is 'a neat encapsulation of the sense of a self-contained community – perhaps even a nation – within London' (2006: 220). Jack Dapper sees Trapdoor and Tearcat as alien, yet English – Tearcat is 'a strange creature – a fat butterbox – yet speakest English' (x, 101–2). 'Butter-box' is a derogatory term for a Dutchman, and so Tearcat responds in bastardised Dutch. For the upper class Dapper it is 'jobbering' – Tearcat speaks a subversive, counter-language that puts his upper class opponent at a disadvantage, leaving him open to gulling. Moll, however, is multilingual. Her privileged knowledge of this world is signified by the play on 'book of horners', referring both to the hornbook which taught children their alphabet and 'horns for the thumb' (x, 141), a piece of horn shaped like a thimble which is used to protect the thumb from the knife when the purse is cut. The audience, onstage and offstage, observes Moll deciphering and reading these criminal types like her ABC, and the ABC she proceeds to give us is the ABC of cant, just like a canting dictionary.

Moll delivers the invitation to cant like an invitation to join her in song or a dance, foregrounding the fact that the audience is watching a piece of entertainment. Dekker, in *Lanthorn and Candlelight*, traced the etymology of canting: 'very aptly may *canting* take his derivation from *a cantando* "from singing" because amongst these beggarly consorts . . . the language of *canting* is a kind of music and he that in such assemblies can *cant* best is counted the best musician' (Middleton and Dekker 1997: 139). Just as the audience has paid their penny to see the play, Lord Noland pays these performers 'their pay' (x, 240). The audience, like Dapper, Ganymede and Noland, take on the role of tourists in this foreign world who pay the natives to perform for them. The threatening presence of this underworld is 'elided by the appropriation and commodification of the rogues themselves; canting and the speakers of it are made into commodities which can be purchased and exchanged' (Forman 2001: 1,553–4).

Mary Frith, via her stage persona, Moll, is herself made into a commodity by Middleton and Dekker. Middleton's epistle plays around with the slippage between the 'real' and the 'fictional' Moll: 'Worse things, I must needs confess, the world has taxed her for than has been written of her; but 'tis the excellency of a writer to leave things better than he finds 'em' (20–3). The reality of Mary Frith, it is suggested, could undo the fictional Moll that the writers have constructed in the play – Frith's appearance before the church courts for 'immodest and lascivious' behaviour would seem to confirm this. As Garber argues, 'the historical figure herself functions as an unmasterable excess' (1991: 221), capable of resisting and undermining her appropriation and commodification as Dekker and Middleton's *Roaring Girl.*

A CULTURE OF CONSUMPTION: SEX, SHOPPING, AND THE HOUSEHOLD

Buying and selling are at the heart of city comedies. The genre is said to be defined by the way it dramatises the changing commercial organisation of London, the transition from the communal medieval marketplace to the private shop and the market economy with its ethos of competitive individualism (Wells 1981: 38–40). The set for Kyle's 1983 RSC production of *The Roaring Girl* was dominated by cog-wheels to emblematise the advent of capitalism in the early modern period (Middleton and Dekker 1997: xxvi). Kyle moved the opening scene set in the Wengrave household to later on in the play so that the curtain opened on the city streets with their shops and customers. We do, however, need to be cautious about using models derived from a capitalist economy when analysing plays and other texts from this period: as we have seen, the credit-based early modern economy continued to centre on the community rather than individual (see above, pp. 28–9). Even so, in the sixteenth and seventeenth centuries opportunities for shopping increased dramatically. The establishment of trading companies, such as the East India Company, greatly facilitated the importation of spices and luxury goods. There were places to shop and be seen – Paul's Walk, with its tradesmen and shops in the cloisters and churchyard; the Royal Exchange, the first purpose-built trading and shopping centre in London where luxury goods could be bought; and London streets, such as Cheapside, immortalised in Middleton's *Chaste Maid in Cheapside*. The result was a 'culture of display', epitomised in city comedies by the gallant and in its depiction of 'an urban milieu in which people could be judged by what they could buy, even though such acquisitiveness was often morally condemned or subject to satiric treatment' (Howard 2007: 13). There are two loci for this culture of display and consumption in *The Roaring Girl*: the aristocratic household of Sir Alexander Wengrave and the citizens' shops on the streets of London. Critical attention has tended to concentrate on the latter and the increasing range and availability of consumer goods. The play also dramatises the effect of this culture of consumption on the aristocratic household, one of the main purchasers of the new goods and services available in early modern London.

Sir Alexander Wengrave's house is a particularly rich instance of the dramatisation of the new gentry household on stage. Sir Alexander is an example of the new, acquisitive gentry as distinct from the old landed baronial gentry represented by Sir Guy Fitzallard. The actor playing Sir Alexander in the 1983 RSC production adopted a provincial accent to signify his status as 'new money'. 'The design of the Wengrave household', Comensoli argues, 'confirms Wengrave's successful climb to the landed gentry, while his status-seeking is the focus of the play's sharpest satirical attack' (1987: 253). The play opens by delineating traffic in goods and services within the early modern elite household. The upper-class heroine of the romantic comedy plot, Mary Fitzallard, arrives at Wengrave's house disguised as a sempstress, supposedly to fit the young master, Sebastian, with a set of 'falling bands' (i, 16) or flat collars. She is admitted by the servingman, Neatfoot. 'Neat' denotes a preciseness and elegance of form, indicating perhaps that the character would move trimly on stage, like an early modern dancing master. When used adjectivally in relation to speech, as Angel Day pointed out in his *English Secretary*, it signified 'Aptness of words and sentences . . . that they be neat and choicely picked' (1586: A2v; *OED* 3b). Neatfoot's speech is anything but clear and concise: 'is it into his ears, sweet damsel, emblem of fragility, you desire to have a message transported, or to be transcendent?' (i, 2–4). Neatfoot is using a rhetorical device called *synonymia*, the expression of the same meaning by different words or phrases. It is a means of amplification (*amplificatio*) since the different words or phrases introduce additional meanings. The Renaissance rhetorician George Puttenham called *synonymia* 'the figure of store'. It is a figure of speech particularly appropriate to a culture of accumulation.

'Neat' operates satirically in this scene to provide us with a lesson in how social class functions through language. The word's association with elegance and refinement is naturalised when it refers to an elite culture. However, when applied to a lowly servingman it signifies an unnatural disjunction between style and substance. Neatfoot is neat because his manner and speech are affected and mimic that of his social betters. Since he is not entitled to use this linguistic style, his speech and behaviour are parodic – put simply, it does not come naturally to him. The upper-class Mary says she 'could smile/To see this formal ape play antic tricks' (i, 30–1). The servingman Neatfoot is a performing ape, ludicrously counterfeiting the form and gestures of his social superiors in a manner that entertains but does not convince. The difference between animal and human is used as a guide to the differences between servants and masters, the elite and the lower classes. Yet the ape is a particular kind of animal, and was chosen to denote this kind of behaviour precisely because, unlike other animals, it was able to mimic human behaviour with a degree of accuracy. Apish behaviour has as much to do with proximity as distance. It suggests that servants' over-familiarity with their masters' speech, habits and clothes fosters these kinds of apish tricks unless class distinctions are rigorously policed. It also suggests that when this type of apish servant appears in plays it is to signify there is a problem with the ethos of the household.

In the two opening scenes the social space of the household is dramatised both spatially and temporally with extraordinary richness. Mary has arrived at dinner time – she is invited by Neatfoot, *'with a napkin on his shoulder, and a trencher in his hand, as from table'* (i, s. d.), either to eat in the hall with servingmen or in the buttery with the waiting-women. Sebastian is called from the master's table – in the next scene, we discover it is the 'inner room' (ii, 6). Such care is taken because the Wengrave household is novel. The sixteenth century witnessed a social change in the architecture of the houses of the aspiring middling classes, gentry and aristocracy. The use of the spacious medieval hall as a communal space where all members of the household would gather to dine, servants as well as masters, slowly began to disappear. The great house instead now included smaller chambers – specific dining rooms, such as in Wengrave's house, so that masters and servants ate separately, as well as other rooms where individuals could sit privately (James 1974: 183–7). The Wengrave household represents a departure from the older baronial values identified with Mary and her father, the elderly knight Sir Guy Fitzallard. Sir Alexander opposes the marriage between Mary and Sebastian because he is motivated by money rather than aristocratic codes of honour. These corrupting acquisitive values are dramatised by the new interior spaces of Sir Alexander's household. The characters in the second scene enter the stage from the dining room, praising the lavish feast. Sir Alexander invites his guests, and the audience, to admire these new rooms, with their expensive furnishings: 'Th'inner room was too close; how do you like/This parlour, gentleman?' (ii, 6–7). Older rituals of hospitality, such as feasting, that were intended to cement social bonds within the community are debased through their use as an occasion for ostentatious display and conspicuous consumption. This city house is the type of edifice 'built to envious show' Ben Jonson criticised in the opening line of 'To Penshurst' (Jonson 1985: 282).

The notion of 'service' is dangerously compromised within this new acquisitive environment. Older feudal models of service are often nostalgically idealised in the figure of the steadfastly loyal and honest servant. Servants in *The Roaring Girl* are not of this type. While the 'formal ape' Neatfoot testifies to the ostentation of Sir Alexander's household, his employment of the criminal Ralph Trapdoor in his plot to get rid of Moll signifies a further debasement. The service that Trapdoor will provide is 'To be a shifter under your worship's nose of a clean trencher, when there's a good bit upon't' (ii, 195–6). The image Trapdoor uses to define the subservience he offers derives from the communal, mixed dining of old medieval hall. Sir Alexander responds accordingly that he is an 'honest fellow' (ii, 197). Yet the metaphor also suggests that Trapdoor will take this opportunity to steal from under his master's nose. The dangerous openness of the aristocratic household to criminality through this new acquisitive culture is set out in scene viii when Sir Alexander displays luxury objects in his private chambers that he hopes Moll will steal. The valuables are put on display as in a shop. The act of consumption is not simply associated with temptation and illicit desires, but brings together the worlds of the aristocratic household and the criminal underworld. Gentry and their households are now open to the criminal classes because the market in luxury consumer goods has created a new 'black' economy (Forman 2001: 1,546–8). The real Mary Frith, as we have seen, moved between these two worlds and capitalised on this market by acting as a fence who 'returned' stolen goods, such as watches, to their owners for a fee. The play similarly suggests the dangerous proximity of these two worlds from a different angle – the downward mobility resulting from the gentry over-extending themselves financially to maintain face within this culture of display. Jack Dapper's prodigality causes his father to hatch a plot to have him imprisoned in the Counter, a debtors' prison, to tame his 'follies' (vii, 73). The Counter is imagined as a reform school for gentlemen to discipline their prodigal ways, as Sir Alexander advises: 'Sir Davy, send your son to Wood Street College;/A gentleman can nowhere get more knowledge' (vii, 107–8; Howard 2007: 73–5). The name of Jack Dapper's companion, Lord Noland, suggests that he has consumed his lands in order to live as a city gallant, in a similar fashion to Master Salewood in *Michaelmas Term*.

The commerce between the gentry and the citizen merchants is dramatised in scene iii. The action moves to the commercial streets of London and the shops of the citizens and their wives. Three booths are set on stage in a row – the Gallipots' apothecary shop, the Tiltyards' feather shop, and the Openworks' sempster shop. This is a crowded street scene, with ten actors on stage at the one time. The group of gallants – Laxton, Dapper, accompanied by his page, Gull, Goshawk and Greenwit – move from one shop to the next, mimicking the random and leisurely movement of shopping (Womack 2006: 205). The 1983 RSC production emphasised the dark, satiric edge to this scene by adding a crippled beggar, who dragged himself around the stage, thus setting out a structural link between an acquisitive culture and social deprivation. The director also highlighted the speech delivered by Gull, Jack Dapper's young servant, which foregrounds the disparity between the rich lifestyle and diet of the wealthy and the poverty of those who serve them. Gull complains about the pittance he receives to feed himself after his master's excesses the previous night: 'Three single halfpence? Life, this will scarce serve a man in sauce . . . He could spend his three pound last night in a supper amongst girls and brave bawdy-house boys' (iii, 128–9, 133–4).

The scene opens with a city siren's song of commerce: 'Gentlemen, what is't you lack? What is't you buy? See fine bands, and ruffs, fine lawns, fine cambrics. What is't you lack, what is't you buy?' (iii, 1–3). Dekker uses a similar song in *The Shoemaker's Holiday*, when the sempstress Jane calls to Hammon: 'Sir, what is't you buy? / What is't you lack, sir? Calico, or lawn, / Fine cambric shirts, or bands, what will you buy?' (xii, 21–3). The song promises that desire, 'lack', can be sated by the process of buying and consuming goods. Sex and shopping are made analogous – the citizen-wives are viewed by their male customers to be on sale as much as their goods. The 'intermingling of venereal and economic pursuits' in this scene transforms the city into an 'erotic terrain' (Howard 1992: 174). Laxton's arrangements for his sexual assignation with Moll bring together the new forms of leisure and sexual commerce – he promises to 'hire a coach with four horses', a new and expensive form of travel, to take her 'out o' town', including a supper at Brentford, and, in a complex financial and sexual trans-action, he uses the money he has been given on the promise of sex with Mistress Gallipot to secure Moll's promise to 'be merry and lie' with him (iii, 285–312). Forman argues that Laxton invests in these processes of exchange with Gallipot and Moll, which are based on the deferral of sex, to compensate for the lack that he embodies within this culture of display (2001: 1536). One of the items closely identified with Laxton and consumed in this scene is tobacco, a newly fashionable imported commodity that similarly symbolises lack and the folly of consumption through its narcotic effects and the fact that it goes up in smoke.

Although shopping is gendered and satirised as a characteristi-cally feminine activity in contemporary plays, such as Jonson's *Epicoene*, in *The Roaring Girl* the consumers are the male gallants. Conspicuous consumption, as we have seen, is concentrated in the figure of Jack Dapper, and signifies a form of male excess, a lack of manly discrimination and loss of self-control. Dapper's taste for feathers – a 'spangled feather' (iii, 162) – symbolises his 'unmanly degeneration'. The 'young men in this age', Barnaby Rich lamented, 'that is not *strumpet* like attired, doth think himself quite out of *fashion*'. Fashionable and effeminate dress was a vice particularly associated with youth; writers of conduct manuals argued that it 'disqualified young men from claiming manhood' (Shepard 2003: 29). His father attempts to cure his son of his unmanly prodigality so that he is fit to take up his patrimony. Yet, even though Dapper is clearly associated with male excess, the play refuses to condemn him, and instead the prodigal and effeminate young man triumphs over his father with the aid of Moll. Jack Dapper has an affinity with Moll in that both signify 'unmasterable excess' (Garber 1991: 221; Comensoli 1987: 261), which in turn is identified with their taste in apparel. Clothes were a complex signifier on the early modern stage: '[C]ostumes (often cast-off aristocratic attire) both determined character status and functioned as fluid props interchanged among multi-role actors, who were of course of low rank . . . clothes, onstage and off, were a floating signifier, signalling changeability, not stability' (Hutchings and Bromham 2008: 48).

The Roaring Girl certainly satirises a culture of fashion, and yet it is also possible to argue, along with Howard, that the play views the 'ability to transform one's appearance by the sartorial possibilities afforded by the market place [as] . . . a potentially liberating phenomenon' (Howard 1992: 180). This ambivalence structures Middleton's prefatory epistle when he compares the 'fashion of play-making . . . to nothing so naturally as the alteration in apparel' (1–2). *The Roaring Girl* is not only cut according to new fashion for the summer, but is advertised as a leisure activity that will occupy the gallant, since it is 'good to keep you in an afternoon from dice, at home in your chambers; and for venery you shall find enough, for a sixpence, but well couched an you mark it' (12–14). Such a reflection on the theatre – and the printed playbook – as part of a new entertainment industry is evident when Sir Alexander asks his guests to 'look into my galleries' (ii, 14). His account of his pictures is a metatheatrical device that turns our attention to the audience in the tiered galleries of the Fortune Theatre: 'Within one square a thousand heads are laid/So close that all of heads the room seems made' (ii, 20–1). The scene constitutes a defining moment when the theatre recognises itself as entertainment, as a new leisure activity.

NOTES

1. Dialogic is a term that derives from the works of the Russian literary theorist Mikhail Bakhtin, who contrasted 'monologic', in which the author's controlling perspective dominates, with 'dialogic' or 'polyphonic', in which individual voices are not harmonised within the author's point of view, but express independent viewpoints often challenging each other.
2. Galen was an ancient Greek physician whose theories of the human body and the humoural system dominated medical understanding of the body in the Renaissance.

CHAPTER 4

Tragicomedy and the City: *Chaste Maid in Cheapside* and *No Wit, No Help Like a Woman's*

Chaste Maid in Cheapside and *No Wit, No Help Like a Woman's* appeared on the public stage soon after *The Roaring Girl* – the Oxford *Collected Works* suggests a date for the first performance of *No Wit, No Help Like a Woman's* in summer 1611, and *Chaste Maid in Cheapside* in spring 1613 (Middleton 2007: II, 371, 373–5). Both are London plays, and yet are departures from his earlier satiric comedies for the Children of Paul's. *Chaste Maid in Cheapside* is frequently hailed as Middleton's finest comedy, surpassing his earlier city comedies through its 'marvellous unity of tone and headlong vitality' (Middleton 2002: xv). *Chaste Maid* keeps in play four wittily interrelated plots. The main plot is the comic love story in which the union of the young gentleman, Touchwood Junior, and Moll Yellowhammer is opposed by her parents, the goldsmith Yellowhammer and his wife, Maudline, who instead have arranged a marriage with the debauched nobleman, Sir Walter Whorehound. It is mirrored in the subplot in which a marriage is arranged by the Yellowhammers between their son, Tim Yellowhammer, and the Welsh Gentlewoman, who is in fact Whorehound's mistress. The other two plots involve two households linked in terms of character (Whorehound) and thematically: that of the Allwits, in which Master Allwit is the willing cuckold of Whorehound, who keeps Mistress Allwit in a continual state of pregnancy, while the second household consists of the childless Lord and Lady Kix, the latter of whom is serviced by Touchwood Senior.

No Wit, No Help Like a Woman's is similarly energetically inventive in its plotting and has two interlaced intrigue plots. Kate Lowwater hatches a plan to restore her husband to his fortune, which has been lost through the double-dealing of the usurer Goldenfleece, recently deceased. Kate disguises herself as a young man and courts and then marries his widow, Lady Goldenfleece. She tricks her 'bride' on her wedding night into a compromising situation and forces her to restore her husband's stolen estate. Lady Goldenfleece also possesses a secret that is key to the second plot which involves lost mothers and substituted daughters. This romance plot focuses on the fortunes of two sets of lovers, Philip Twilight and Grace, and Sandfield and Jane, whose unions are blocked, unwittingly, by the father, Sir Oliver Twilight. Jane and Grace have been substituted at birth, Grace and her 'mother', Lady Twilight, are then lost at sea to pirates. Philip, sent to pay the ransom for his mother and sister, instead squanders the money, marries Grace, and passes her off as his lost sister. The resulting complications, which veer towards tragedy when the mother returns and claims her 'daughter', are finally resolved through the agency of Lady Goldenfleece, the *deus ex machina*, who reveals the secret of the substitution of the infants.

Chaste Maid in Cheapside and *No Wit, No Help Like a Woman* are unsettling and exuberant plays. They disturb our sense of how dramatic conventions should function, just as their witty perversity disrupts the commonplaces of early modern society. While the liquidity celebrated in *Chaste Maid* has attracted critics interested in gender and the symbolic economies of early modern London, *No Wit* has received little critical attention. Yet its plotting of the disruptive effects of desire and use of the cross-dressed heroine not as an erotic object for men but for women are features which place it alongside plays, such as *The Roaring Girl*, that offer challenging perspectives on early modern culture.

EXPERIMENTATION IN THE THEATRE: TRAGICOMEDY AND BURLESQUE

Chaste Maid in Cheapside was first performed at the Swan Theatre by Lady Elizabeth's Men probably sometime in spring 1613

(Middleton 2007: II, 373). The playing company is significant because it prompts questions about one of the dominant concerns of the play – children. Soon after the Lady Elizabeth's Men began performing in London in the Christmas season of 1612–13, they merged with the Children of the Queen's Revels, a company of boy actors. The company had lost royal patronage in 1606, because of a series of satiric comedies whose mocking references to leading courtiers caused offence, and finally collapsed around 1608 due to continued indiscretions. The company was revived in 1609, and moved to Whitefriars until their merger with Lady Elizabeth's Men (Munro 2005: 2). This meant that Middleton was writing his play for a company that included the renowned 'boy' actor, Nathan Field, as well as other very experienced older boy actors, such as Joseph Taylor and William Ecclestone. It should be remembered that these 'little eyases' were now young men – we know, for example, that Field was twenty-five in 1613 (Munro 2005: 39–41). Even so, it is likely that the company also included younger boys. This may account, as Ceri Sullivan has speculated, for the two parts for young boys in *Chaste Maid* – Wat and Nick, the bastard sons of Sir Walter Whorehound, who have small speaking parts in Act I, scene ii and Act v, scene i (2007: 174). Older 'boys', such as Field, would have been available for the parts of the young men, Touchwood Junior and Tim, as well as the numerous women's parts in the play – the christening scene in Act III, scene ii, for example, requires at least seven boys on stage at the same time to take the parts of the three Gossips, two Puritans, Mistress Allwit, the Nurse and Tim. The play's thematic focus on children as the embodiment of the play's procreative energies could be read as a festive celebration of the very recent merger of Lady Elizabeth's Men with the Children of the Queen's Revels, as well as a celebration of the legacy of the children's companies, which were such a significant presence on the London stage in the early part of the century, but had now largely disappeared. Middleton successfully collaborated with the Children of Paul's (see above, pp. 19–28); his plays were also performed by the Children of the Queen's Revels (Munro 2005: 28). It may be the case that the value placed on children in *Chaste Maid*, who symbolise the forces of vitality, if not legitimacy, is a reflection on the significance of the children's companies as innovative, creative and often subversive forces on the Jacobean stage.

Attention to the earlier repertoire of the Children of the Queen's Revels may also shed light on Middleton's experimentations with tragicomedy in this period. Middleton wrote three highly self-conscious tragicomedies over a two-year period from around 1615 to 1617: *The Witch* and *More Dissemblers Besides Women*, for Shakespeare's company, the King's Men; and *A Fair Quarrel*, co-written with Rowley for Prince Charles's Company. His interest in tragicomedy is already clearly evident in *A Chaste Maid*. Beaumont and Fletcher had led the fashion for tragicomedy in their plays written for the Children of the Queen's Revels (Munro 2005: Ch. 3). Middleton was therefore collaborating with a company very familiar with performing tragicomedy. Tragicomic conventions are used by Middleton in both *Chaste Maid* and *No Wit* to extend the range of the satiric city comedy.

One of the defining features of tragicomedy is the miraculous reversal. A classic example is the scene in *The Winter's Tale* when the statue of Hermione, whose tragic death was reported in Act III, scene ii, miraculously comes to life; the wife is restored to her husband, and mother and the lost child are re-united. Middleton uses the tragicomic trope of 'miraculous' resurrection in the last Act of *Chaste Maid*. Following a duel between Sir Walter Whorehound and Touchwood Junior, in which both are wounded, Touchwood Junior is said to have died from his wounds. Moll 'dies' of a broken heart upon learning of her lover's death. The transition from death to rebirth is signalled by the intervening scene in which Sir Oliver celebrates his wife's 'miraculous' pregnancy brought about by Touchwood Senior's 'magical' elixir of life. The final scene opens with a funeral procession, with the coffins of Moll and Touchwood Junior carried on stage, accompanied by mournful music. Touchwood Senior delivers the funeral oration, praising the virtues of the young couple, gains the assent of the assembled community to their hoped-for marriage, and immediately calls on the couple to rise up from their coffins and 'take your fortunes,/Make these joyful hearts; here's none but friends' (V, iv, 28–9). As Joanne Altieri notes, there is 'no "wonder"' in the resurrection, rather it is embedded in the quotidian reality of this

London community (1988: 181). The scene does open with elaborate sound and visual effects – the *'solemnly decked'* coffins are
'attended by many in black', recorders play *'dolefully'* and offstage
'there is a sad song in the music room' – that are intended to induce a
sense of pathos. Yet there is little attempt to sustain the tragic affect
or to introduce symbolism to insinuate that a wider, redemptive
pattern is at work. Instead the 'resurrection' is quickly revealed not
to be miraculous at all but a plot hatched by Touchwood Senior and
aided by the servant, Susan, in order to dupe the parents who
oppose the marriage.

The play parodies tragicomic conventions through its insistent
and playful deflation of tragicomic miraculism by securing it in the
material world. Susan is only an 'honest chambermaid' and not an
agent of divine justice like the loyal waiting woman, Paulina, in
Winter's Tale (Altieri 1988: 181; see also Chakravorty 1996: 107–9).
It may be possible to argue that Touchwood Senior does signify
some of the higher, mythic values typically identified with tragicomic agents. Arthur Marotti, for example, describes Touchwood
Senior's 'enormous sexual potency' as symbolising a life-affirming
procreative vitality that exposes the empty, life-denying materialism
of the Yellowhammers, the blocking figures in the play (1969: 67–
72). Certainly the news of Lady Kix's pregnancy, also brought about
by the agency of Touchwood Senior, ushers in the rebirth of the
lovers. That said, bawdy punning means that the audience is well
aware that Lady Kix's pregnancy is anything but miraculous – in Act
III, scene iii, Touchwood Senior sends Sir Oliver Kix on a merry
dance, and then serves Lady Kix her medicine (appropriately
the colour of almond milk) lying down. The contract between
Touchwood Senior and the Kixes is similarly financial and prosaic:
Touchwood Senior needs money to maintain his expanding household, while Sir Oliver Kix needs an heir to prevent Whorehound
from inheriting his estate. The idealising energies of tragicomedy are invoked in order to be jestingly brought down to earth.
'Middleton suggests very strongly that reality transcends our capacity to reconstruct it within *any* mythic frame; he also suggests that
the frames are leaky,' Altieri argues. 'What spills over is the social,
contingent world that seems to escape formalization' (1988: 180–3,
174).

If *Chaste Maid* parodies tragicomic miraculism, then *No Wit, No Help Like a Woman's* directs its subversive energies at conventional romance formulae – the recovery of mothers and children lost at sea and the recovery of lost identities following the substitution of children. Middleton invokes the miraculous and providential pattern of romance early in the play. Mistress Low-water soliloquises on the divine and wondrous powers of redemption:

> The husk falls off in time that long shuts up
> The fruit in a dark prison; so sweeps by
> The cloud of miseries from wretches' eyes,
> That yet, though fall'n, at length they see to rise.
> The secret powers work wondrously, and duly. (ii, 148–52)

The 'wretch' is an image of fallen man redeemed through the mysterious workings of divine providence. It is presumably providence that restores the Low-waters to their fortune, re-unites Sir Oliver Twilight with his lost wife and daughter, and restores the daughters to their true parents and identities, reversing their fateful substitution at birth. This final restitution also averts the tragedy of incest, redeeming the marriage between Philip and Grace and allowing the two young couples to celebrate their unions.

Yet Middleton also travesties romance conventions in *No Wit*. The source for this plot is an Italian play, Giambattista della Porta's *La Sorella*, 'a sentimental Italian comedy'. Middleton lowers its tone considerably through often dark, bawdy humour (Gordon 1941: 400, 404). When Sir Oliver hears the news that his wife and daughter are still alive, in a foreign land, he sends his son, Philip, and faithful servant, Savourwit, with the ransom. The son and servant heartlessly spend the money on prostitutes: 'To lighten us of our carriage because gold/Is such a heavy metal, [we] eased our pockets/In wenches' aprons' (i, 77–9). Philip secretly marries 'a sweet young gentlewoman', but only because she 'would not sell her honour for the Indies' (i, 83–4). On their return, she is passed off as his ransomed sister, while Sir Oliver is told that Lady Twilight is 'gone to heaven./So he believes two lies in one error bred:/The daughter ransomed, and the mother dead' (i, 96–8). All's well that ends well, in that this 'trick' works by 'secret powers', unknown to the tricksters, and makes possible the restoration of the daughters.

That said, the play also reminds us that it is a venal and cruel trick which is initially driven by appetite at the expense of love and compassion for the lost mother and sister. The reconciliation scene between Philip and his mother uncomfortably mixes pathos with farce. Philip does not confess to his mother out of remorse, although he does recognise his 'share of sin and a foul neglect' (v, 16). Instead he follows the counsel of the trickster, Savourwit, to save both their skins by shamelessly exploiting his 'mother's pity': 'Beg, weep, kneel, anything, 'twill break no bones, man./Let her not rest, take breathing time, nor leave thee/Till thou has got her help' (v, 96–8). The theatricality of Philip's act of repentance is heightened by Savourwit's asides. It produces a highly self-conscious and artful mode of spectatorship in the scene. Critics have found this scene uncomfortable (Muir 1983: 155–7). Lady Twilight's too-easy forgiveness of her son's venery as youthful exuberance could be interpreted that the mother is once again being played. She is drawn into complicity in the deception out of over-fondness for her son, rather than a sense of redemptive justice. Attention is drawn to the success of the trick and not the miraculous 'secret powers' of providence, as Savourwit notes in an aside, 'She helps our knavery well; that's one good comfort' (v, 143). The use of Lady Goldenfleece as the tragicomic *deus ex machina* is similarly compromised. She is not a seer-type figure, a mystic keeper of a secret, like Paulina in *Winter's Tale*. Instead she is implicated in the treacherous and mercenary plots of her husband, the usurer Goldenfleece, and must endure a series of humiliations. In the final Act, she too is redeemed by her 'double charity' (ix, 575) – her marriage to Kate Low-Water's brother, Beveril, and her restoration of the fortunes of Kate's husband.

Middleton's interest in parody and burlesque is notable in the banquet in scene iv Weatherwise's banquet necessitates fourteen actors on stage at the same time at one point – five of these are seated around a table set out in signs of the zodiac. The use of such an elaborate conceit, where even the *'banqueting stuff'* (s. d.), – the fruit and sweetmeats brought on stage – is in the shape of zodiac signs, mimics the elaborate artifice and theatricality of the aristocratic feast (Middleton 2007: I, 781). Yet Weatherwise's banquet is in the tradition of burlesque feasts that goes back to the classical writers and Lucian's *The Lapiths* in which the banquet degenerates into a drunken brawl (Jeanneret 1991: 150–1). Weatherwise's 'conceited' feast parodies and debases the courtly neo-Platonic symbolism of the aristocratic feast by turning its ideals into the popular, low forms of the almanac, a staple of cheap print (Middleton 2007: I, 781). The subversive, mocking presence of the Clown at the table acknowledges the debt of this seene to a burlesque tradition (O'Callaghan 2007: 73–6). The meal's high-minded civilising influence dissipates as sexual competition over the widow, which should be sublimated in the interests of civility, overflows – the feast ends in true burlesque fashion with a quarrel and the expulsion of one of the guests, Sir Gilbert Lambstone.

Middleton also includes an elaborate wedding masque in scene ix in which the jilted lovers subvert the harmonising function of the masque, quickly turning it into an anti-masque. This broken wedding masque is a comic version of the masque that closes *Women Beware Women*. These ensemble pieces, the banquet and the masque, demonstrate Middleton's skills in composing and managing complexly choreographed scenes, which come to the fore in his tragedies, particularly *Women Beware Women*.

THE TRAFFIC IN WOMEN: FEMINIST READINGS OF MIDDLETON

The commodified sexual body is a defining feature of city comedies. The marriage, the engine of the comic plot, is translated into the commercial terms of the city. Women are transacted in these plays. *Chaste Maid in Cheapside* opens in a goldsmith's shop in Cheapside or West Cheap. The goldsmith's shop was the centre of the trade in luxury items as well as a type of bank, in that the goldsmith acted as a money-changer: Yellowhammer remonstrates with his wife, 'Has no attorney's clerk been here o'late/And changed his half-crown-piece his mother sent him,/Or rather cozen'd you with a gilded twopence' (I, i, 30–2). As Janelle Day Jenstad notes, 'the early modern goldsmith's shop offers a playwright particularly rich metaphoric possibilities' (2002: 1). Middleton uses the goldsmith's shop as the primary site for the negotiation of marriage contracts, thus establishing equivalence between the trade in gold, coinage and other luxury goods, and the trade in women. A comparable analogy between the trade in goods and the trade in women is established in Middleton's and Dekker's *Roaring Girl* – scene iii opens with a row of shops on stage, with citizen wives selling their wares to gentlemanly gallants. *Chaste Maid* opens with Maudline Yellowhammer in the shop despairing of her daughter. Despite all efforts to add social capital, through music and dancing lessons, and thereby raise the social value of this citizen daughter to make her 'fit for a knight's bed' (I, i, 11), Moll 'dance[s] like a plumber's daughter and deserve[s]/Two thousand pound in lead' for her marriage portion and 'not in goldsmith's ware' (I, i, 21–2). Moll is explicitly portrayed as a commodity in the commercial transaction between the Yellowhammers and the knight, Sir Walter Whorehound. This is not the only marital transaction in this scene. Her brother, Tim, 'must marry/ . . . a match of Sir Walter's own making,/To bind us to him, and our heirs for ever' (I, i, 44–6). There was a structural equivalence between youths and women in the early modern household: children were subject to their parents, and their marriages carefully arranged to secure social relations. The two youths, the Ward and Isabella, in *Women Beware Women* are similarly commodified in the marriage negotiations between his guardian and her father.

Running throughout this opening scene is a complex analogy between women and coinage, which masterfully utilises the significance of the goldsmith's shop as the place where money is converted. For the Yellowhammers, the knight, Sir Whorehound, represents a vector for social conversion from citizenry to gentry. What they do not realise is that Whorehound is on a downward turn. Ironically, it is Yellowhammer who points out that the goldsmith may be 'cozened' by false coin, and 'gilded twopence' (I, i, 32) exchanged for his true gold. This is precisely the piece of 'conversion' Whorehound aims at by marrying his mistress to the wealthy citizen's son, and securing his own fortune by marrying Moll, the 'chaste maid'. As he says to the Welsh gentlewoman: 'I bring thee up to turn thee into gold, wench,/And make thy fortune shine like your bright trade;/A goldsmith's shop sets out a city maid' (I, i, 107–9; Jenstad 2002: 4–5, 20). The conversation between Whorehound and his mistress takes place while Yellowhammer is valuing a customer's gold chain, reinforcing the analogy between the trade in women and gold. Whereas Whorehound has over-valued his mistress, and is trying to pass off false coin as true, a pros-titute for a 'pure virgin', the Yellowhammers have miscalculated the true value of their daughter in this exchange. Earlier in the scene, Moll's value on the marriage market had been described by her mother in terms of lead, as opposed to gold. Touchwood Senior's eulogy in the closing scene appropriately reveals her true value. Jenstad notes Middleton's witty pun on 'chaste' as 'sexually pure' and 'chased' as a 'jewel set in gold or silver': 'Moll is ultimately not base metal or a counterfeit coin, but "Beauty set in goodness . . . that jewel so infixed"' (V, iv, 17–18), a reference that suggests that she is the true 'chased' maid despite her parents' debasement of her' (Jenstad 2002: 16–20). We should remember that Moll's 'jewel' is her virginity; her value as the 'true, chaste' maid is reduced to the status of her hymen. Given that this is the case, does it make a difference that the play closes by seeming to endorse Tim's ability to 'prove/A whore an honest woman' by marrying the Welsh gentlewoman?

Lady Goldenfleece, the wealthy widow of the usurer, Sir Avarice Goldenfleece, similarly is the prize sought by a number of the male characters in *No Wit, No Help Like a Woman's*. The pursuit of the rich widow drives much of the Low-water intrigue plot. Middleton uses this plot device of the rich widow in a number of plays. As we have seen in *Trick to Catch the Old One*, the widow has a high value on the marriage market. Witgood's efforts to secure Joyce, his 'chaste maid', and her fortune, a 'thousand good pound' (I, i, 145–6) is dependent on the success of the Courtesan's disguise as a wealthy widow. The early modern widow was caught between competing imperatives: on the one hand, the Church insisted on 'the chastity of widows', who should remain faithful to the memory of their husbands; on the other, wealthy widows were pursued by suitors because of their economic desirability as the executors of large estates (Jardine 1983: 83–4). Both *A Trick* and *No Wit* make it clear that the rich widow functions as a form of property. Hence the promise of marriage to the Widow Medlar in *A Trick* enables Witgood to raise the credit necessary to gain 'a virgin's love, her portion and her virtues' (I, i, 22). Part of the trick is that Witgood's knowing attempt to keep this valuable property to himself and out of circulation is guaranteed to fail in a rapacious city populated by the likes of Moneylove and Hoard. It is worth noting just how many times variants on the phrase 'Four hundred a year landed' (II, ii, 16) are used as a synonym for the rich widow. Similarly, the 'happy rumour of a rich country widow' (II, ii, 13) circulates across Act II, scene i to Act III, scene i, providing a dramatic and symbolic linkage between the various constellations of characters.

The transaction of the rich widow is sexualised; it is said that 'She lies open to much rumour' (II, ii, 63–4) alluding to the proverbial sexual availability of the widow as well as the way news of the widow is being transmitted in London through the channels of gossip. The name Widow Medlar refers, on one hand, to the fruit of the medlar tree which is best eaten when rotten (*OED*, 2), and to meddle as in 'to have sexual intercourse' (*OED*, 5). The name reveals the Courtesan behind the rich widow, and carries negative connotations in its association of the woman's sexualised body with fleshly decay. That said, just how stable is this image of sexual corruption? Presumably the 'Widow Medlar' is 'tasty' precisely because she is sexually experienced, thus problematising the moral dichotomy between good and bad, pure and corrupt, wife and whore. The stereotype of the lusty widow is invoked when Lamprey, advocating on Hoard's behalf, cajoles the Courtesan into accepting Hoard's marriage proposal, chiding her 'Come, you widows are ever most backward when you should do yourselves most good, but were it to marry a chin not worth a hair now, then you would be forward enough' (III, i, 197–200). The widow's financial and sexual independence within this cultural logic means that she is driven by lust, and hence would choose young men for their sexual performance, rather than older men for the security they offered (Leinwand 1986: 180–2). The problem posed by the widow is that she can take herself out of the homosocial exchanges of the early modern traffic in women and transact her own marriage (see above, pp. 34–5, 41).

The stereotype of the self-ruled lusty widow underpins the courtship of Lady Goldenfleece by Kate Low-water, disguised as a young gentleman, in *No Wit*. Kate woos Lady Goldenfleece by promising her youth and sexual vigour. It is this youthful forwardness that wins the suit against the other competitors. The courtship scene bawdily puns on the language of business and financial transactions. 'I promise you, widow,' says the disguised Kate, committing herself sexually to Lady Goldenfleece, 'were I a setter-up, such is my opinion of your payment I durst trust you with all the ware in my shop' (vi, 124–6). 'His' shop is 'his' penis; since 'he' has nothing to offer her but sex, financial liquidity is replaced by phallic potency. When Lady Goldenfleece urges her new husband towards the marriage bed, the rapacious sexual appetite of the lusty widow is equated with the extortionate practices of her dead husband, Sir Avarice Goldenfleece, 'Now like a greedy usurer, alone/I sum up all the wealth this day has brought me;/And thus I hug it' (ix, 208–10).

The joke is that the young gentleman is a young gentlewoman. Middleton exploits the jest by folding same-sex desire into the stereotype of the lusty widow. The jilted Sir Gilbert Lambston bitterly satirises the sexual appetites of this figure:

> Rich widows that were wont to choose by gravity
> Their second husbands, not by tricks of blood,
> Are now so taken with loose Aretine flames
> Of nimble wantonness and high-fed pride,
> They marry now but the third part of husbands –
> Boys, smooth-faced catamites – to fulfil their bed,
> As if a woman should a woman wed. (ix, 86–92)

The perceived desire of 'rich widows' to maintain financial and sexual independence after marriage is condemned as narcissistic. Women-on-top only want toy boys or dildos. They want the sex, 'the third part of husbands', but not their governance. The 'smooth-faced catamite' is a visual pun on the boy actor playing Kate Low-water, who in turn plays the part of a youth. The proximity between a youth and a maid, and the widow's unwitting marriage to a woman is collapsed into the closing image of the lesbian marriage. The joke is at the expense of the widow. The laughter is the laughter of ridicule that directs its violence at the 'high-fed pride' of widows. Lady Goldenfleece is punished in the play by being hit where it hurts: the 'physic [that] will pay't home' (ix, 293) is her new 'husband's' refusal to have sex with her, and she is subjected to further sexual humiliation when she is tricked into a compromising position with Beveril.

Lady Goldenfleece, however, is not all bad. Theodore Leinwand suggests that Middleton's depiction of the widow is complex and complicated: 'Middleton seems to be struggling with the stereotype of the sex-craved widow – one moment he stages the type uncritically, but in the next moment he uncovers the very human needs and desires which are traditionally distorted by the stereotyped monster' (Leinwand 1986: 184). The play does invest the speeches of Lady Goldenfleece in the final scene with pathos:

> Have I yet married poverty, and missed love?
> What fortune has my heart? That's all I craved,
> And that lies now a-dying. It has took
> A speeding poison, and I'm ignorant how.
> I never knew what beggary was till now. (ix, 284–8)

There is the suggestion that marriage with an effeminate youth would lead to mutuality and companionship. She is not a venal character like her failed suitor, Sir Gilbert Lambston, who flees in shame at the close of the play. It is, however, possible to argue that these contradictions arise because her character is over-determined by the plotting, rather than by the play's efforts to evoke sympathy for her plight. Lady Goldenfleece must be 'physicked' and redeemed in this final scene in order to make her a fit wife for Kate Low-water's brother, Beveril, and so that she can function as the *deus ex machina* in the tragicomic plot. And yet the representation of women is shifting, complex and complicated in *No Wit*. Middleton's plays are not simply responsive to the contradictory demands of early modern gender ideologies, but search out points of instability and place dramatic pressure on them. One of the way these 'facetious' plays destabilise conventions is through the forms of the carnivalesque.[1]

FLESH AND FLUIDS: CARNIVAL AND THE CARNAL

Chaste Maid in Cheapside is set during Lent, a period of 'carnal strictness' (II, ii, 75). The play devotes Act II, scene ii to Lenten restrictions against eating meat which had been tightened in 1613 (Middleton 2002: xiv). Under the promoters, whose office it was to ensure that the Lenten restrictions were enforced, carnival persists in debased carnal forms. The promoters are imagined by Allwit as crows pecking on 'dead corpses of poor calves and sheep,/Like ravenous creditors' (II, ii, 62–3) intent on beggaring the city, taking goods out of necessary circulation to fatten their own households. Images of death and corruption cluster around the promoters (Marotti 1969: 70). That said, the scene ends with a baby and a feast, prompted by the trick played by the Country Wench, who leaves the promoters with the care of her illegitimate child. To commiserate, the promoters will 'go to the Checker at Queenhive,/And roast the loin of mutton till young flood;/Then send the child to Brentford' (II, ii, 186–8). Images of rebirth are associated with the baby, and are echoed in the promise of 'young flood', but the infant is also a product of the sins of the flesh. As the promoters rummage in the basket, the baby's head is mistaken for a lamb's, alluding to the symbolism of the Lenten pascal lamb, yet also carrying uncomfortable connotations of cannibalism, extending the earlier imagery of carrion crows to this vision of promoters hoping to feed off young flesh. This is 'realist, urban grotesque', as Rick Bowers has noted, in which 'Carnival and Lent collide and reconfigure themselves with unsentimental comic tension' (2003: 1, 6). The nature and function of the carnivalesque energies of *Chaste Maid* have received a great deal of critical attention, and much of that is divided. This section will set out key readings of comedy and carnival in *Chaste Maid* since they encapsulate the variety of approaches available for elucidating the issues at stake.

For Arthur Marotti, the carnivalesque energies of the play are a celebration of the flesh and the triumph of life forces over death. As this formulation suggests, he offers a Freudian reading of the play as dramatising the dialectical and primal struggle between eros and thanatos, the sex and death drives. The 'unusual number of pregnancies and onstage infants' is a material sign of the play's affirmation of fertility and regenerative sexuality. The children of Mistress Allwit and the Country Wench do not function to condemn male libertinism but instead amplify the 'theme of procreative vitality'. This priapic play discloses the source of comedy in the ancient forms of phallic song: 'If Eros is the "presiding genius of comedy", he exists here in his properly comic avatar Priapus in the character of Touchwood Sr., who, in his enormous sexual potency, most vividly symbolizes the power of fertility present in Middleton's dramatic world' (Marotti 1969: 66–7, 70). The erotic energies of *Chaste Maid*, Marotti argues, are communal in orientation and anti-materialist, and so work to deride the avaricious and deathly commerce of the Lenten promoters as well as the materialism of the Yellowhammers. Marotti's reading is idealising in that his model of carnival privileges the mythic over the materialist. And it also interprets the play as an unproblematic celebration of virile masculinity.

Gail Kern Paster's feminist reading looks at the woman's part in this celebration of (male) fertility. She concurs with Marotti that phallic potency does drive the play, but locates its symbolism within the power relations of a patriarchal society:

> Middleton creates a wonderfully comic context for his male fertility gods by linking the biological fact of male potency to the far more reliable social facts of the play – that is, to the ingenious social and discursive arrangements by which male authority in Cheapside masks and serves its sexual drive and social ambitions. (Paster 1993: 57)

The myth of male potency has a material investment in maintaining homosocial relations (see above, pp. 34–5, 41). Hence, Paster argues, the play sets up a series of productive alliances between men: Allwit and Whorehound, Sir Oliver Kix and Touchwood Senior, and Touchwood Senior and Junior. If male liquidity denotes phallic power and its processes of transmission, then female liquidity represents its inverse – loss of control and lack of self-control.

The key scene in this reading is the christening scene in Act III, scene ii. This scene is set in Mistress Allwit's bedchamber, during her period of lying-in. There is a 'bed thrust out upon the stage', in which Mistress Allwit has pride of place, and Maudline Yellowhammer, Lady Kix, Gossips and the Puritan women all take stools around the bed, as the Nurse passes around the baby girl to be admired. This is an overtly feminine space, and the scene opens by jesting about paternity. Men are part of the scene, but are clearly uncomfortable and marginalised among this company of women. Female liquidity in this scene is urinary as well as sexual. The spectacle of wine being consumed is accompanied by other liquids. Allwit complaining of the gossips' pocketing food, the excesses of female consumption, notes with disgust: 'Now in goes the long fingers that are washed/Some thrice a day in urine' (III, ii, 53–4). One of the Gossips, her tongue loosened by drink, speaks incontinently about her daughter's 'secret fault' (III, ii, 95), that 'she's too free' and 'cannot lie dry in her bed' (III, ii, 98–9). Allwit surveying the drunken women, complains in disgust that 'They have drunk so hard in plate/That some of them had need of other vessels' (III, ii, 179–80), 'How hot they have made the room with their thick bums' (III, ii, 193), and is concerned about the wet under the stools. He views the women and this feminine space with disgust and loathing, venting his spleen at the way they have 'shuffled up the rushes .../With their short figging little shuttle-cork heels!/These women can let nothing stand as they find it' (III, ii, 201–3). This is the 'body embarrassed'; emotions of shame and disgust, as well as the laughter of ridicule are directed at the incontinent female body. By translating female liquidity primarily in shameful, urinary terms, the play sets out the ideological differences between male and female fluids. The 'construction of women as leaky vessels' in the play serves the 'powerful interests of patriarchal ideology' in that it becomes the task of men to keep women under control and their 'holes plugged' (Paster 1993: 58).

Paster's reading of the christening scene allows us to see how the jokes function in terms of notions of shame and disgust, which in turn direct the violence of derision against the female body. One difficulty with her reading of this scene, as others have noted, is that she takes Allwit as the play's ideal spectator, a stable moral point-of-view, through whose eyes we see the action. Bowers points out that the danger of promoting 'Allwit to the status of choric commentator' is that it 'confer[s] normative values on to Allwit and misrepresent[s] the sharp comedy involved' (2003: 12). Paster does give a very 'straight' reading of *Chaste Maid* that does not adequately take into account the witty perversity of the play and sidesteps the formal and discursive issues raised by the use of travesty and burlesque, particularly in the christening scene (Newman 2006: 244–5). Malcolm McKay's 1997 production of the play for the opening season of the Globe Theatre emphasised the grotesque elements of the scene for a modern audience by having the gossips played by male actors in drag (Middleton 2002: xxxii). That said, Paster does make an important point that the majority of the jokes in this scene are directed at the woman's body through images of the *female* grotesque. Bowers, following Altieri, draws attention to the importance of the use of Aristophanic models of comedy in *Chaste Maid* when analysing Middleton's version of the carnivalesque. Aristophanic comedy delights in parody and burlesque; it is not an idealising form since its energies are directed into subverting norms through travesty; it challenges conventional categories by violating them (2003: 18–20; Altieri 1988). This has particular repercussions for the stability of key patriarchal norms and institutions in the play, such as primogeniture. The tactical wit of *Chaste Maid* introduces play and instability into the very 'foundations of power' (de Certeau 1988: 37–9).

Altieri draws attention to the complex ways in which 'the intense specific sociality' of Middleton's plays fixes the mythic dimension of the carnivalesque in the material world (1988: 173). Models of carnival, following through the implications of the work of Bakhtin, tend to confine the materialism of the carnivalesque to bodily forms. Bakhtin's carnivalesque, with its language of the lower bodily stratum, belonged to the older communal and pre-capitalist marketplace, a 'place of both trade and celebration' (Wells 1981: 38) For Karen Newman, the carnivalesque energies of the play do not represent market forces as life-denying, but rather celebrate the liquidity of the early modern London marketplace, 'a place of never-ending exchange and circulation'. The 'leaky vessels' of the play, both male and female are not contained, instead 'the circulation of waters . . . continues unabated' (2006: 245). Newman considers how this playful liquidity operates at structural level in the play and its impact on the audiences' ability to locate stable moral vantage points. *Chaste Maid*, as we have seen, has a complex multiple plot which is structured analogically, in that constellations of characters and lines of action in one plot are mirrored in another. Does this structural doubling affect the audience's ability to make clear moral distinctions between the different characters and plots? Richard Levin, in his study *The Multiple Plot in English Renaissance Drama* argues that the analogical structure of the play sets up clear moral antitheses, for example, between the sexual contract that brings together the Allwits and Whorehound and that between the Kixes and Touchwood Senior (1971: 95–6). Yet it is also possible to argue, along with Newman, that the complex and insistent analogical structure of the plot is designed to foreground similarities, 'equivalences [which Middleton] . . . presents in comically explicit economic terms' (2006: 242).

The way that the patterns of equivalence, exchange and circulation structure the play impacts on the nominal subject of the play – the chaste maid. What is the valuation placed on chastity within a symbolic economy that privileges circulation? The sexual circulation of women, as we have seen in *Trick to Catch the Old One*, *Mad World, My Masters*, as well as *Chaste Maid*, does not seem to render these women worthless within the carnivalised patriarchal economy of these plays. Do they, instead, accumulate value? The trick that converts the Courtesan into a rich widow, and Whorehound's mistress into the Welsh Gentlewoman, runs parallel to the trick that propels the romantic comedy plot and concludes in both plays with the double marriage. The libertinism of this doubling is foregrounded in the closing speeches of *Chaste Maid*. The mock-scholastic dimension of travesty is signalled by Tim's carnivalised Latin: '*Flectere si nequeo superos, Acheronta movebo*' (V, iii, 99) – this is a line from Book VII of Virgil's *Aeneid*, 'Since I cannot move the powers above, I shall work on the lower regions' (Middleton 2002: xx). This scholarly joke draws attention to the playful downward movement of travesty and burlesque – although its playful meaning is restricted to those in the audience able to understand Latin. Tim is a parody of the new university man, the type of learned fool (see above, p. 8). His function in this scene is to deride the forms of logic and set in its place a facetious wit. Tim and his tutor may not be able to prove the Welsh Gentlewoman 'honest' by logic, but as she points out 'There's a thing called marriage, and that makes me honest' (V, iii, 111), to which his mother responds, 'there's a trick beyond your logic, Tim' (V, iii, 112). Maudline's merry 'trick' homophonically echoes Tim's earlier '*meretrix*' (V, iii, 109), the Latin for whore. We do have to ask ourselves, when did marriage become a trick and not a legitimating practice? Tim's final speech throws everything up in the air: 'I perceive then a woman may be honest according to the English print, when she is a whore in the Latin; so much for marriage and logic! I'll love her for her wit, I'll pick out my runts there; and for my mountains, I'll mount upon [. . .]' (V, iii, 113–17). Wit here has a sceptical quality in that it destabilises the traditional humanist equation between the rhetorical forms of argument and moral judgement and conventions (see pp. 2, 147). According to the mocking 'logic' of *Chaste Maid*, it seems not to matter if your wife is a whore or your children are bastards.

In *No Wit, No Help Like a Woman's*, woman's wit similarly has a structural function. As D. J. Gordon notes, each plot is an 'illustration' of the 'thesis' set out in the play's title that there is 'no wit, no help like a woman's': 'it is Mistress Low-water who tricks her enemy and helps her brother; it is Lady Twilight who rescues her son from the mess he has got into'; and 'it is Lady Goldenfleece who finally resolves the lovers' difficulties' (1941: 414). As in Middleton's other comedies, the female trickster is given a driving role in the plot. That said, the female wits of *No Wit* are arguably less destabilising than their comic counterparts in Middleton's city comedies. Female wit functions in this play to secure homosocial interests: Kate Low-water chastises the widow, Lady Goldenfleece, restores her husband's fortune, and finally succeeds in marrying her brother to a rich widow. Yet the emphasis on female wit is accompanied by a carnivalised patriarchy, and the agency accorded to Kate in the play is predicated on disempowered male characters. The carnivalesque unleashes energies – social, political, textual and dramatic – that are difficult to control and contain.

MASCULINITY: SEX AND THE SOCIAL ORDER

As we have seen in *The Roaring Girl*, the problem in Middleton's comedies is not so much unruly women as unruly or deficient men (see above, pp. 53–4). The instability inherent in representations of masculinity in these plays alerts us to the distinctions between patriarchy and forms of manhood. Patriarchy in the early modern period meant, quite specifically, 'rule by fathers': 'the government of society by male household heads', which involved 'the subordination of younger men as well as women' (Shepard 2003: 3). Early modern patriarchy set up an equivalence between male youths and women that is frequently placed under erotic pressure in comedies through the figure of the cross-dressed boy, from Mary Fitzallard in *The Roaring Girl* to Kate Low-water in *No Wit*. As this implies, gender identities should be understood less in terms of a rigid binary between male and female, than as a spectrum in which the effeminate youth enjoyed a close proximity to the nubile woman. An awareness of the differences between men and boys also alerts us to 'the gender differences *within* each sex'. There was a multiplicity of gender identities available in the period. While some formulations of manhood were complicit with patriarchy, other modes of masculinity ran counter to patriarchal imperatives (Shepard 2003: 4–5; see above, pp. 54, 65). Middleton's plays are populated by unruly men – Laxton is a good case in point – who not only threaten the domestic realm, but as simultaneous embodiments of excess and lack, threaten to undo dominant discourses of masculinity that promote self-possession.

Primogeniture is turned into a joke in *Chaste Maid*. 'Touchwood Senior's whole portrayal', Altieri writes, 'is . . . a carnivalesque attack on primogeniture, on the sanctity of bloodlines, an attack consistent with the play's social iconoclasm' (1988: 181–2). Touchwood Senior is structurally mirrored in the play in Sir Walter Whorehound in that both are variations on the unruly sexuality of the libertine: both have illicit sexual contracts with married couples; their excessive virility is evident in their over-production of children; and if Whorehound has his Welsh Gentlewoman, then Touchwood Senior has his Country Wench. The difference between the two men is that Touchwood Senior's libertinism is communal in impulse as opposed to the acquisitive individualism identified with Whorehound. Touchwood Senior will use the money from supplying the Kixes with an heir to maintain his own family and so restore himself to his household. Whorehound represents a threat to the Kix's estate since it passes to him if they remain childless. Lady Kix laments to her husband that their barrenness makes him fat: 'None gets by your not-getting but that knight;/He's made by th'means, and fats his fortunes shortly/In a great dowry with a goldsmith's daughter' (II, i, 157–9). As his name indicates, Whorehound is a negative stereotype of the unruly male whose lechery turns him into a dog, less than man and the embodiment of bestial appetite.

Patriarchs, heads of households, are deficient in *Chaste Maid*. Allwit is a willing cuckold, more than happy to vacate his position at the head of the household and turn the role of husband and father over to another man. Sir Oliver Kix is similarly a deficient male; his sexual inadequacy is expressed through his inability to govern his wife, turning the household into a battleground. His manhood is restored at the end of the play: 'Ho, my wife's quickened; I am a man for ever!' (V, iii, 1). Yet it takes a bastardised form given that Sir Oliver is reliant on the sexual services of Touchwood Senior for his heirs, effectively turning him into a version of Allwit. The play does not censure either Allwit, who is able to set up 'shop' with his wife elsewhere in London, or Sir Oliver whose contract with Touchwood Senior is a key element of the restoration of community at the end of the play. Bastard children are similarly portrayed in a favourable light – one of the Puritan Gossip admits 'I would not care what clown my husband were too, so I had such fine children' (III, ii, 30–1). In the case of these 'fine children', the sins of the father are not visited on the children, and the conventional association between moral deformity and physical ugliness is not maintained. In the case of the contract between Sir Oliver and Touchwood Senior, bastard children function as a positive sign of the social exchanges between men in the play thus endorsing a bastardised, carnivalised patriarchy.

Patriarchs, in the case of the Low-water plot in *No Wit*, as Jowett points out, are either 'dead (Goldenfleece), ineffectual (Low-water) or contemptible (the Widow's suitors)' (Middleton 2007: I, 779). Low-water, in particular, is defined by his failure to respond adequately to patriarchal imperatives. His name signifies poverty, yet, given Middleton's delight in the language of liquidity, it suggests it is not just his fortunes which are at a low ebb. The homosociality of a culture of credit meant that male self-worth was predicated on men's creditworthiness, their ability to generate wealth and protect their fortune. Low-water has clearly failed this 'social and economic assessment of men' (Shepard 2003: 191). His witty wife, seemingly possessed of greater intellectual capital, must take his place. The play stages her entry into the male fray at a definitive homosocial event, the banquet, where she enters into sexual competition with the other men for the widow, while her husband takes on the socially subordinate role of servant. Philip Twilight has some of the characteristics of the unruly male. His early libertinism, however, is contained within the romantic plot and directed towards marriage. And yet marriage is itself destabilised in the play. Two 'false marriages' link the two plots: the same-sex marriage between Widow Goldenfleece and Kate, and the incestuous marriage between Philip and Grace. Both short-circuit the generational role of marriage: 'Incest doubles the family upon itself, and same-sex marriage denies the possibility of progeny . . . [both] undermine male control of reproduction and inheritance' (Middleton 2007: I, 781).

Gender instability is a feature of Middleton's comedies in general. For a Calvinist writer, Middleton has a positive fascination with libertinism, from the licentious and sceptical wit to the priapic champion of *Chaste Maid*, Touchwood Senior.[2] One feature of Middleton's 'witty muse' is an interest in exploring modes of masculinity that undermine or are in tension with patriarchal imperatives. But, as we shall see in his tragedies, it does not prevent his plays from mobilising deeply misogynist responses to female sexuality. There is a level of violence to Middleton's wit that is disturbing even in his comedies and tragicomedies and adds a dangerous edge to his satire. Lyn Gardner, in her review of McKay's 1997 production at the Globe for *The Guardian*, criticised the way it turned the play's 'very precise satire' into 'broad farce' by creating 'a gallery of loveable rogues rather than a cast of despicable villains who'd happily slit your throat on a dark night and enjoy watching you bleed to death. This is all too pleasant by half. You miss the sour stench of Middleton's poisonous humour' (Middleton 2002: xxxii).

NOTES

1. 'Carnivalesque' is a term that derives from carnival, a ritual period of revels, feasting and entertainment, which symbolise the momentary subversion of forms of authority, through figures such as the Lord of Misrule. Mikhail Bakhtin coined the term in his *Rabelais and his World* (1965) to describe the incorporation of the subversive structures and energies of carnival into language and literature, exemplified by burlesque, parody and satire and other forms of 'low' literature, which privilege the disruptive effect of the body and material world on 'higher' forms.

2. On Calvinism, see above p. 18.

CHAPTER 5

The Playwright as Craftsman: Middleton's Civic Pageants

Middleton's first involvement with civic pageantry came in 1604, with the entertainments for the entry of James I into the City of London. The event had been delayed by plague, but this did not mar the magnificent spectacle the governors of London staged for the new King. Free wine flowed from the water conduits, and the streets were thronged with people. The arch at Fleet Street was designed by Dekker, and Middleton provided the speech the figure of Zeal addressed to the King. Dekker and Ben Jonson devised the entertainments for the royal entry – Jonson was responsible for the first and last arches, and Dekker for the rest (Bergeron 2003: 83–4, 71). It is likely that Dekker commissioned his new associate, Middleton, to assist him with his part of the dramas. Zeal's speech begins with a lament that Elizabeth's death put the order of the cosmos out of joint, it is James who has realigned the globe and renewed the state: 'Our globe is drawn in a right line again,/ And now appear new faces and new men' (*The Whole Royal and Magnificent Entertainment*, Middleton 2007: I, 2,130–1).

Middleton was one of the 'new faces and new men' on the London scene in the early seventeenth century. As David Bergeron argues, the 'London entertainment for James is a pivotal moment in civic pageantry' because it takes the form to a new level of magnificence and sophistication. Civic pageantry 'achieves a new status', attracting established dramatists eager to explore the possibilities of the medium. Middleton was the dramatist who took the pageant form to these new levels, and did more to shape the form than his contemporary, Anthony Munday, the most prolific writer of pageants (2003: 88). From 1613 to 1626, he was employed by the City governors and guilds to produce various entertainments. His civic pageants are experimental, transforming the medium from a simple emblematic device into a complex allegorical drama. At the same time, his immersion in a pageant tradition feeds into his later plays, particularly his great tragedies, *Women Beware Women* and *The Changeling*. Civic pageantry can tell us much about Middleton's work as a playwright, from collaboration to staging spectacles.

STAGING LONDON: CIVIC ENTERTAINMENTS AND CIVIC IDEOLOGY

Middleton was a valued and committed servant of the City of London. The first and arguably the most important Lord Mayor's Show Middleton produced was *The Triumphs of Truth*, devised for the inauguration of the Grocer, Sir Thomas Myddleton, in 1613. It was not only 'the most expensive mayoral pageant' of this period, but set the standard, a very high standard, for subsequent pageants (Bergeron 2003: 88, 179). In 1616, he provided two scenes for the entertainments sponsored by the City of London, *Civitatis Amor*, to mark the investiture of Prince Charles as Prince of Wales. The next year, he was again commissioned by the Grocers and devised *The Triumphs of Honour and Industry* (1617) for the mayoral inauguration of George Bolles. Two years later his pageant, *The Triumphs of Love and Antiquity* (1619), was chosen, this time by the Skinners' Company for the instauration of Sir William Cokayne. In 1620, Cokayne and his successor, Sir Francis Jones, commissioned Middleton to write entertainments for grand feasts or other events, which he gathered together and published in a volume entitled *Honourable Entertainments*. This was the year he was awarded the new office of city chronologer in recognition of his service to the City of London. Over the next six years, he produced four more shows: *The Sun in Aries* (1621) for Edward Barkham and the Drapers; *The Triumphs of Honour and Virtue* (1622), again for the

Grocers, this time for the inauguration of Sir Peter Proby; he collaborated with Anthony Munday on *The Triumphs of Integrity* (1623) for Martin Lumley of the Drapers; and his final show was *The Triumphs of Health and Prosperity* (1626) for another Draper, Cuthbert Hacket. It is likely that the furore over *A Game at Chess* (1624) meant that he was not considered a politic choice for the mayoral pageant of 1624, and in 1625 the Lord Mayor's show was cancelled due to plague.

Middleton enjoyed the patronage of wealthy city merchants. The Myddleton brothers employed Middleton to devise not only the mayoral show for Sir Thomas, but also an earlier entertainment to mark the opening of the New River, a project to bring fresh water into the city, sponsored by Sir Hugh Myddleton. Both Sir Thomas and Sir Hugh were wealthy enterprising merchants. Sir Thomas had gained much of his wealth through trade enterprises in Europe, and had invested as well in expeditions in the Indies. He acquired substantial landholdings in his native Wales when local gentry defaulted on loans made by him – there is an intriguing echo here of the plight of Master Easy in *Michaelmas Term*, the gentleman who loses his land to a merchant (see above, pp. 30–2). Sir Hugh began his city career as a goldsmith and similarly prospered. Heinemann has argued that the Myddleton brothers were part of a group of 'Parliamentary Puritans' who were 'discreetly opposed on occasion to the policy of the Crown'. Middleton gained their patronage, she argues, because of a shared religious politics (Heinemann 1982: 126).

It is the case that *The Triumphs of Truth* (1613), devised for Sir Thomas Myddleton, is notable for its promotion of godly Protestantism. The epistle calls on the forces of 'Almighty Providence', and sees public office in distinctly Calvinist terms as necessitating purity of conscience: '[A]ll pollution,/Sin, and uncleanness must be locked out here,/And kept sweet with sanctity, faith, and fear' (188–90).[1] The pageant is a sustained allegory in which Error, identified both with religious error (Catholicism) and corruption of office (flattery, bribery), is driven out of the city by the Protestant forces of Zeal and the Angel of Truth. Both these figures are militaristic, they are God's soldiers, and, as such, identified with Sir Thomas in his office as Lord Mayor. The streets of London, from the Cross in Cheap to St Lawrence Lane, become a battleground between the forces of Truth and Error – the pageant ends with a firework display by Humphrey Nichols in which Error's chariot is 'blown up' by a flame shot from the head of Zeal. In a spectacular display, the Lord Mayor and his fellow governors are presented as the godly and righteous forces that will drive out abuses in the commonwealth (Bromham 1995). The figure of 'Perfect Love' advises Myddleton that the good health of the commonwealth can be secured only by a strict dietary regimen of Truth.

Heinemann's study, *Puritanism and Theatre*, was important for drawing attention to the politics of pageantry. That said, the details of its argument have been challenged by historians and literary critics. One difficulty raised by reading Middleton's civic entertainments solely as vehicles for promoting the oppositional agenda of the 'Parliamentary Puritans' is that not all the lord mayors he wrote for fit this profile. *The Triumphs of Love and Antiquity* was devised for Sir William Cokayne, a merchant-courtier who 'earned his knighthood by feasting and bestowing lavish gifts on the monarch' (Middleton 2007: I, 1,397). He was responsible for the disastrous 'Cokayne Project', which had a severe impact on the English cloth trade. Middleton's pageant for Cokayne takes the trade of the Skinners – basically skinning 'beasts bearing fur' (105–6) – as the grounds for his story of Orpheus's civilising influence over the beasts. Cokayne is the careful and 'wise magistrate', who has tamed the wilderness of the commonwealth, and reformed its 'oppression, coz'nage, bribes, false hires' (151) through his virtuous civilising influence. Middleton does not shy away from honouring Cokayne's dependence on the court and his reliance on royal favour for his schemes: 'Never was man advanced yet waited on/With a more noble expectation' (133–4). His mayoral pageant for Sir Peter Proby, *The Triumphs of Honour and Virtue* (1622), similarly honoured the alliance between court and city, reminding London, that 'You have a courtier now your magistrate' (145). Middleton's work for Cokayne did not end here, and so it cannot be seen simply as expediency on Middleton's part. In April 1620, he again celebrated this merchant prince's alliance with the court with an entertainment to honour Cokayne's partnership with the King in a scheme to restore St Paul's Cathedral, which also doubled as a wedding entertainment for the marriage of Cokayne's daughter to the son and heir of Charles Howard, Earl of Nottingham (Middleton 2007: I, 1,431).

While it is difficult to sustain the argument that Middleton's civic entertainments are motivated by an ideological opposition between the city and the court, it is possible to argue that he fashions and promotes a civic ideology that champions trade and industry through his pageants. A number of the lord mayors for whom Middleton devised pageants had interests in overseas trading companies, such as the East India and Virginia Companies. This was the case with *The Triumphs of Honour and Industry* (1617) written for the investiture of George Bolles, who, along with many of his fellow Grocers, was an investor in the East India Company. The 'First Invention' presented in this pageant consisted of a company of young Indians, who are first shown labouring and then dancing around spice trees and other exotic plants. India is, itself, personified; this 'seat of merchandise' (53–4) is depicted accompanied by allegorical figures for Merchandise and Industry (55–6). Middleton returns to these figures for overseas trade in *The Triumphs of Honour and Virtue* (1622). Paul's Churchyard is transformed into 'the Continent of India', once again depicted metonymically through spice plants and 'a black personage representing India, called, for her odours and riches, the Queen of Merchandise', who is 'attended by Indians in antique habits' (39–45). The allegorical figures of Commerce, Adventure and Traffic, 'habited like Merchants' (46–47), present her with the emblem of Knowledge. The Black Queen explains that she is spiritually 'beauteous in my blackness' (58) because she was 'By English merchants first enlightened' (81). This pun on spiritual enlightenment relies on separating 'skin colour' from 'moral qualities', which means that the Black Queen/India can then be enlightened, made white by commerce with the English merchants (Middleton 2007: I, 1,715). Religion and commerce join together in a justification of the morality of English trading practices. India provides the English merchants with material goods – spices and other luxury goods – and, in return, they give her superior spiritual qualities, so that she is obliged to 'confess/All wealth consists in Christian holiness' (78–9). The Black Queen/India in this 1622 triumph is an extended version of the King of the Moors (the Ottoman Empire) that was presented in a river pageant in *The Triumphs of Truth* (1613). This figure similarly provides an opportunity to unpick the distinctions between white and black, Christian and Moor, to justify trade with other nations and other religions. The King confronts the potential prejudices of his audience that 'I being a Moor, then, in opinion's lightness,/As far from sanctity as my face from whiteness', and assures them that in this 'land/Where true religion and her temples stand' (421–4), 'However darkness dwells upon my face,/Truth in my soul sets up the light of grace' (429–30). Both figures offer the promise of the conversion of the infidel to Christianity to legitimise 'English trading practices overseas' (Middleton 2007: I, 1,715).

Middleton's model of honour is civic-minded, in that it is consistently, and even aggressively, meritocratic. The clearest expression of civic meritocracy is given in *The Triumphs of Integrity*, devised for Martin Lumley, a Grocer, in 1623:

And 'tis the noblest splendour upon earth
For man to add a glory to his birth,
All his life's race with honoured acts commixed,
Than to be nobly born, and there stand fixed,
As if 'twere competent virtue for whole life
To be begot a lord: 'tis virtuous strife
That makes the complete Christian, not high place,
As true submission is the state of grace. (76–83)

The argument that those men who achieve 'glory' through their 'honoured acts' are truly noble derives from the way the ideal citizen is described in a classical republican tradition. This discourse of citizenship was revived in the sixteenth century to validate the processes whereby men of relatively lowly birth were holding offices at court and in the city and rising through the ranks to become gentlemen and even knighted. These men were profitable to the commonwealth because they promoted the common good through their 'honoured acts', unlike those who were 'nobly born' yet added nothing to their name since they did not act with a view to the common good. 'The public good was, therefore,' as Markuu Peltonen sets out, 'not totally dependent on the qualities and abilities of the prince, but also, and perhaps in particular, on the virtuous civic participation of the people as a whole' (1995: 39). In *The Triumphs of Honour and Industry* (1617), Justice corrects the over-liberality of Reward, reminding the audience that Reward must be earned, and is dependent on merit rather than birthright (195–214). The eyewitness account of this pageant provided by Orazio Busino, the chaplain to the Venetian ambassador, recognised the civic ideal of citizenship promoted by mayoral pageants and began his account by turning London into a city-state and presenting its affinity with the republic of Venice: 'The city itself is more like a republic of merchants than anything else: idlers are banished, and noblemen and foreigners are excluded from its government' (*Orazio Busino's Eyewitness Account of* The Triumphs of Honour and Industry, Middleton 2007: I, 8–11).

In Middleton's pageants, this civic ideology has a distinctly Protestant aspect. *The Triumphs of Honour and Industry* (1617) describes the active virtue required for civic government in terms of a spiritual battle against the forces of envy: ''tis no mean fight/That wins this palm' (202–3). As we have seen in *The Triumphs of Truth* the godly citizen is imagined as one of God's soldiers fighting in the battle against the forces of Error, typically identified in the Protestant imagination with Spain and Catholicism. Middleton's entertainment for the opening of the New River draws on the idiom of Protestant chivalry, which had its most famous expression in Spenser's *The Faerie Queene*. Music and spectacle turn this citizen into a knight, who is ennobled by his virtuous civic acts rather than by birth: '[T]he warlike music of drums and trumpets liberally beats the air, sounds as proper as in battle, for there is no labour that man undertakes but hath a war within itself, and perfection makes the conquest' (*The Manner of his Lordship's Entertainment*, Middleton 2007: I, 20–3). The citizen's working life becomes a psychomachia in which he daily engages in spiritual battle through his labours for the commonwealth. The closing pageant for *The Triumphs of Honour and Virtue* (1622) is a highly sophisticated expression of the ideal of Protestant magistracy that turns inward to contemplate the religious virtues necessary for good government. The pageant presents 'eight bright personages most gloriously decked, representing . . . the inward man, the intentions of a virtuous and worthy breast by the graces of the mind and soul, such as Clear Conscience, Divine Speculation, Peace of Heart, Integrity, Watchfulness, Equality, Providence, Impartiality' (241–6).

Heinemann's account of Middleton's mayoral pageants, and subsequent work in this field by critics such as Tony Bromham, foreground the need to take historical context into account when analysing the symbolism of their extended allegories (Bromham 1995). This is particularly the case with *The Triumphs of Integrity*, presented in 1623, which ends on an avowedly godly and militantly Protestant note:

The cloud that swells beneath 'em may imply
Some envious mist cast forth by heresy,
Which, through his happy reign and heaven's blest will,
The sunbeams of the Gospel strikes through still. (293–6)

Middleton presents an image of James as the Protestant Prince, the champion of the godly in his fight against the forces of Catholic 'heresy' on the continent. He was able to do so because of recent events. The belligerent tone of this pageant is in tune with the wave of anti-Spanish and anti-Catholic feeling that greeted the safe return from Spain of Prince Charles and Buckingham and the failure of the marriage negotiations with Spain. In late 1623, the mood at court and in the city was belligerently anti-Spanish and pro-war. The next summer, Middleton would write his *A Game at Chess* (1624), an allegorical drama that mercilessly satirised the Spanish court and celebrated the return of Charles and Buckingham from its clutches (see below, pp. 154–66).

Middleton's mayoral pageants consistently magnify civic authority; however, this does not preclude expressions of loyalty and devotion to the King. Even though *The Triumph of Integrity* ends on a militaristic note, the pageant includes a 'thrice-royal Canopy of State' (255) which is adorned with James's motto *Beati pacifici*, as the narrator explains, 'so is it comely and requisite in these matters of triumph, framed for the inauguration of his great substitute, the Lord Mayor of London, that some remembrance of honour should reflect upon his majesty, by whose peaceful government, under heaven, we enjoy the solemnity' (267–71). James's pacific rule provides the conditions under which trade and commerce can flourish. What this vision of unity elides is the King's constant interference in trade, particularly overseas trade, and the conflict over whether James's pursuit of peace was in the best interests of England's Protestant allies on the continent. There is also a potential for conflict between the King and 'his great substitute, the Lord Mayor'. Who has ultimate authority over the City of London? This tension is conveyed in an anecdote relating to Bolles's tenure as Lord Mayor. To enforce the message of his *Book of Sports* (1618), which gave royal support for festivities against the Puritan ban on recreation on Sundays, James had his carriages drive through the streets of London on Sunday during church services. Bolles had them stopped. James angrily complained that, 'He thought there had been no more kings in England but himself', to which Bolles replied, 'Whilst it was in my power, I did my duty; but that being taken away by a higher power, it is my duty to obey' (Middleton 2007: I, 1,254, n. 12). Bolles may have acknowledged his duty to the King, but its expression was double-edged. Middleton's civic pageants similarly tend to resolve rather than foreground this conflict – the ideal they promote is co-operation between court and city, an ideal often difficult to maintain in practice.

MAKING 'SPECTACLES OF STATE'[2]: THE PLAYWRIGHT AS CRAFTSMAN

'More than his Jacobean contemporaries', according to Bergeron, Middleton used the printed text of his first pageant, *The Triumphs of Truth*, to set the aesthetic agenda and 'to defend his "art"'. In doing so, he played on the notion of the poet as 'craftsman' to foreground the fact that the word 'art' 'can be applied, comfortably, both to the literary works of a poet and to the work of the city's trades and craftsmen' (Middleton 2007: I, 964). Civic pageants did, of course, bring the arts of the dramatist and the artisan into alignment in a practical as well as aesthetic sense. The working relationship between the two is described by contemporaries in terms of the unity between body and soul: the painting and carpentry constitute the mechanical body and the poetry and allegory are the poetical soul. This way of thinking about the allocation of parts was drawn from emblem books, yet it also speaks to an organic understanding of the collaboration between poet and craftsman in the production of civic pageants (Bergeron 2003: 236).

At the end of printed texts of his pageants, Middleton is always careful to acknowledge the work of his fellow artisans in devising the pageant. John Grinkin, who was the artificer for *Triumphs of Truth*, made extremely sophisticated machinery for the pageant – ships, the chariots of Error and Truth, and the islands. Middleton, accordingly, commends him warmly for 'the proper beauties of workmanship, most artfully and faithfully performed' (784–5), as well as Humphrey Nichols, 'a man excellent in his art' (783), for his firework display which ends the pageant. In both cases, the devices are absolutely integral to the allegory and its success; machinery and poetry work in harmony. Middleton's closest relationship was with Gerard (or Garret) Christmas, who also worked as a naval carpenter. They first collaborated in 1619 on *The Triumphs of Love and Antiquity*, and then again in 1621, 1622, 1623 and 1626. Middleton always stresses the interdependency of the 'body' and 'soul': 'For all the proper adornments of art and workmanship in so short a time, so gracefully setting forth the body of so magnificent a triumph, the praise comes, as a just due, to the exquisite deservings of Master Garret Christmas' (*The Triumphs of Integrity*, 311–14). If Middleton took the mayoral pageants to new levels of sophistication, then Christmas, along with his sons, was responsible for developing the role of artisan into the architect of the pageant (Bergeron 2003: 244–7).

The emblematic qualities of Middleton's later plays, in particular, are often noted, from his use of staging to his dramatic allegories and use of keywords as visual and dramatic emblems (see below, pp. 144–8). In Middleton's emblematic theatre, we can see the cross-fertilisation between civic pageantry and the stage: Middleton uses the skills he is developing in pageants in his plays, and transfers techniques developed in the theatre to his pageants. Bergeron has observed how 'Middleton's speech for Zeal in the 1604 royal entry pageant lingers in his artistic consciousness' to return in *No Wit, No Help Like a Woman's* (1611) (2003: 8; Bergeron 1985). For *The Triumphs of Truth*, Middleton draws on the themes and structure of the morality play tradition, and gives the pageant dramatic unity by having the main protagonists, Truth and Error, appear throughout (Bergeron 2003: 185). Unlike Munday's pageants, which 'segregate performance and explication' of the allegorical devices, Middleton integrates narration, explication and performance, so that 'dramatic action, however rudimentary, is embedded' in the allegorical substance of the pageant (Middleton 2007: I, 1,251–2). The game of chess in *Women Beware Women* is like a show, or invention within a pageant. The audience is asked to interpret the game played on the lower stage as an allegory for the dramatic action – the seduction and rape of Bianca that is occurring on the upper stage (see below, pp. 125–8). This type of emblematic theatre, in which there is a sophisticated integration of diachronic dramatic action, that occurs over a period of time, and synchronic allegory, in which forward movement is suspended to concentrate on a single heavily symbolic moment, culminates in *A Game at Chess*. The play's central conceit is, once again, the chess game, and the play understands it as a metaphor that is thoroughly actable. The chess game is the dramatic and allegorical medium taken by political, religious and sexual intrigue; each chess move is the result of elaborate plotting that is skilfully integrated within the overarching dramatic action of the play.

Middleton also developed his dramatic repertoire through writing masques. In 1614, he was commissioned by the Lord Mayor, Sir Thomas Myddleton, to write the now lost *Masque of Cupids* for the marriage of Sir Robert Carr and Lady Frances Howard. The text of the masque, unusually, was not printed, but Middleton characteristically recycled songs from the masque in his plays, *The Witch*, *Chaste Maid*, and *More Dissemblers Besides Women* (Middleton 2007: I, 1,027). Interestingly, cupids also appear in the broken wedding masque of *Women Beware Women*. Given the subsequent controversy surrounding Carr and Howard, questions are raised by the way parts of their wedding masque circulate across these plays (on the Overbury scandal, see below, pp. 155–7) – is it just the pragmatism of a working playwright, or might there be political resonances? One of the key figures of his next masque, *The Masque of Heroes*, written for performance at the Inner Temple during their 1618–19 Christmas revels, is Doctor Almanac, a figure that clearly draws on his earlier play *No Wit, No Help Like a Woman's* – this play was given the title *The Almanac* for a performance at court. The elaborate banquet scene in this play draws on both the civic pageant and the court masque (see above, pp. 73–4). *The Masque of Heroes* similarly mixes high and low, bringing together the 'popular culture of almanacs [and] folk plays' with the high-minded aesthetics of the masque (Middleton 2007: I, 1,321).

Civic pageants, most notably *The Triumphs of Truth*, often adapt devices from the medieval morality play to structure the procession through the streets of London, halting at key sites, such as Paul's Churchyard, for the staging of shows. To an extent, these Protestant civic entertainments take the place of the pre-Reformation mystery cycles – mayoral shows were performed on the morning after the feast day of St Simon and St Jude. The two forms had co-existed in Catholic England, but in post-Reformation England the mystery cycles were banned (Happé 1999: 19–20). One reason for the ban was the hostility of reformers to images and image-making, which they identified with Catholicism and idolatry. The Protestant preacher, Philip Stubbes, in his *Anatomy of Abuses*, extended the notion of idolatry to the stage: 'Do they not maintain bawdry, insinuate foolery, and renew the remembrance of heathen idolatry? Do they not induce whoredom and uncleanness?' (cited in Heinemann 1982: 20). For Protestant poets, fictional art raised particular problems of how to discriminate between 'true' and 'false' images. Stubbes complains that the theatre induces a lack of discrimination; instead of godly self-government, the audience succumbs to sins of the flesh.

Middleton's civic pageants frequently present images of the impaired vision of fallen man through the devices of clouds or the 'envious mist cast forth by heresy' (*The Triumphs of Integrity*, 294). One of the closing shows in *The Triumphs of Honour and Virtue* (1622) is a device of 'eight personages' representing the Protestant 'inward man'. To illustrate the fallen nature of man a 'cloud of frailty' rises from the ground, and the figures fall back into the globe 'showing, that as the brightest day has his overcastings, so the best men in this life have their imperfections' (249–54). To reform faulty vision, Middleton instructs his audience through 'true' images, such as the device of the crystal Temple of Integrity in *The*

Triumphs of Integrity (1623). The deity of the Temple of Integrity calls for the multitude to look at her temple with 'greedy eyes' (205), and then corrects their fleshly sight through a reformed vision based on the conceit of the transparency of the crystal mirror: 'There's no disguise or hypocritic veil,/Used by adulterous beauty set to sale' (211–12). Middleton's Calvinism obviously does not translate into a rejection of fictional art as necessarily deluding. Rather, as John King says of that other Protestant poet, Edmund Spenser, he 'assumes the existence of a complex dialectic in which a destructive attack against "false" images gives rise to a corresponding movement to construct acceptable forms of "true" literature and art' (King 1990: 7).

This 'complex dialectic' in the production of dramatic images or spectacles can be seen at work in *The Changeling*, performed the year before his *Triumphs of Integrity*. The play opens with a discussion between Alsemero and Beatrice-Joanna on problems of seeing clearly with eyes unclouded by 'false' images. Yet Beatrice-Joanna herself is a 'false' image, disguised by a 'hypocritic veil'; her 'true' inner depravity is slowly discovered as the distinctions between the beautiful Beatrice and her ugly servant, De Flores, collapse (Neill 1997: 194). The moment of revelation is her death scene in which Beatrice-Joanna is offered to the audience as a spectacle of damnation (see below, pp. 146–7). The Reformation did away with Catholic rituals for remembering the dead, and so gave rise to an alternative 'theory of *memoria*', as Nigel Llewellyn explains, 'which stressed the didactic potential of the lives and deaths of the virtuous' (cited in Neill 1997: 39). The virtuous had their funeral monuments, and the unregenerate were memorialised on the stage through tragic and didactic spectacles of dying badly. The masque in *Women Beware Women*, for example, is wittily didactic in that characters' deaths are emblematic of their sins (see below, pp. 123–4). In the case of *The Changeling*, Beatrice-Joanna turns herself into a negative exemplum, dispelling the veil of ignorance and hypocrisy, so that the audience can see her clearly for what she is. The play draws attention to simultaneous function of this scene of dying both as a revelation and as a negative memorial. Vermandero exclaims at the sight of his damned daughter: '[M]y name is entered now in that record/Where till this fatal hour 'twas never read' (V, iii, 180–1) – that 'record' is the heavenly book listing the saved and the damned. The tragic end of Beatrice-Joanna is in keeping with Middleton's reformist definition of tragedy in his early work, *Wisdom of Solomon Paraphrased*. Middleton understands tragedy, as Deborah Shuger argues, not in terms of

> extraordinary calamities nor the fall of princes nor Fortune's caprice; it has no politics and no heroes. Instead, in *The Wisdom of Solomon* 'tragedy' signifies something close to the Calvinist state of fallen nature . . . Middleton's tragic creatures are sinful, hopeless, and agonizingly mortal. (Middleton 2007: I, 1,918)

The Protestant response to fictional art was diverse and complex. John Stachniewski has drawn attention to the Calvinism that infuses Middleton's tragedies (see below, pp. 145–8). Middleton himself wrote Calvinist tracts throughout his career, from *The Wisdom of Solomon Paraphrased* (1597) to *The Two Gates of Salvation* (1609), reissued in 1620 as *The Marriage of the Old and New Testament*. His civic pageants are exercises in Protestant emblematic theatre, yet his tragedies suggest a more complicated response to spectacle. In Middleton's 'obsessive focus on the ruined world' of fallen man in his tragedies (Middleton 2007: I, 1,918), Calvinist sobriety is coupled with a fascination with the grotesque, with bizarre and unstable images of fallen nature, and with the forms of 'horrid laughter'.

NOTES

1. On Calvinism, see above p. 18.
2. Ben Jonson, 'An Expostulation with Inigo Jones', in Jonson, 1985: p. 463, l. 42.

CHAPTER 6

Plotting Revenge: *The Revenger's Tragedy, Women Beware Women* and *The Lady's Tragedy*

Middleton's violently witty tragedies draw on his experience working across a range of dramatic genres, from satiric city comedies to civic pageants, and disturbing tragicomedies to masques and entertainments. This chapter will concentrate on two plays that experiment with the conventions of revenge tragedy: *The Revenger's Tragedy* and *Women Beware Women*. It should be acknowledged from the outset that the authorship of *The Revenger's Tragedy* remains uncertain. In attributing the play to Middleton, I follow the majority of critics, including the editors of the recent Oxford *Collected Works*.[1] *The Revenger's Tragedy* was performed by the King's Men at the Globe Theatre around 1606. This was a time when Middleton was writing satiric London comedies for the Children of Paul's. The company had been in decline since mid-1606; performances became increasingly intermittent and finally ended in mid to late 1608 (Gair 1982: 172). It is therefore possible that Middleton, looking for work at other theatre companies, began writing plays for the King's Men during this period. The anonymous *The Lady's Tragedy*, also now thought to be Middleton's, was written for the King's Men in 1611 (Gurr 1992: 164).[2] *Women Beware Women* may also have been a King's Men play. Its date is uncertain. Some place it in years 1612 to 1614, alongside *Chaste Maid in Cheapside* and *The Witch*, as well as his Lord Mayor's Show, *The Triumphs of Truth*. Others, including the editors of the Oxford *Collected Works*, advocate a later date of 1621, grouping it with his other great tragedy, *The Changeling* (Middleton 2007: II, 414–15).

Placing *The Revenger's Tragedy* alongside *Women Beware Women* allows us to see how Middleton gave a distinctive twist to the conventions of revenge tragedy. The plays are comparable in the way that they respond inventively to the challenges of the revenge plot through witty and complex plotting. Middleton's plays in general, as we have seen, are distinguished by their inventive, often virtuoso plots; a testimony to this playwright's skill in creating and managing complex multiple plots. *The Revenger's Tragedy* multiplies the revenge action. Vindice, the primary revenger, is avenging the murder of his betrothed, Gloriana, by the Duke, and the attempted prostitution of his sister, Castiza, by the Duke's son, Lussurioso. The judges seek legal retribution against Junior, the Duchess's son, for the rape of Antonio's wife, while Antonio and his fellow noblemen seek their own revenge for this act. The Duchess and Spurio, the Duke's illegitimate son, engage in an incestuous liaison as an act of revenge against the Duke. The Duchess's sons plot against their step-brother, Lussurioso, while Lussurioso seeks to avenge his father's cuckolding by his wife and bastard. This layering of plots is designed to lead to confusion and mistaken identity; it also adds a particular wit to the way justice is meted out. Middleton multiplies the revengers in *Women Beware Women* as well, although in this case revenge is dealt in the final scene, in the masque, when the niece murders her aunt, the sister kills her brother, and the wife accidentally murders her husband. There is a self-conscious theatricality to Middleton's treatment of the revenge plot. These plays draw attention to their own glittering artifice and murderous excesses. Such highly stylised drama provocatively and deliberately works against the notion that moral retribution and divine justice can be enacted through revenge.

ITALY AND REVENGE: BLOOD AND HONOUR

Revenge has an Italian character. There is a distinct sub-genre of revenge tragedies set in Italy, which includes *Revenger's Tragedy* and *Women Beware Women*, as well as Webster's *The White Devil*.

Early modern Englishmen had an ambivalent response to Italy. 'On the one hand, Italy's culture and civility, its agricultural and mercantile riches are to be emulated,' Cathy Shrank notes, 'on the other, its "popery", perceived lasciviousness and habits of deceit are to be renounced.' Early modern humoural theory explained different national characters in terms of climate: the warm airs of Italy were thought to heat the blood, producing the fiery, passionate temperament of the Italian (Shrank 2004: 37–43). The Italian was therefore thought to have a greater innate susceptibility to crimes of blood. Thomas Nashe included a discourse against travel in his *Unfortunate Traveller* that used the example of the Italian's native propensity for revenge as an argument for staying at home in the safety of England. So extreme is the Italian's sense of honour, and so quickly and hotly do they take offence, that the unsuspecting Englishman only has to 'lend half a look' to an Italian's wife or respond negatively to one of his jests and 'thou shalt be sure to be visited with guests in a mask the next night, when in kindness and courtship thy throat shall be cut, and the doers return undiscovered' (1985: 342; Clare 2006: 92–3).

The Italian setting in *Revenger's Tragedy* is less of a precise locale than a climate made known through the heated blood of the play. The characters are given allegorical Italianate names, whose meanings could be found in John Florio's Italian–English dictionary, *A World of Words* (1598): Vindice (a revenger), Lussurioso (lecherous, luxurious, riotous), Spurio (bastard, a counterfeit), Ambitioso (ambitious), Supervacuo (superfluous, vain, to no use). These are typical Italianate courtiers: as Nashe wrote, the Italian courts 'maketh a man an excellent courtier, a curious carpet knight; which is, by interpretation, a fine close lecher, a glorious hypocrite' (1985: 345). Italian principalities, such as Milan, Florence and Parma, were ruled by Renaissance despots; the courts of the Visconti of Milan and the Medici of Florence were admired for their magnificence, and identified with violent intrigue, usurpation and murder. *The Revenger's Tragedy* conveys the ambivalence of the English towards Italy through the use of the classical Roman story of the rape of Lucrece to signify the degeneration of the Italian state from its idealised Roman past. Middleton produced a female-voiced complaint on this theme, *The Ghost of Lucrece* (1600), and it provides the source for the 'noble' suicide of Antonio's 'virtuous lady' (I, iv, 6) whose dead body is discovered to an audience of noblemen as a sign that 'Violent rape/Has played a glorious act' (I, iv, 3–4). 'Lucrece', as Catherine Belsey states, 'tells a story about possession'; a story about women as the property of fathers and husbands, in which the woman's body becomes the site of struggle between men. In political terms, Lucrece's chastity signified the strength of Roman republican values against the corrupt tyranny of Roman monarchy (2001: 315–16, 320–1). Hence, the rape of Antonio's wife by the Duke's son, Junior, symbolises the political and moral degeneration of the Italianate royal court.

One of the sources of *Women Beware Women* is the story of the Italian despot, Francesco de Medici, and his mistress, Bianca di Cappello. At the age of sixteen, Bianca, a wealthy Venetian gentlewoman, had eloped to Florence with a 'penniless Florentine', Pietro Bonaventuri. Pursued by her family, who were intent on revenge, the young couple sought the protection of Francesco. The story had been published in Venice in 1609 in a collection of short stories, *Ducento Novelle*, by Celio Malespini, loosely based on actual events. The stories about the Medici family stimulated the imagination of English writers and dramatists – Francesco de Medici also appears in Webster's *White Devil*, and Fynes Moryson told the story of Bianca and Francesco in his *Itinerary* (Mulryne 1975: 70–4). Middleton's recasting of the story changes the source of threat to the happiness of the young lovers from the vengeful parents, intent on claiming their lost possession, to the lustful Duke, who takes Bianca as his seignorial right as Duke of Florence. In the opening scenes of the play, we view Bianca entirely through this language of possession. Middleton holds up for inspection not simply a Renaissance despot, but also suggests the insecurities of the type of honour culture, frequently identified with Italy, in which men have such a political and emotional investment in their claim to the right to possess women's bodies.

Ann Rosalind Jones, in her seminal essay on this topic, 'Italians and Others', describes how Italy functioned in English imagination as the 'other' country, 'a fantasy setting for dramas of passion, Machiavellian politics, and revenge' (1991: 251). Italy was a site onto which the English projected their own dangerous fantasies of sexuality and power. Illicit desires were thereby safely ascribed to the foreigner and used to affirm the Englishman's difference from the Italian. Watching or reading plays about Italy was a form of armchair tourism, which enabled the audience to enjoy these foreign dramas of corruption, passion and revenge from a safe distance; spectators could vicariously experience 'foreignness' but 'without suffering' the debilitating 'self-transformation' that threatened the English traveller in Italy (Barbour 2003: 109). Italian revenge tragedies thus allowed English dramatists and theatregoers to '[nourish] . . . a fantasy of irresistible evil, imaginable at length because it is located elsewhere' (Jones 1991: 260).

We can see this English depiction of the luxury and illegitimacy of the despotic Italian court as one of the ways in which the 'foreignness' of Italy was imagined and, as a consequence, the superiority and legitimacy of the English state asserted. England not only had a centralised monarchy, rather than rival principalities, but the sovereign claimed the throne through patrilineal laws of descent. Royal power was sacralised through the notion of the divine right of kings, which identified the monarch as God's magistrate on earth. It should be said, that in the case of both Elizabeth I and James I, the line of succession which brought them to the throne was by no means clear-cut; the charge of bastardy hung over Elizabeth, and James's mother was Mary, Queen of Scots, viewed by many English Puritans as a Catholic whore. James's court was criticised for its luxury and for bestowing lavish favours on unworthy courtiers. The emergence of a political language of court corruption, which identified venal practices with the decay of the state, coincided with the popularity of Italianate tragedies on the Jacobean stage. Heinemann interpreted the defiant figure who populates Jacobean tragedy, 'prepared at all costs, for good or ill, to vindicate his honour', as an expression of 'the aristocratic and intellectual . . . revolt against the corruption and oppression of Stuart absolutism' (1982: 173). The comforting fiction of diabolical Italian tyranny as opposed to godly English monarchy might not have been so secure.

SEXUAL POLITICS: DESIRING BODIES AND TYRANNICAL STATES

The revenge plot frequently relies on a corrupt state in which the instruments of justice are tainted or implicated in the injustices they should redress. Criminality is situated at the heart of power, in the royal court itself. In the trial scene, which opens the second scene of *The Revenger's Tragedy*, justice at first seems to proceed smoothly as the Judges prosecute the rape case against Junior, and their words overrule the pleas of his mother, the Duchess, for clemency. At the last moment, just as the Judge is about to pronounce the final judgement, the Duke intervenes and defers the sentence. With the full authority of the law suspended, revenge plots proliferate in the resulting legal vacuum. A tyrant makes the law dependent on his perverted will and lust. Introduced in the first scene as the 'royal lecher' (I, i, 1), the Duke is true to the stereotype. One issue of the Duke's lust is, of course, his bastard Spurio, 'true-begot in evil' (I, i, 3). Spurio embodies the unfixing of social identity in a tyrannical state ruled by lust – he is 'an uncertain man,/Of more uncertain woman' (I, ii, 133–4). Through his bastard, the Duke destroys the very heart of the patriarchal state that should be the basis of his authority. Hence, by the end of the second scene, Spurio and the Duchess have embarked on a revenge plot aimed at the foundations of a patriarchal honour culture – their incestuous coupling intensifies the cuckolding of the Duke.

The tyrant is a tragic character type that allows the dramatist to explore the interdependence of power and desire, sex and politics. By giving free rein to his lust and perverse appetites, the tyrant is enslaved by his own passions. Rebecca Bushnell has described tyrants as 'terrifying machines of desire, consuming and annihilating everything in their path' (1990: 32). In revenge tragedies, the violence of desire resonates across the dramatis personae; it is not simply confined to the tyrant, but infects all involved in court politics, including those who seek to redress its injustices. The distinction between the all-consuming sensual appetites of the tyrant and the all-consuming retributive justice of the revenger is frequently blurred – both are driven to excesses and become terrifying machines of annihilation. 'The revenger,' as Katharine Maus points out, 'seems compelled to take purgative action – to cleanse the world of a terrible wrong – but the only way to do so magnifies the original atrocity' (1995: ix).

The 'original atrocity' in *The Revenger's Tragedy* is the Duke's poisoning of Vindice's betrothed, Gloriana:

> Because thy purer part would not consent
> Unto his palsy lust; for old men lustful
> Do show like young men – angry, eager, violent,
> Outbid their limited performances. (I, i, 33–6)

The sense of the moribund state of the royal court under his rule is conveyed by this image of 'his palsy lust'. Decrepitude and illness pervert sexual desire which, in such a sick state, can be expressed only through the violent destruction of youth, beauty and virtue. The set designs for the 1987 RSC production portrayed the 'corruption of power politics' by hanging the gallery fronts and rear wall with 'dark, torn hangings, obviously concealing inner chambers and hiding places for intruders'. The costumes, wigs and makeup were experiments in grotesquerie, appearing luxurious but on close observation 'dusty, gaudy, deliquescent, hoar-frosted with sequins and cheap glass, rotting into the wearer's skin', '[w]hat looked like make-up was actually pustules on the skin'. The aim was to demonstrate that 'only a society in the worst condition of decay could really stoop to this kind of violence and brutality and animal ambition' (Mulryne and Shewring 1989: 31, 78–81). This was also the thesis behind Alex Cox's 2002 film of the play which justified its setting in a post-apocalyptic Liverpool of 2011. Such a dystopian setting made sense of the juxtaposition of seventeenth-century and twenty-first-century Britain, and foregrounded the carnivalesque and grotesque aspects of the play – also a key feature of the costumes and settings in this production (Spiller 2003: 3). Like Cox's other films, it has an 'anarcho-punk sensibility', which finds a 'revolutionary message' in Middleton's depiction of the corruption of political systems: compared to Shakespeare, whose 'politics are fairly square' and the 'greatest crime in a Shakespeare play is to murder the king. For Middleton it's like, "Kill the king? Why not?" Its inspirational – nobody is above being brought down' (quoted in

Davies 2002). Melly Still's 2008 production of *The Revenger's Tragedy* used a whirling, revolving stage, along with digitised images of a skull and contemporary dance music, and juxtaposed visual referents from club culture with Renaissance art – Caravaggio's painting of St Jerome in his study, with a skull on the table, and erotic paintings in Titian's fleshly style. The effect was in keeping with Jonathan Dollimore's description of the way the play captures 'the frenetic activity of an introverted society, encompassed by shadows and ultimately darkness' (1984: 143).

Critics have drawn attention to the similarities between *Revenger's Tragedy* and *The Lady's Tragedy*, an anonymous play also attributed to Middleton. The Tyrant in this play is a dramatic emblem – his name denotes his nature. His first act following his usurpation of the rightful king, Giovanni, is to lay claim by right of conquest not just to his throne but also to his betrothed, the supremely virtuous Lady. When the Tyrant attempts to have her taken by violence, the Lady defends her honour by taking her own life. The Duke in *Women Beware Women* similarly uses his political power for sexual ends. His rape of Bianca is an act of conquest that insists on taking by force rather than by consent:

> I affect
> A passionate pleading 'bove an easy yielding,
> But never pitied any – . . .
> I can command –
> Think upon that – (II, ii, 358–62)

What he offers Bianca is 'wealth, honour/. . . a duke's favour' (II, ii, 368–9), and what he offers her cuckolded husband in recompense is 'the captainship/Of Ruinse citadel' (III, ii. 39–40). Leantio responds to the Duke's show of 'favour' with a potent image of the corruption of the court and its systems of patronage:

> All preferment
> That springs from sin and lust, it shoots up quickly,
> As gardeners' crops do in the rotten'st grounds.
> So is all means raised from base prostitution
> E'en like a sallet growing upon a dunghill. (III, ii, 48–52)

Corruption is understood in the conventional sexual and political terms defining the tyrant's rule; its source is right at the very centre of royal government. While the court retains the veneer of political health, the social relations radiating from the centre, which should ideally bind the commonwealth, reproduce this 'base prostitution'. The Duke's rape of Bianca initiates a series of corrupted and corrupting social relations in the action of the play: the father prostitutes his daughter by perverting the godly purpose of the marriage, and the aunt, in order to satisfy her brother's incestuous desires, acts as bawd to her niece. The play ends with the image of the Tyrant delineated in the Cardinal's warning: 'Two kings on one throne cannot sit together,/But one must needs down, for his title's wrong;/So where lust reigns, that prince cannot reign long' (V, i, 264–6).

In scenes such as these, when characters gather on state occasions, we can clearly hear a discourse of tyranny and court corruption in the language of *Women Beware Women*. That said, it is not the dominant language of the play. As Heinemann points out, *Women Beware Women* is not a tragedy of state, but rather a 'city tragedy'. The action of the play is less concerned with the high politics of statecraft than with the interpersonal sexual politics of those who live within the city state of Florence (Heinemann 1982: 180–7). If we compare the families in *The Revenger's Tragedy* with those in *Women Beware Women* then it is noticeable just how bourgeois, as opposed to aristocratic, the depiction of family life is – domestic scenes in *Women Beware Women* are less concerned with issues of blood, honour and chastity than with money, property and marriage. This means that the sexual politics of this play are of a different order and register from *The Revenger's Tragedy* and *The Lady's Tragedy*. One way to examine these differences is to compare the sexual politics which inscribe women's bodies across these plays.[3]

In both *The Revenger's Tragedy* and *The Lady's Tragedy*, male relations of power are articulated through a masculine aristocratic honour code, which obsessively invests itself in the woman's body and fixates on female chastity. Such male investment in notions of female sexual purity leads to an idealisation of the chaste woman which, in turn, means that chastity becomes the sole avenue for expression of female agency and virtue. By taking her own life, Antonio's wife turns the shame of her rape into her glory. Her dead body is self-consciously turned into a set of signs, a text to be read: her cheek rests on a prayer-book and in 'her right hand' is a book 'with a leaf tucked up/Pointing to these words:/*Melius virtute mori, quam per dedecus vivere*' ('Better to die in virtue than to live with dishonour') (I, iv, 15–17). As Dollimore points out, the 'affected grief' of the assembled male audience in the scene celebrates 'not her innate virtue but her dutiful suicide' (Dollimore 1984: 142). The suicide of the Lady in *The Lady's Tragedy* has a very similar effect. Giovanni apostrophises over the Lady's dead body:

> hast thou, valiant woman, overcome
> Thy honour's enemies with thine own white hand,
> Where virgin-victory sits, all without help?
> Eternal praise go with thee!   (III, i, 175–8)

Castiza's rejection of Lussurioso's sexual advances similarly sends Vindice into rapture:

> O, I'm above my tongue! Most constant sister,
> In this thou hast right honourable shown.
> Many are called by their honour that have none.
> Thou art approved for ever in my thoughts. (II, i, 45–8)

Chastity is not simply understood as the locus of masculine honour, but is given a transcendent, spiritual value that surpasses codes of honour deriving from hereditary title. Notice how hereditary honour is spoken of only its negative, satiric form, represented by those 'call'd by their honour that have none', in order to amplify the value accorded to female chastity. Vindice values his sister's chastity so highly because it secures family honour on this higher moral plane, above the corrupt world of the court, and so stands for the integrity of older, aristocratic honour codes that have been marginalised at court.

Vindice is obsessed with his sister's virginity. As Peter Stallybrass explains, he 'tirelessly seeks to find in woman's body the privileged container of an impermeable honor' (1991: 216). Ironically, the threat to the sanctity of this body comes from within the family. Gratiana attempts to prostitute her daughter to the Duke's son, momentarily opening the family to the corruption of the court, *and* the agent of the court is her own son, Vindice, who is compelled to contaminate his ideal even as he upholds it. The mother is violently forced to repent the error of her ways and the breach in the family is repaired. The family reunion is symbolically marked by two kisses: the first between Gratiana and her two sons ('I'll kiss you now. Kiss her, brother./Let's marry her to our souls, wherein's no lust,/And honourably love her' (IV, iv, 57–9)); and the second between mother and daughter ('O mother, let me twine about your neck/And kiss you till my soul melt on your lips' (IV, iv, 146–7)). The kiss is described in neo-Platonic terms as the chaste union of souls, and is to be read as one of the signifiers for the transcendent values of an honour culture (Stallybrass 1991: 210–11). That said, it bears an uncanny resemblance to the earlier hellish 'incestuous kiss' (I, ii, 173) between the Duchess and Spurio. The scene in which Vindice as Piato tries to seduce first his sister and then his mother suggests how deeply family relations are contaminated in the play. Antony Sher's interpretation of Vindice in the 1987 RSC production blurred the line between incestuous lust and familial love in these scenes: '[A]s we worked on them it became apparent that there is an element of incest on Vindice's part towards his sister, and maybe even towards his mother, which makes the scenes absolutely gripping and quite unhealthy in a way' (Mulryne and Shewring 1989: 121). There are other kisses in this play that tell of the corruptions of the flesh, and illustrate how this valuation of woman's body has its flipside in disgust at woman's fleshly nature (Stallybrass 1991: 211–12, 218).

The poisoned kiss unites *Revenger's Tragedy* and *The Lady's Tragedy*. In both cases, the dead mouth of the beloved is painted with poison, and so becomes a potent figure for exploring the theme of the sins of the flesh. In the case of *Revenger's Tragedy*, the woman's body is reduced to a skull, one of the starkest images of death. Its first use in the play is as a *memento mori*, a visual reminder of death. Since Gloriana is a victim of the Duke's lust, the skull is an emblem of the interdependence of lust and death. Even in this first scene, when the skull of Gloriana is held up as a symbol of the righteousness of Vindice's cause, his idealisation of his chaste mistress is troubled by an underlying misogynist view of woman's nature. Still's 2008 production featured a computer-generated image in this first scene in which Gloriana's beautiful face decays into a grotesque mouldering skull with a writhing grey worm for a tongue, capturing the way the play is obsessed with the deathly decay and sexual corruption lurking beneath female beauty. (Donatella Martina Cabras plays both the Whore and Gloriana in this production.) Gloriana's beauty, rather than an uncomplicated sign of her inner purity, is cited only in terms of its potential to incite lustful thoughts and actions even in 'the uprightest man – if such there be/That sin but seven times a day –' who would break 'custom,/And [make] up eight with looking after her' (I, i, 23–5). The opposition between chastity and lust the play seems so determined to secure is here undercut. The purity of Gloriana's beauty is similarly contrasted to the artificiality of cosmetics: ''twas a face/So far beyond the artificial shine/Of any woman's bought complexion' (I, i, 20–3). Cosmetics feature prominently in misogynist discourses as a signifier for female vanity, the sin of pride, and also the artifice that incites lust and disguises the essential corruptions of the body (Stallybrass 1991: 218).

In Act III, scene V, Gloriana's skull, now *dressed in tires* and painted in readiness for the seduction of the Duke, prompts a series of meditations on sin, death and the woman's body that culminates in a diatribe against cosmetics:

> Does every proud and self-affecting dame
> Camphor her face for this? And grieve her maker
> In sinful baths of milk, when many an infant starves
> For her superfluous outside – all for this? . . .
>   See, ladies, with false forms
> You deceive men, but cannot deceive worms –
>   (III, v, 84–7, 97–8)

The painting of the Lady's corpse in *The Lady's Tragedy* similarly provokes a meditation on cosmetics. The duality that structures the symbolism of Gloriana's skull and the Lady's corpse discloses the misogyny at work in the idealisation of woman's chastity. The insistence on female sexual purity is motivated by a belief that the woman's body is the gateway to sin and damnation; only by closing it off can the threat be averted. This misogynistic reading of the woman's body is similarly present in the 'one incestuous kiss [that] picks open hell' (I, ii, 173) – the pun on opening hell refers to the moment both when the Duchess makes her body sexually available to Spurio and when the incestuous revenge plot is unleashed. The revenge plot, as this suggests, has a particular symbolic, psychological and misogynistic investment in the woman's body. Still's 2008 production had Cabras, the actress who plays Gloriana, take the place of the dummy used to poison the Duke, so that when the murderous violence Vindice inflicts on the Duke reaches its bloody climax, Gloriana rises and moves off, all the while holding Vindice's gaze, who, imploringly, holds out a hand for her to stay, before returning to finish the deed. On the one hand, we could see Gloriana, here, as Eurydice to Vindice's Orpheus, but there is also a darker reading available in which she is a vengeful ghost who demands blood and cannot rest until she achieves full retribution. Desire and revenge meet in a sadistic orgy of violence.

Just as Vindice turns his dead mistress into a painted whore that poisons the 'royal lecher', so too Giovanni turns the dead body of his beloved into a painted idol that poisons its idolater. The use of a corpse as an erotic object brings into play the perverse desires of necrophilia, thereby dramatically heightening and intensifying the association between sex and death. *The Lady's Tragedy* is a sustained study of necrophilia; the Tyrant is so fixated on the Lady that her death seems to intensify rather than end his sexual obsession. The transgressiveness of his desire is conveyed by the reactions of his hardened soldiers to his order to break open the sanctity of her tomb. While the Tyrant's passions may be extreme and perverse, the use of the dead body as an erotic object draws on scriptural discourses that view sex as an act of carnal fornication which leads to spiritual death (Zimmerman 2002: 218–19, 230–2). The destruction that attends sex is grotesquely portrayed in *The Revenger's Tragedy* through the fate of the Duke's body following the poisoned kiss: first his 'teeth are eaten out' (III, v, 160), then his tongue.

Women Beware Women also uses the poisoned kiss to signify the spiritual dangers of lust. Bianca knowingly kisses the lips of her beloved, the Duke, whom she has unwittingly poisoned:

> Give me thy last breath, thou infected bosom,
> And wrap two spirits in one poisoned vapour.
> Thus, thus reward thy murderer, and turn death
> Into a parting kiss. My soul stands ready at my lips,
> E'en vexed to stay one minute after thee. (V, i, 234–8)

Once again, we have the connection between lust and death. Yet there is something more complex going on in this speech than the straightforward condemnation of carnal fornication. Since Bianca looks forward to the union of her soul with her beloved in death, this poisoned kiss incorporates the symbolism of the neo-Platonic kiss. The poisoned kiss in *Women Beware Women* has a different function from its counterpart in *The Revenger's Tragedy* and *The Lady's Tragedy*. It is part of the tragic spectacle that signifies the downfall of 'Pride, greatness, honours, beauty, youth, ambition' (V, i, 259) through lust, and thus the deathliness of carnality. That said, the sexual politics of *Women Beware Women* draws on a different idiom from these other tragedies. There is an investment in woman's body in the play, not so much as 'the privileged container of an impermeable honor' (Stallybrass 1991: 216), but rather as an object to be possessed and transacted within a sexual economy. Instructive parallels can be drawn with Middleton's city comedies, in particular, *Chaste Maid in Cheapside*. The plots of city comedies are frequently driven by the trade in women on the marriage market (see above, pp. 74–9). Chastity, in this context, is significant in terms of its exchange value rather than its exclusivity. Touchwood Senior, when giving the 'true' valuation of Moll, the 'chaste maid' of the title, as we have seen, uses the metaphor of 'jewel so infixed' (V, iv, 18). As Kathleen McLuskie points out, this metaphor draws on scriptural proverb, 'the price of a good woman is above rubies'. When used in the context of city comedies, this lapidary metaphor is used to denote the exchange value of women in the sexual economy. Chastity, like a jewel, has value only when it is open to trade (1989: 127–8).

When Leantio introduces his new bride to his mother in the opening scene of *Women Beware Women*, he speaks of her repeatedly as a priceless jewel, a 'treasure' of 'the most unvalued'st purchase' (I, i, 14, 12), and of her 'hidden virtues' which lie 'locked up', 'Like jewels kept in cabinets' (I, i, 55–6). The degree of Leantio's objectification of Bianca, and expression of love in terms of ownership, is striking. To an extent, Leantio's commercial vocabulary is in keeping with his occupation as a factor or mercantile agent of an estate. Yet it also introduces us to the commodified sexual body familiar from city comedies. The tragedy arises from the fact that Leantio has stolen his bride, rather than negotiated the marriage contract through the proper channels of exchange – parents and friends. His theft brings into play class difference, since only through theft could such a poor man possess such a rich prize; this gives the trade in women an illicit dimension, that will have tragic consequences. Since Bianca is stolen property, she must remain hidden, and Leantio will need to 'take heed' that this 'jewel is cased up from all men's eyes' (I, i, 169–70). Bianca is objectified in such an extreme way in the earlier scenes of the play in order to set her up for her rape by the Duke, when Leantio's stolen jewel is itself stolen (McLuskie 1989: 127–8).

The opening scenes of *Women Beware Women* concentrate on the trade in women. Act I, scene ii, opens with Fabritio and Guardiano arranging the marriage of Guardiano's ward (the Ward) and Fabritio's daughter, Isabella. It is the presence of the Ward, in particular, that foregrounds the commercial aspect of marriage and gives the scene its negative, satiric aspect. On the death of their parents, heirs to aristocratic estates became royal wards. The buying and selling of wardships was a constant grievance in Jacobean England (Heinemann 1982: 192). Wardships were incredibly lucrative, and were sold by the monarch as a means of raising revenue. Guardians had control of the orphan's estate and could arrange their marriages, frequently to their own advantage, until the time when the ward reached the age of majority. We can see this commercial aspect of wardships in the way Guardiano says he wishes to 'tender him a wife' (I, ii, 6); the irony is that there is no affection involved in any aspect of the match, and the term is used by Guardiano only in its contractual sense. The father, Fabritio, is similarly a satiric type, a 'foolish old man' (I, ii, 12), who is intent upon forcing his daughter into marriage, and sees no need to secure her liking to the match. That he understands her value only in economic terms is made clear in the comic play on 'dear' when Fabritio introduces his 'dear child' at court: when the Duke reminds him 'That must needs be; you say she is your daughter', Fabritio corrects him: 'Nay, my good lord, dear to my purse, I mean' (III, ii, 106–8). The patriarchal politics of the play are complicated by age and class, which cut across gender lines. The Ward, the youth 'owned' by a guardian, and Isabella, the daughter 'owned' by the father, occupy an equivalent position within the patriarchal household – both are relatively powerless and subject to paternal authority. Class operates in a similar way. Leantio, the lower-class male, is placed in a similar position to Bianca once he enters the upper-class world of the court. Just as the Duke has taken sexual possession of Bianca, Livia buys Leantio, who becomes a kept man. The young lovers introduced at the start of the play may become bitter enemies, yet they share the same condition: both are the pampered possessions of older, wealthier, more powerful lovers; a point that is brought home in Act IV, scene i, when the two mock each other's fine clothes and 'good' fortunes.

In *Women Beware Women*, the female characters are so degraded by the commerce in sex that they transact their own bodies, capitalising on the value that they possess. Hence, Bianca following her rape, unlike Antonio's wife or the Lady, does not choose suicide but pragmatically embraces her corruption. Isabella laments the plight of women within the patriarchal marriage, which functions solely in the interests of men. Even in the case of love marriages, women 'do but buy their thraldoms, and bring great portions/To men to keep 'em in subjection' (I, ii, 172–3), concluding with the adage that 'Men buy their slaves, but women buy their masters' (I, ii, 178). Isabella's lament is not anti-marriage; she does acknowledge that the fundamental inequality of the marriage may be ameliorated by 'honesty and love' which makes marriage 'next to angels', the most blest estate' (I, ii, 179–80). The play insistently draws attention to the degradation involved in arranged marriages through the figure of Isabella and her fool of a father, on the one hand, who speaks of his daughter solely in commercial terms, and her fool of a husband, the Ward, on the other, who looks over his prospective wife as if she were a horse, checking her teeth and her gait.

Conventional discourses of love are redeployed as vehicles for illicit desires and the values they encode are disturbed. The play seemingly is sympathetic towards Hippolito and Isabella, consistently contrasting Hippolito's cultivation with the Ward's animalism. Their union is initially presented in idealising neo-Platonic terms. On seeing the couple, Guardiano opines, 'O affinity,/What piece of excellent workmanship art thou!/'Tis work clean wrought, for there's no lust, but love, in't' (I, ii, 69–71). But Hippolito already has carnal desires, and the line between affinity and incest, sanctioned love and illicit desire, is blurred, suggesting that it was not clearly drawn in the first place. Our view of these characters is subsequently compromised and muddied. Isabella becomes complicit in her own 'sale' in order to continue her love affair with her uncle under the cover of marriage. In the 2006 RSC production of *Women Beware Women*, when the Ward and Sordido look up Isabella's skirts in Act III, scene iii, the actress playing Isabella, Emma Cunniffe, expressed indignation, and attempted to resist their dehumanising attentions by snatching her skirts together. The action maintains the audience's sympathies for Isabella in this scene. Yet, the play arguably is less kind, and suggests that Isabella lets the Ward have a good look to whet his sexual appetite: 'I shall be glad to fetch a walk to your love, sir./'Twill get affection a good stomach, sir' (III, iii, 125–6). At the end of the display, she asks invitingly, 'And how do you like me now, sir?' (III, iii, 133).

Both *Revenger's Tragedy* and *Women Beware Women* draw attention to the intimate and violent relationship between sex and power. The 1960s saw a revival of Middleton's dark, sexual tragedies on the professional stage – *The Changeling* in 1961, followed by *Women Beware Women* in 1962 and *Revenger's Tragedy* in 1966. These revivals were made possible by changing attitudes towards the performance of sexuality on stage, which 'coincided with the last, successful, phase of the effort to remove [theatrical] censorship'. Just as Cox found Middleton more politically radical than Shakespeare, the theatre critic Kenneth Tynan, writing of the ground-breaking 1962 performance of *Women Beware Women*, found Middleton more sexually liberated and, unlike Shakespeare, willing to tell 'the truth about sexuality' (McLuskie 1989: 19). Anthony Page's 1962 RSC production turned Livia into 'the play's most powerful, enigmatic, and multifaceted dramatic role' (Middleton 2007: I, 1,491). In Laurence Boswell's 2006 production, Penelope Wilton presented Livia as cold and calculating in her game-playing, delighting in the power she can wield behind the scenes, and yet also invested the role with pathos, drawing on contemporary sensibilities in her poignant portrayal of the love of a middle-aged woman for a younger man. Howard Barker's 1986 revisioning of *Women Beware Women* for London's Royal Court Theatre gave the play a different ending that similarly focused on Livia and Leantio. Barker read Middleton's play as a powerful study of the way that sexuality sustains power. By rewriting the play so that the upper-class Livia is sexually and politically awakened by her lower-class lover, Leantio, Barker gave it a revolutionary ending that presented sex as the site for political liberation. Livia organises the rape of Bianca to destroy the Duke and the political system he represents, since he uses the mythos of Bianca's chastity to secure his power (McLuskie 1989: 19–21). In a similar way, Cox's film *Revengers Tragedy* emphasised the way Antonio, exploiting all the resources of modern media, uses his wife's chastity – and her rape and suicide – to promote his own political image.

Barker's revisioning of *Women Beware Women* does present the sexual power politics of the play in bold type, yet in doing so he arguably flattens out its complex and nuanced representation of desire and sexuality. More problematically, Barker privileges the phallus as a source of power in his version of revolutionary sexual politics, in that it is the violent male penetration of women's bodies that is presented as liberating. Arguably, this reworking of Middleton's play replicates the politics of rape without sufficiently critiquing its violent subjection of women's bodies (McLuskie 1989: 22). *Revenger's Tragedy* and *Women Beware Women* raise important questions about the way women's bodies are inscribed within patriarchal discourses. Both plays mobilise misogynistic discourses to produce their images of corruption as well as their sharp, satirical jests. But as we have seen in the carnivalised homosociality of *Chaste Maid at Cheapside*, it is often difficult to identify precisely what is being endorsed in the play. Patriarchal structures are themselves subject to subversive energies if not sustained critique.

PARODY AND PLAY: THE THEATRICALITY OF REVENGE

Middleton's tragedies have provoked very different, even polarised responses from critics. One school, which dominated Middleton studies in the twentieth century until the 1980s, read his plays within a morality tradition. These critics argued that allegorical figures, verbal and visual puns, peripeteia or ironic reversal, as well as the characters' invocation of divine or diabolical forces, relied for their meaning on an orthodox world view (Ribner 1962). In Middleton's great tragedies, *The Changeling* and *Women Beware Women*, T. S. Eliot discovered a universal moral essence that went well beyond the 'conventional moralizing of the epoch' to reveal profound truths about 'permanent human feelings' (Eliot 1990: 136). Yet, critics also found aspects of Middleton's tragic style distasteful. William Archer, writing in 1923, thought his plays were 'spoilt' 'by a wilful and quite unnecessary dragging to the front of the physical incidents of depravity' (Archer 1990: 133). The play that has attracted the most opprobrium is *The Revenger's Tragedy*. Eliot did not think that the play could be Middleton's; while he praised 'its amazing unity – an intense and unique and horrible vision of life', the 'cynicism, the loathing and disgust of humanity' were so excessive it could arise only out of an immature mind (Eliot 1990: 34–5).

Nicholas Brooke was one of the earliest critics to engage seriously with the 'horrid laughter' that characterises Jacobean tragedy. He did not deny that Middleton had the 'subtlest moral intelligence of the Jacobeans', but this did not make his plays orthodox. Orthodox moral viewpoints are held up for inspection in *Revenger's Tragedy* and *Women Beware Women*, yet the playful stylisation and the 'monstrous humour' of these tragedies makes such a didactic view of the action impossible to sustain. Brooke focused critical attention on the formal, dramatic qualities of the plays: the 'quality' of *Revenger's Tragedy*, for example, was concentrated 'in its superb theatricality' (1979: 47). In the late 1960s, Antonin Artaud praised the 'artistic self-consciousness' of *Revenger's Tragedy*, and championed the play as an early exemplar of theatre of the absurd (Maus 1995: xviii). Such heightened dramatic self-consciousness refuses to naturalise the moral absolutes of tragedy; instead, a play like *Women Beware Women* critiques the 'moral force' of tragedy through parody and tragi-farce (Brooke 1979: 106–8). Jonathan Dollimore, in the early 1980s, took these arguments a step further as part of a broader refutation of the school of humanist criticism that had dominated not simply Middleton studies, but literary studies more generally. The 'horrid laughter' of *The Revenger's Tragedy* becomes in Dollimore's account 'subversive black camp' that 'celebrates the artificial and delinquent', and 'through parody . . . declares itself radically sceptical of the ideological policing though not independent of the social reality which such scepticism simultaneously discloses' (1984: 149).

Heightened theatricality, parody and grotesque humour, in varying degrees, are distinctive features of revenge tragedy as a genre. There is a certain decorum to revenge – the punishment should fit the crime. It is here that the wit of the dramatist and that of the revenger come into alignment. The 'royal lecher', the Duke, is murdered by a poisoned kiss and becomes in his death throes an emblem of the spiritually corrosive effects of lust. The deaths in *Women Beware Women* are similarly apt: Livia is finally outwitted by one of her victims, Isabella, and falls through her ambition; Isabella is murdered through a shower of flaming gold in her lap, a 'conceit' which is ironically read by father as symbolising the 'prosperity [that] overjoys us all' (V, i, 158), and so signifies the deadly commodification of her body within the sexual economy; Guardiano is also fatally outwitted and caught in his own trap; Hippolito's punishment for incest, 'a fearful lust in our near bloods' (V, i, 193), is to be literally inflamed when he is shot by Cupid's poisoned arrows; and Bianca's lips, eaten away by the poisoned kiss, are a sign of her spiritual deformity: 'A blemished face best fits a leprous soul' (V, i, 246). Each death may function as a 'moral emblem', yet, as the bodies pile up on stage, the grotesquely heightened theatricality of the scene complicates the notion that this is 'appropriate retribution' according to 'the perspective of orthodox Christian dualism' (Batchelor 1990: 218). Instead, these speaking pictures, a macabre and artful combination of visual and verbal effects, turn the act of revenge into a self-consciously stylised and frequently parodic game, which demands that the audience recognise and admire the wit, the *sprezzatura* of the dramatist. The violence the revenger visits on the convulsing body of the victim is aestheticised just at the point when the audience is asked to recognise the spiritual and physical pain of all-too human sinners. In the case of *The Revenger's Tragedy*, Vindice is so pleased by the aesthetics of revenge and his own wit as revenger that, like the dramatist, he asks his audience to applaud his ingenuity: 'We may be bold/To speak it now. 'Twas somewhat witty-carried,/Though we say it. 'Twas we two murdered him' (V, iii, 96–8). In modern productions, these lines are greeted with laughter, generated by such self-conscious and audacious play with the dramatic vocabulary of revenge.

Revenge tragedies are the ultimate tragedies of blood. Since they deal in the excesses of emotion and violence, their view of human nature is inclined towards the monstrous – men and women make themselves worse than beasts by acting on their lusts. To represent the monstrous onstage dramatists turned to the grotesque. Its hybrid literary forms enabled dramatists to hold the polarities of laughter and revulsion in dynamic tension. The result is 'horrified laughter': as Brooke says of *The Revenger's Tragedy*, 'Revulsion *and* fascination meet in a very nasty joking' (1979: 24). The 'horrified laughter' of *Women Beware Women* and *The Revenger's Tragedy* relies on carefully balancing the diverse elements of tragi-farce that, in turn, requires 'great comic control' on the part of the dramatist and actor. Until Trevor Nunn's groundbreaking production of *The Revenger's Tragedy* for the RSC in 1966, its hybridity had meant that it was 'neglected as unplayable for three centuries', as Ronald Bryden noted in his review: 'Balancing terror and absurdity, it points the way back to a kind of theatrical response killed off by naturalism and the novel: the suspension not only of disbelief, but of belief, too' (*The Observer*, 9 Oct. 1966). As a sign of changing theatrical fashions, Antony Sher, who played Vindice in the 1987 RSC production, argued that the play was so effective on stage because it was written 'as a comedy':

[I]t's wildly, grotesquely funny in a way that's ahead of its time. It has one-liners in it that are like Joe Orton. The audi-

ence would constantly check with us afterwards whether we
had slipped those in or whether they were in the script – lines
like the Bastard's 'Old Dad, dead'. That gets a huge laugh and
people just can't believe that [Middleton] actually wrote that.
Or the last few moments of the play when Lussurioso is dying,
and as he's dying Vindice finally tells him the truth – saying
'Tell nobody'. It's terrifically funny in a grotesque way.
(Mulryne and Shewring 1989: 171)

The brilliant comic timing of the play is evident in the confusion of
the two plots of Ambitioso and Supervacuo to save one brother and
kill the other. These scenes, as Brooke notes, 'verge on camp
comedy' (1979: 21). The comic bewilderment of Ambitioso and
Supervacuo at the surprise entrance of Lussurioso in the 1987 production was greeted with howls of laughter from the audience. The
closing masque of death in *Women Beware Women* when the protagonists are wittily dispatched is similarly 'terrifically funny in a
grotesque way'. One-liners follow in quick succession and the stage
action often verges on slapstick. Hippolito realising Isabella has
been murdered strikes the floor in his anguish; and the Ward, like
the fool he is, releases the trap as planned, but sends Guardiano to
his fate. Then come the rapid one-liners: Hippolito, bewildered by
the sudden disappearance exclaims, 'How's that?'; the other fool,
Fabritio notes delightedly, 'Look, there's one of the lovers dropped
away'; and the Duke is just confused (V, i, 165–7)
    Staging in this final scene is very complex; a situation that is
compounded by minimal stage directions in the first 1657 edition
of the play. We do know that the deaths of the Duke and Bianca
occur on the upper stage, and the Cardinal's final speech is also
delivered from here. *Women Beware Women* makes extensive use of
the upper stage throughout the play to an extent 'that is unusual if
not unique in Renaissance drama' (Thomson 1986: 331). The play
is also notable for using the upper stage emblematically – here
Middleton could draw on his experience in designing elaborate allegorical civic pageants for the City guilds. We can see this in operation at the end of the first Act of the play when Bianca and the
Mother appear in the upper stage space, which represents the
window to Leantio's house, and the state procession of the Duke

and his court passes below, across the main stage. Refusing the Mother's offer of the stool, Bianca stands framed in the window. One way to read the window is to see it as a liminal dramatic space positioned between the private domestic interior of the house and the external public world of the street; Bianca is standing on the cusp between the bourgeois domestic world of her husband, which she is about to leave, and the opulent aristocratic world of the Duke, her soon-to-be lover. There is another level of meaning to this particular use of the upper stage. The framing of Bianca in the window provides a complex reflection on artifice. This framing device reminds us of the ways in which Bianca is consistently objectified in the play. It looks forward to her rape by the Duke amongst the gallery of paintings and statues in Livia's house. Bianca is like a beautiful painting that he desires to possess, an analogy made explicit when the Duke describes her delicate beauty as 'such as bless the faces / Of figures that are drawn for goddesses / And makes art proud to look upon her work' (II, ii, 340–2; Hopkins 1996: 5). And it recalls the lapidary language her husband, Leantio, uses to describe her earlier in the scene: she is a jewel that needs to be 'cased up from all men's eyes' lest other covetous men see her and realise that 'a gem' of 'that great value' 'were kept . . . under this plain roof' (I, i, 170–2). This is, of course, what happens. The level of stylisation in these opening scenes makes possible a meditation on the objectification of women within a patriarchal economy (McLuskie 1989: 127–8). The upper stage denotes the idealisation of Bianca – she is literally placed on a pedestal. Given her fate, the play could be said to reveal how such idealisation results in the dangerous and deathly objectification of women.

The famous chess scene again uses the upper stage in combination with the game of chess played on main stage, to produce an elaborate and extended gest, or speaking picture. Like his later *Game at Chess*, Middleton uses chess as an extended dramatic metaphor. The game of chess is the key strategy in Guardiano's and Livia's plan to entrap Bianca since it is used to distract the Mother from her role as custodian of her daughter-in-law. Chess was reputed to 'serve as a cover for sexual intrigue', which adds a sexual charge to moralising arguments against games as organs of idleness (Taylor and Loughrey 1984: 345). Livia calls on Bianca to comment on the act of game playing as a contest between women: 'Look you, lady, here's our business./Are we not well employed, think you? – an old quarrel/Between us that will never be at an end' (II, ii, 261–3). Bianca's response ironically clarifies and extends this analogy between chess strategy and gender politics that is then further developed by Livia. In response to Bianca's comment on the game that there are 'men [i.e. pawns] enough to part you [i.e. women]', Livia points out that, in fact, it is women who are men's pawns and used for their sexual purpose without regard for women's needs: 'Ho, but they set us on! Let us come off/As well as we can, poor souls; men care no further' (II, ii, 264–6). Women should beware women, but it is men who call the shots (Taylor and Loughrey 1984: 346). Hence, in order to secure the Duke's patronage and so safeguard her social standing, Livia entraps Bianca.

Social niceties are carefully observed within this scene – the courteous exchanges between the aristocratic Bianca, Guardiano and Livia contrast delicately with the homely gratefulness of the socially lower Mother. Social realism coexists in this scene with elaborate stylisation. Social and power relations are translated into the different positions available in a chess game. Livia is the 'queen'/quean who has moved her 'duke' or Rook (Guardiano) into position so that he 'Will strike a sure stroke for the game anon./Your pawn [Bianca] cannot come back to relieve itself' (II, ii, 300–1). The chess game prefigures the action on the upper stage as Bianca is taken by the Duke (the Black King) through the work of the 'duke' or Rook (Guardiano), who as the Mother unwittingly notes has 'done me all the mischief in this game' (II, ii, 415). The Mother herself has been given the 'blind mate twice' (II, ii, 391), an elaborate play on her blindness in the sense of actual poor sight, as an inferior chess and social player, in terms of her inability to foresee the entrapment of Bianca and, relatedly, her lack of foresight and vigilance in general, given that Livia admits she has deliberately prolonged the game, in effect, to allow for the rape of Bianca (Taylor and Loughrey 1984: 343–4). The language of game-playing in the play turns sexual politics into a highly stylised game that is dependent on the skill and wit of those who play it (McLuskie 1989: 128). The highly sophisticated sexual politics of the courtly chess game contrasts with the vulgar bawdiness of the common games played by the Ward. This contrast is made explicit in Act II, scene ii, when the game of chess is preceded by the appearance onstage of the Ward and Sordido with a shuttlecock and battledore or racket, which then provide the occasion for bawdy sexual innuendo. The deadly games played in the closing masque fail because they are overdetermined; with too many wits working at cross-purposes, game-playing implodes into farce.

The 1987 RSC production of *The Revenger's Tragedy* used dance in a similar way to equate the play's action with a highly stylised social game. The performance opened with a pavanne, a courtly Renaissance dance, in order to convey a strong sense of physical energy being constrained and oppressed by the restrictive hierarchy of the court world. The director, Di Trevis, chose the pavanne because 'of all the dances [it] . . . requires such a slow and held control . . . that's what so immensely difficult about it and also gives it this undertug of intrigue, because the upper body doesn't move, but you're aware all the time of moving with other people, and having to keep in columns and lines' (Mulryne and Shewring 1989: 78). The movement of the pavanne is echoed in the revenger's dance in Act V, scene iii, which reiterates the deadly nature of these courtly games. Nunn's 1966 production opened with an elaborate dumb show, complete with torches, that similarly focused the audience's attention from the start on the highly stylised, violent and corrupt court games: 'The glittering, silvery courtiers of the Duke's household surge forward from a deep black box, brandishing masks and torches: as they swish in patterns about the stage, like brilliants juggled on black velvet, we get a clue about who's being raped, who's in charge, who's paying court to whom' (D. A. N. Jones, *The Listener*, 4 Dec. 1969). Still's 2008 production similarly began with a highly stylised and lengthy opening, which turned the opening emblematic pageant into a contemporary take on the masked ball. As the stage revolved, the violent rape of Antonio's wife was played out to frenetic contemporary dance music, while the Duke was fellated just behind the wall, thus disclosing the dark, libidinous energies pulsing beneath the surface.

Vindice, in the 1966 production, appeared on stage in the opening scene as author and director, describing his enemies as they 'silently introduce[d] themselves' to the audience (D. A. N. Jones,

The Listener, 4 Dec. 1969). It is frequently noted by critics that Vindice is the consummate performer, able to inhabit the role of Piato, the minion of Lussurioso, so effectively that even his mother and sister do not recognise him. Janet Clare has argued that Vindice is 'all actor', who conveys 'very little sense of identity, either social or psychological'. He so fully inhabits 'the part he is playing; if he discloses little of himself outside the part, that is because there is nothing to disclose' (2006: 66). Dollimore views Vindice as the arch-parodist, who 'is invested with a theatrical sense resembling the dramatist's own'. The most telling example is the treatment of thunder in Act V, scene iii. The end of the revengers' dance, the choreographed murder of the new Duke, Lussurioso and his nobles, is marked by thunder, which prompts Vindice's lines: 'Mark, thunder!/Dost know thy cue, thou big-voiced crier?/ Dukes' groans are thunder's watchwords' (V, iii, 42–4). Vindice invokes the traditional role of thunder as a sign of God's retributive justice, his judgement of the guilty. But he does so in a way that parodies the convention and reveals it to be a device, a sound-effect produced offstage in the tiring-house in response to an onstage 'cue', the 'Dukes' groans' which are the signals, 'watchwords'. 'At precisely the moments when,' Dollimore argues, 'if the providential references are to convince, the dramatic illusion needs to be strongest, Vindice (as playwright) shatters it' (1984: 140).

These critical readings put forward the argument that the play's self-conscious theatricality disables any attempt to attribute a coherent morality to the play or to read Vindice as a psychologically credible character. While modern productions want to foreground the artifice, they are less comfortable with its implications for characterisation. Sher approached Vindice as a character that has been psychologically damaged by the 'tragedy of Gloriana' so that 'the whole play is really a process of redemption for him': 'What finally released the part was the realisation that Vindice must have some kind of joy in it all, otherwise it's too ghastly to contemplate.' Sher does not clarify the nature of this 'joy', but it seems to be synonymous with the concept of horrified laughter, the way the play is written 'with great comedy' (Mulryne and Shewring 1989: 121). Such juxtaposition of theatricalised grotesque humour with psychological realism is also a feature of Cox's *Revengers Tragedy*. As

Christopher Eccleston, a tautly witty and vengeful Vindice, tells the story of the murder of his beloved Gloriana at their wedding reception, relayed through flashback, the film cuts from images of the emotional intimacy the couple shared to close-ups of Eccleston, his face anguished and eyes wet with tears. The audience is immediately asked to reconcile the pathos of this scene with the grotesque playfulness of his subsequent use of Gloriana's skull in the same scene as the dummy in his deranged ventriloquist act. It is the logic of revenge that brings psychologically credible anguish into an uncomfortable alliance with horrified laughter: 'these old bones will have no peace/Until they have – Revenge!' (quoted in Spiller 2003: 5).

Whereas Sher's self-consciously artful performance, and his brilliant mastery of comic timing, brought the play's black comedy to the fore, Still's 2008 production tried for a different effect. The grotesque humour was still there, but it was less artful. The play was given a psychological coherence via the opening sequence which stages the traumatic rape of Antonio's wife and a closing scene in which we see Antonio delivering news of the execution of Vindice and Hippolito to their mother and sister, and their inconsolable grief. Rory Kinnear's Vindice is an impassioned revenger, who has a touch of Joe Orton, as one critic noted, but a lot more of Hamlet.[4] His performance gave an anguished and credible introspection to Vindice; maddened by the corruption that surrounds him, his Vindice loses himself in sadistic violence, before recalling himself to his purpose and embracing his death in his closing speech.

Since their revival on stage in the 1960s, both *The Revenger's Tragedy* and *Women Beware Women* have been appreciated as wickedly comic tragedies that dramatise the manifold corruptions of diseased and decadent societies. Philip Prowse's production of *Women Beware Women* for Glasgow's Citizens Company in 1995 'hung rotting corpses from meathooks above the action' (Michael Coveney, *Observer* 12 Feb. 1995). Contemporary critics and directors tend to pay attention less to the morality of corruption than to its politics, whether sexual politics or the way the plays starkly dramatise social tensions between the ruling elite and those it has disempowered. In either case, productions, whether for stage or screen, in the case of *The Revengers Tragedy*, continue to realise the ways in which these plays are 'unnervingly relevant' (Mulryne 2005).

NOTES

1. *The Revenger's Tragedy*, although published anonymously, was entered in the Stationers' Register alongside *Trick to Catch the Old One* in 1607. Edward Archer attributed the play to Cyril Tourneur in 1656; a year later, Nathaniel Richards gave a line from *The Revenger's Tragedy*, 'A drab of state' (IV, iv, 72) when praising Middleton's dramatic art in his verse before *Women Beware Women*.
2. Also known as *The Second Maiden's Tragedy*. For clarity, I will follow the title given in the Oxford Middleton.
3. The use of the term 'inscribe' is meant to foreground the way that gender ideologies function through language and discourse.
4. See Paul Taylor's review for *The Independent*, 6 June 2008. The essays by Gary Taylor ('Middleton, Shakespeare, and Carravagio') and Celia R. Daileader ('Middleton's Vindication of Women') in the programme notes to the production make this connection with Hamlet: Taylor argues that the play 'audaciously rewrites *Hamlet*' (p. 9), while Daileader calls it 'Middleton's feminist *Hamlet*' (p. 14).

CHAPTER 7

Partners in Tragedy: Middleton and Rowley, *The Changeling*

The Changeling, although co-written with William Rowley, is regarded as '*Middleton's* greatest play' (my italics), in the words of T. S. Eliot, 'which more than any play except those of Shakespeare has a profound and permanent moral value and horror' (Eliot 1990: 134, 137). First performed at the indoor Phoenix Theatre in May 1622 by Lady Elizabeth's Men, the play continued to be popular onstage until the closure of the theatres in 1642, and was revived after the Restoration. It was revived once more in 1961, and was performed regularly until the 1980s in Britain – it returned to the stage in 2006. The play continues to be considered 'the finest tragedy outside Shakespeare' (Paul Taylor, *The Independent*, 23 Feb. 2006). It is admired for the psychological intensity and subtlety of its portrait of the anti-heroine, Beatrice-Joanna, a 'woman dipped in blood' (III, iv, 129), and the perversity of her misalliance with the servant, De Flores. But *The Changeling* is also the triumph of another partnership, often elided in these arguments for Middleton's tragic genius, that between Middleton and Rowley. Middleton co-wrote plays with William Rowley over a ten year period from 1613 to 1623. They began writing together for Prince Charles's Men – *Wit at Several Weapons* (1613), *A Fair Quarrel* (1616), *The Old Law* (1618), and a masque, *The World Tossed at Tennis* (1620) – before writing for Lady Elizabeth's Men. Heather Hirschfeld argues that their partnership was unusual because they worked together across companies, suggesting that writing together was a deliberate rather than necessary undertaking – they did not write with each other because they had to, in that they were part of a writing team within the company, but because they wanted to (2004: 202–3).

STRUCTURE: PLOTS AND DOUBLES

The Changeling is a play of two halves. The main plot is set in the citadel of Alicante, where Beatrice-Joanna, the daughter of the governor, Vermandero, has fallen in love with a visiting nobleman, Alsemero, and hires her father's servant, De Flores, to murder her betrothed, Alonzo, so that she can marry her new beloved. De Flores demands her virginity as his reward for the murder of Alonzo; her diabolical alliance with De Flores proves her downfall. The main plot is mirrored in the sub-plot set at a hospital for lunatics run by Alibius. His new young wife, Isabella, is pursued by gentlemen of the castle who have disguised themselves as madmen; unlike Beatrice-Joanna, Isabella does not fall, but rather proves the folly of her jealous husband. The sub-plot did not fare well in the play's early critical history and was summarily dismissed for its perceived vulgarity and absurdity. A. C. Swinburne, writing in 1886, thought the sub-plot 'very stupid, rather coarse, and almost vulgar' (Swinburne 1990: 129). Its lowly reputation was compounded by its attribution to Rowley, which meant that it could be conveniently dismissed as 'not-Middleton', and so not worthy of critical attention. The BBC 1993 production for television, starring Elizabeth McGovern as Beatrice-Joanna, Bob Hoskins as De Flores, and Hugh Grant as Alsemero, excised the sub-plot altogether. Playing-time was probably a key factor motivating these cuts; yet it also followed the lead of earlier criticism which insisted that Rowley's comic sub-plot detracted from the tragic intensity of Middleton's main plot.

The skill Rowley is traditionally said to have brought to the partnership with Middleton is the writing of comic scenes – Rowley was the leading comic actor for Prince's Charles's Men. He has long been credited with the first and last scenes, and the comic plot set in the hospital for lunatics. Middleton is usually thought to have been responsible for the tragic scenes set at the castle in Acts II, III and IV. Michael Mooney argues that the two dramatists employed a distinct 'collaborative procedure' which he termed 'framing' that they had also used for an earlier play, *The Fair Quarrel*. Hence Rowley can be credited with sole authorship of the opening and closing scenes and the sub-plot (Mooney 1979: 128). Framing argues for sole authorship of particular scenes. The problem posed by *The Changeling* is that keywords, themes and images echo across the play, leading Mooney to ask a series of questions – 'Was a set of words, a prepared lexicon, used by the playwrights to develop their themes? Were these images added or reinforced in a final joint revision?' – before concluding that answers to 'these questions are inherently uncertain' (1979: 136). Yet, as Richard Nochimson points out, the question of whether the technique of framing was used is just as uncertain, since there is no external evidence to support the assumption that this is how the play was co-written. Moreover, the notion of framing derives from editorial assumptions that privilege sole authorship over collaboration. *The Changeling* is 'a play marked by a thematic consistency that makes the concept of two playwrights working independently of each other on separate shares of the play seem highly improbable' (Nochimson 2001: 52).

Nochimson's displacement of authorial authority with textual authority in his study of collaboration does not answer all the historical and conceptual questions raised by collaboration, particularly in the light of recent work on early modern authorship. What happens if we think about collaboration not as an 'author'-less activity, but as multi-authored? One consequence of this approach for *The Changeling* might be attention to the notion of doubling, to the play's complex dialectic between similarity and difference. Recent criticism has drawn attention to the sophisticated and subtle mirroring of the play's double plot. Hirschfeld notes the art, the technical skill and inventiveness, with which the playwrights interlace the two plots; by having characters across the two plots 'echo or steal one another's language', the double plot is 'a clear demonstration of the playwrights' ability to weave story lines and themes together' (2004: 104). As her use of the word 'steal' indicates, with its connotations of property and ownership, Hirschfeld is interested in the way dramatists negotiated issues raised by distinctive, individual styles as they engaged in shared, collaborative writing practices. It is possible to see the structural, thematic and linguistic use of doubling in *The Changeling*, as well as the figure of the changeling, as a self-conscious study of the arts of collaboration. Doubling and echoing result in a play that is thematically and linguistically unified, and yet composed of distinct parts.

The play sustains two independent lines of action in the two plots, maintained through the distinct dramatic spaces of the castle and asylum, and builds in complex linkages in terms of character, theme and structure. Declan Donnellan's 2006 production for Cheek by Jowl theatre company used a sparse set – the main props were easily moveable red plastic chairs – which meant that the distinctions between castle and asylum could easily be blurred, and scenes set in the castle and asylum slid into each with little interruption. Parallels between the two plots were reinforced by having the principal actors double as asylum inmates in the madhouse scenes. As Paul Menzer points out, 'Seeing our De Flores and Beatrice Joanna double as lunatics literalized the play's figurative analogy between its two main plots and settings' (2007: 96)

The two plots take distinct generic forms. The plot set in the asylum is very familiar from bourgeois city comedies of the period – the old husband jealously guards the beautiful young wife, who is pursued by gallants under his unsuspecting nose. The aristocratic castle plot is cast in the higher mode of tragedy, and incorporates elements of the fashionable revenge tragedy in its focus on blood and betrayal and Tomazo's desire to avenge his brother's murder. What interrelates the two plots are sophisticated mirroring devices that function at the level of character and theme. Pairs and trios of characters, that constellate around the main female protagonists, Beatrice-Joanna at the castle and Isabella in the asylum, are counterpointed. In terms of character types, the servant Lollio is a 'comic reflection' of De Flores, while, in the case of the standard blocking-figure, Alibius counterpoints Vermandero (Hutchings and Bromham 2008: 85).

Counterpointing extends from characters to sets of scenes. The first two scenes are set in the castle and asylum respectively, establishing these spaces as the two sites of action. The first scene ends with De Flores thrusting his fingers into the sockets of Beatrice-Joanna's glove; an uncomfortable image of sexual possession that is echoed in the following scene as Alibius and Lollio play on the wedding ring as a sign of Alibius's ownership of his wife's body – Lollio jestingly warns Alibius that 'You must keep it [the ring/his new wife] on still, then; if it but lie by, one or other will be thrusting into't' (I, ii, 30–1) The next five scenes are set at the castle and end dramatically with De Flores' murder of Alonzo. At Act III, scene iii, the action moves to the asylum – this scene marks the midpoint of the play. Mirroring is achieved through the device of the love-test that formally links the two plots. With the sexual virtues of the two women put to the test, an elaborate dynamic is put in place that contrasts Beatrice-Joanna–Alonzo–Alsemero–De Flores with Isabella–Alibius–Antonio and Franciscus–Lollio. The counterpointing is foregrounded through the repetition of scenes across the two plots in which the servant aims at the sexual blackmail of the mistress (Levin 1971: 35–6). Whereas Beatrice-Joanna cannot resist because she is now a 'woman dipped in blood' (III, iv, 129), since Isabella is not sexually fallen, she can call on her chastity and superior social standing. In the second half of the play, the set of castle scenes culminates in Beatrice-Joanna's successful faking of the virginity test, which is then restaged in the testing of Antonio through Isabella's performance of madness. Whereas Isabella has the perspicacity to judge the truth of Antonio's professed love, Alsemero's pseudo-scientific method is comically flawed.

Most famously, the two plots mirror each other through the theme of madness, in particular, the folly or madness of love. Franciscus is reputed to have fallen mad through love, while Antonio when he reveals himself to Isabella announces 'This shape of folly shrouds your dearest love' (III, iii, 133). Alibius's madhouse is said to literalise the metaphorical madness of the main plot. The folly of love is a conventional theme of romantic comedies. *The Changeling* darkens its treatment considerably by using it to traverse the two plots. Michael Attenborough's 1992 RSC production sexualised the dance of the madmen and fools at the end of Act IV, scene iii, turning it into an antimasque of copulating lunatics which visually mirrored the 'dumb show' of Beatrice-Joanna and De Flores copulating at the beginning of Act IV, scene i.

Characters from the two plots come together in Act V, scene ii, which brings to fruition carefully established points of crossover. Alibius and Isabella appear before Alibius's patron, Vermandero, who is accompanied by Tomazo, with news that two gentlemen of Vermandero's household, Antonio and Franciscus, have been discovered by Isabella at the madhouse and the 'time of their disguisings agrees justly,/With the day of the murder' (V, ii, 77–8). Alibius, Isabella, Franciscus and Antonio then reappear at the castle in the final scene in time for the revelation of the true murderers, which ends with a riff on the figure of the changeling – Alibius's part in this set piece is to promise to 'change now/into a better husband' (V, iii, 213–14). The comedic function of these speeches does seem unsettling following on from the deaths of De Flores and Beatrice-Joanna and the pathos of her parting words: 'Forgive me, Alsemero, all forgive:/'Tis time to die when 'tis a shame to live' (V iii, 178–9). The incongruity is an effect of the play's generic hybridity. There are moments in *The Changeling* that do approximate the 'horrid laughter' of *The Revenger's Tragedy*, such as the grim humour of De Flores's efforts to remove the ring from Alonzo's finger: 'What, so fast on?/Not part in death? I'll take a speedy course then:/Finger and all shall off' (III, ii, 24–6). That said, *The Changeling* stops short of the witty tragi-farce of either *Revenger's Tragedy* or *Women Beware Women*.

The final scene integrates the comic and tragic plots through the figure of the changeling (Hutchings and Bromham 2008: 76). At a general level, the term signifies 'one given to change; a fickle or inconstant person' (*OED*). From the moment Beatrice-Joanna announces that she 'shall change my saint, I fear me; I find/A giddy turning in me' (I, i, 158–9) she is identified with the figure in the title in specifically gendered terms, in that she exemplifies the dangerous changeability of women. Her identification of herself as tainted blood that must be removed, purged from her father's body, associates her with the second meaning of 'changeling' which derives from folklore – the child, often deformed or an idiot, exchanged for the 'true' child by the fairies. Her comic counterpart is Antonio, who is named as the changeling in the list of characters, and passes himself off as a changeling – the idiot son of a noble family. To an extent, Diaphanta, who takes the place of Beatrice-Joanna in the bed-trick, also plays the part of the changeling, although as a manifestation of the shape-shifting associated with diabolical women, like Beatrice-Joanna.

There is a further rhetorical meaning to the figure of the changeling. George Puttenham, in his *The Arte of English Poesie*, called 'hypallage', the rhetorical figure denoting the transference of attributes from their proper subjects to others, typically by 'revers[ing] the natural relation of two terms in a sentence', the 'Changeling'. Hypallage describes the union of Beatrice-Joanna and De Flores in that loathing is perversely transformed into love, and his outward deformity describes the beautiful Beatrice-Joanna's inward corruption (Slater 1983: 429–40; Chakravorty 1996: 164–5). Or rather, it could be said that the figure of the changeling describes the inherent propensity for female beauty to become monstrous, given women's 'true', inward nature. We can also see how this rhetorical figure operates more generally in the play through the notion of misapprehension, of mistaking one thing for another. Misapprehension is explored through the failure of 'intellectual eyesight' and, as we shall see, through word play and punning, in which key words carry and accrue double or multiple meanings, that characters at different moments in the play either mistake or fail to apprehend fully.

THEATRICAL SPACE: CASTLES, CLOSETS AND CABINETS

The Changeling was performed at the Phoenix Theatre as well as at court, as part of the 1623–4 Christmas festivities. It is therefore possible that the play was specifically designed to take full dramatic and symbolic advantage of indoor staging. Certainly, a number of scenes benefit from a darkened stage and the use of candle-light. More generally, the enclosed space of the indoor theatre adds to the often claustrophobic interiority of this play and may have encouraged the dramatists to experiment with the dramatic and emblematic use of space. The play takes full symbolic advantage of the motif of enclosed spaces through its scenes set at the castle and the asylum, as well as its use of the interior, curtained-off spaces of the stage for its closet scenes (Hutchings and Bromham 2008: 83).

The symbolism of the castle derives from a conceit often found in Petrarchan love poetry that imagines the chaste mistress as a fortress besieged by her importuning lover (Berger 1969: 37). The range of this conceit is established right at the start of the play, when Beatrice-Joanna asks her father if Alsemero can 'see your castle' (I, i, 163). Vermandero replies:

> Yet there's an article between: I must know
> Your country; we use not to give survey
> Of our chief strengths to strangers. Our citadels
> Are placed conspicuous to outward view
> On promonts' tops; but within are secrets. (I, i, 165–9)

This speech sets out the interchangeability of Vermandero's castle and his daughter. The equation relies on the patriarchal analogy between the family and the state. As governor and father, Vermandero controls the access to his castle just as he controls access to his daughter; the integrity of its walls and her maidenhead are vital to his social standing. The power to grant access to the castle is immediately identified with Vermandero's choice of son-in-law, Alonzo de Piracquo. Beatrice-Joanna is the 'tie' (I, i, 223) that will bind these two men together. Vermandero's rights over his daughter's body and the role of marriage as a homosocial exchange of property and status are made explicit in this opening scene (Malcolmson 1990: 330–1).

The fact that Beatrice-Joanna, like the citadel, is 'placed conspicuous to outward view', and yet strictly regulated, has led to Alsemero's fatal misapprehension. The play points out that Alsemero's birth and qualities give him as much right of access to the castle (and hence Beatrice-Joanna) as the 'complete' gentleman, Alonzo. Notice the way a play on 'will' and 'want', carrying the double sense of desire and lack, is introduced in this first scene. When Vermandero announces that Alonzo shall be bound to him through marriage or 'I'll want/My will else', Beatrice-Joanna retorts in an aside 'I shall want mine if you do it' (I, i, 223–4). Her veiled insistence on the primacy of her own desires provides the audience with an indication of what the dangerous 'secrets' lurking within her 'outward view' of chastity, modesty and obedience might be. This misogynist view of wilful female duplicity informs the symbolism of 'secret' spaces throughout the play. Alsemero's own aside, interestingly, initially makes him complicit in the transgression: 'How shall I dare to venture in his castle/When he discharges murderers at the gate?/But I must on, for back I cannot go' (I, i, 226–8). 'Murderers' are the small cannon guarding the entrance to the fortress. The image of the Petrarchan lover who lays siege to his beloved is given a murderous twist. Alsemero betrays Vermandero's hospitality by entering his castle as an enemy, an underminer. It implies Alsemero's own culpability in the murders, along with Beatrice-Joanna, and reveals traces of its Calvinist source text, John Reynolds's *The Triumphs of God's Revenge against . . . Murther* (1621), in which Alsemero does not escape God's vengeance for his sins and is killed in a duel with Tomazo (Middleton 1990: xiii).

Alsemero's pun on 'murderers' draws attention to the violence of the siege metaphor in that the logic of taking the citadel by force is the logic of rape. The sequence of dramatic action in this scene associates Alsemero's entrance into Vermandero's castle with the sight of De Flores thrusting his fingers into Beatrice-Joanna's glove. De Flores introduces a further dimension to equation between Beatrice-Joanna and the castle. This trusted servant acts as the keeper of the castle, possessing full knowledge of all its secret places. Having the liberty of the castle, De Flores is a troublingly mobile figure. Beatrice-Joanna at the start of the play complains that she finds his presence invasive. For his part, De Flores's recourse to the motif of love as a hunt, 'Must I be enjoined/To follow still whilst she flies from me?', gives an indication that he does not maintain his proper social distance, and instead chooses 'all opportunities' to 'please myself with sight' of Beatrice-Joanna (I, i, 101–4). His mastery of the inward, secret spaces of the castle is dramatised in the murder scene; appropriately, De Flores begins his murderous attack by clubbing Alonzo with the key. Similarly, the murder of Diaphanta is achieved through his knowledge of the house. Mastery of the castle, and knowledge of its bloody secrets, translates into possession of Beatrice-Joanna's body. The vulnerability of Beatrice-Joanna to the predations of a servant describes the fatal permeability of her body, as well as the dangerous openness of the castle to underminers (Malcolmson 1990: 332).

Sexual access is one of the themes traversing the castle and mad-house scenes. Alibius's opening words to his servant, Lollio, are: 'I must trust thee with a secret,/But thou must keep it' (I, ii, 1–2). His young wife, Isabella, is his 'secret'; Alibius makes Lollio her jailer in order to keep her away from the 'quick enticing eyes' of the gallants who daily come to see his 'brainsick patients' (I, ii, 55, 53). While Alibius does attempt to police his wife's body, we need to consider whether the madhouse functions as metaphor for the female body in the way that the castle does. Given that Alibius's household is a hospital for lunatics we could see the madhouse as literalising the folly of the jealous husband. Regulatory bodily images are employed in the representation of the madhouse, but they are parodic rather than explicitly gendered. The early modern medical language of dietary regimens, intended to regulate the body, is carnivalised. Lollio gives a parodic daily regime for the madhouse that is metonymically body-centred in comic fashion:

for every part has his hour: we wake at six and look about us, that's eye-hour; at seven we should pray, that's knee-hour; at eight walk, that's leg-hour; at nine gather flowers and pluck a rose, that's nose-hour; at ten we drink, that's mouth-hour; at eleven lay about us for victuals, that's hand-hour; at twelve go to dinner, that's belly-hour. (I, ii, 71–7)

Lollio also plays with the language of the school-room; this is another way in which the madhouse scenes parody early modern humanist discourses of discipline.

The heightened sense of social spaces in *The Changeling* increases the dramatic attention to the role of servants in managing, even governing the household. This is the case with the male servants, De Flores and Lollio. Diaphanta, Beatrice-Joanna's waiting woman, has a less commanding, but no less significant role. Alsemero draws attention to the importance of the lady's maid as keeper of her mistress's secrets: 'These women are their ladies' cabinets;/Things of most precious trust are locked into 'em' (II, ii, 6–7). The cabinet, like the lady's maid, was particular to elite households. Both, in a sense, are signifiers for the private life of the gentry and aristocracy in that they are typically represented on stage and in literary texts as the keepers or repositories of secrets.[1] We need to be wary of simply conflating modern notions of private life with early modern. These devices shed light on one particular configuration of privacy in this period. In this case, privacy is understood in class terms – the ability to afford private rooms, set off from more communal, public areas, as well the ability to employ others to take on household labour, meant that certain experiences of privacy were confined to the social elite. Privacy in this scene is also gendered. Diaphanta speaks of the secret part of the castle, where she brings Alsemero for his assignation with Beatrice-Joanna, as 'my charge' (II, ii, 1), thus denoting a specifically feminised space that is simultaneously identified with concealment. At this point in the play, Alsemero is confident that he has unique access to Beatrice-Joanna and her 'cabinet', and so interprets her inwardness in terms of 'precious trust'. Nonetheless, the sexualising of Beatrice-Joanna's private world means that it carries latent associations with the dangerous unknowability and uncontrollability attributed to female desire.

The play neatly contrasts 'ladies' cabinets' and their secrets with Alsemero's 'physician's closet', complete with phials and ' "The Book of Experiment,/Called *Secrets in Nature*" ' (IV, i, 20, 24–5). This cabinet belongs to the disciplines of knowledge parodied in the madhouse scenes. It is a mode of knowledge held up to ridicule because its method, the play argues, is fundamentally flawed (Stachniewski 1990: 234–6). Since it locates truth in material rather than spiritual signs, it is easily deceived by false appearances; hence Beatrice-Joanna can fake the virginity text. Beatrice-Joanna is very good at 'faking it' in her encounters with Alsemero – first in the virginity test and then the bed-trick. Marjorie Garber argues that the concern with women's ability to 'fake it' speaks to anxieties about the unknowable nature of female desire; hence Alsemero's cabinet promises, yet fails to discover the 'secrets' of women's sexual nature. At the same time, the ability to 'fake it' empowers women since it 'protects the privacy and control of pleasure' (Garber 1994: 19–38). There is an interesting parallel use of the closet in the sub-plot. Alsemero's closet was probably a curtained-off area of the stage that functioned to signify interior or 'secret' off-stage spaces of dramatic action. In Act IV, scene i, Beatrice-Joanna gains possession of Alsemero's key to his closet; this action is mirrored in Act IV, scene iii, when Isabella takes the key of Lollio's 'wardrobe', and exits, probably into the same curtained-off area that signified Alsemero's closet, to disguise herself as a madwoman in order to test Antonio. Given the mirroring effect, how are we to interpret Isabella's act of 'faking it' in the following 'mad' scene?

Beatrice-Joanna's moment of self-mastery is brief; its end is marked by the transformation of Alsemero's closet into another form. The earlier humanist, pseudo-medical function of the closet is given a religious dimension in the final scene, which realises its 'true' function as a mechanism for revelation of biblical proportions. Alsemero locks Beatrice-Joanna and De Flores in his closet, inviting them to:

> rehearse again
> Your scene of lust, that you may be perfect
> When you come to act it to the black audience
> Where howls and gnashings shall be music to you.
> Clip your adulteress freely; 'tis the pilot
> Will guide you to the *Mare Mortuum*.[2] (V, iii, 114–19)

The recurrent association of cabinets and closets with woman's secret nature and female sexuality coalesce in Alsemero's conventional misogynist naming of female genitalia as the gateway to hell. The play seems to want to localise damnation in the body of Beatrice-Joanna. Yet, this evocative dramatic use of the closet, with its echoing of other 'secret' places in the play, casts its shadow over the space of the castle itself, giving the uncomfortable impression of a city of the damned.

DRAMATIC LANGUAGE: PUNS AND KEYWORDS

The Changeling is praised for its psychological intensity. As we have seen in its complex layering of dramatic action and emblematic use of stage space, it is a superbly crafted play. Visual and dramatic representations of 'secret', private places on stage are mirrored in the language of the play. *The Changeling* is remarkable for its reliance on asides. Asides are a dramatic representation of levels of speech. In *The Changeling*, asides do not simply signify the demarcation of public and private speech, but associate the latter with often negative ethical values, such as the concealment of intent or the expression of illicit desires that cannot safely or acceptably have open, public expression. When assessing the status of the aside as a dramatisation of interiority we need to be aware that, particularly in early modern religious discourses, expressions of selfhood did not necessarily have positive value, but more often than not carried negative connotations. Christopher Ricks's seminal essay on double-meaning in *The Changeling* argues that its puns are intrinsic to the psychology of the play to the extent that the 'verbal structure . . . exactly provides the moral structure of the play'. *The Changeling*'s puns take a particular form. The predominant feature of puns in the play is that 'the character who speaks them is not intending a double meaning' (1990: 169, 160). This type of punning discloses a tragically divided self, frequently manifested through the processes of misapprehension which reveal a lack of self-knowledge or comprehension of the workings of wider external forces.

Ricks formulated a list of five keywords, repeated across the play, that are subject to this kind of punning. High on the list, not surprisingly, is 'blood', followed by 'will', 'act', 'deed' and 'service'. He identified a further subset of keywords: 'forward', 'modesty', 'honour', and 'honesty'. 'Blood' is first used in the opening scene when Jasperino, punning on the language of early modern medicine, propositions Diaphanta, offering to show her 'such a thing with an ingredient that we two would compound together, and if it did not tame the maddest blood i'th'town for two hours after, I'll ne'er profess physic again' (I, i, 144–6). Here, blood refers to the passions, to sexual desire. The word is not used again in the play until Act II, scene ii, when Beatrice-Joanna dissuades Alsemero from challenging Alonzo to a duel since 'Blood-guiltiness becomes a fouler visage' (II, ii, 40) – 'blood' here, as well as later in the scene at line 120, prefigures De Flores's murder of Alonzo. When De Flores uses the word, after agreeing to the murder, 'O my blood!' (II, ii, 148), it returns darkly to its earlier meaning of sexual arousal, stimulated by both the bloody deed he has been asked to perform and its hoped-for reward. In this scene, 'blood' first becomes part of a cluster of words that accrue meaning in relation to 'service', 'act' and 'deed'. The nasty joke is that Beatrice-Joanna in appealing to De Flores's manhood has raised his blood, unwittingly sexualising the language of service, and does not yet comprehend that De Flores has applied other meanings to her words.

The full meaning of service is slowly revealed to Beatrice-Joanna in Act III, scene iv, beginning with the moment when De Flores offers Alonzo's severed finger – still bearing the diamond ring that Beatrice-Joanna sent to Alonzo as a betrothal gift – as a love token and sign of the bloody deed. With this act, Beatrice-Joanna and De Flores are united in blood (III, iv, 129), which overpowers the other meaning of 'blood' (III, iv, 134), signifying birth and status, that should keep him at a 'distance' (III, iv, 133) and in his social place as a servant. The severed finger illustrates how, as Ricks points out, these puns 'are thoroughly *actable*' (1990: 169). It is a visual emblem of the bloody deed, a speaking picture that signifies the unholy union of De Flores and Beatrice-Joanna; as De Flores says, parodying the marriage service, the act that has 'made you one with me' (III, iv, 143; Lomax 1987: 162–5).

John Stachniewski does not disagree with Ricks and others about the psychological power of the play; but he does warn against anachronistically adopting Freudian readings that privilege sexuality and its drives when deciphering its keywords, and instead insists on the 'Calvinist psychology' that gives the play its particular moral logic.[3] This reading would have us see Beatrice-Joanna as damned from the very outset. Her status as the changeling points to the existence of 'secret' identity, hidden in the recesses of her soul, that neither she nor her kin are aware of, but nonetheless marks her out as reprobate (Stachniewski 1990: 229). This renders Alsemero's first vision of Beatrice-Joanna at the church, when he imagines their marriage will reverse the effects of the Fall, since it 'admits comparison/With man's first creation, the place blest,/And is his right home back, if he achieve it' (I, i, 7–9), deeply and darkly ironic. If Beatrice-Joanna is irredeemably fallen, then she is comparable to Eve only in the misogynist sense that she will bring sin and death into this world. This reading makes sense of the recurrent association of De Flores with the serpent, most tellingly when Beatrice-Joanna is brought to the awareness of her predestined fallenness by De Flores: 'Was my creation in the womb so cursed,/ It must engender with a viper first?' (III, iv, 168–9; Frost 1990: 223–4).

'Calvinist psychology' brings a different cluster of keywords relating to sight and judgement to the fore. These keywords are established in the first scene when the question of eyesight is particularly prominent. Beatrice-Joanna warns Alsemero:

> Be better advised, sir:
> Our eyes are sentinels unto our judgements,
> And should give certain judgement what they see;
> But they are rash sometimes, and tell us wonders
> Of common things, which when our judgements find,
> They can check the eyes, and call them blind. (I, i, 71–6)

Both Alsemero and Beatrice-Joanna have problems with their eyesight. Thomas Wright, in his *Passions of the Mind*, said of those possessed by the 'Passion of Love' that it 'blindeth their judgement', meaning that they mistakenly 'judgeth all things that occur in favour of that passion to be good and agreeable with reason' (Hamlin 2005: 226). Antonio fails to see Isabella through her disguise as a madwoman, earning her scathing mockery: 'You, a quick-sighted lover?' (IV, iii, 139). Yet it is only Beatrice-Joanna's eye that is darkened in the scriptural sense: 'But if thine eye be evil, thy whole body shall be full of darkness' (Matthew 6: 23). Her blindness derives from 'self-ignorance'; as Stachniewski points out, this is not so much hypocrisy or 'conscious pretence . . . as an inability to distinguish between the outward (flesh) and the inward (spirit)' (1990: 242; see below, pp. 168–71). It is important to point out that both Alsemero and Beatrice-Joanna mistake physical beauty for spiritual worth, and we need to consider why it is Beatrice-Joanna that is marked out as damned in the play. Part of the reason lies in the misogyny driving this Calvinist psychology that genders fallen nature feminine.

A different set of keywords structure the madhouse plot – folly, madness, the lunatic and the lover. It too uses highly sexualised word play. Yet, unlike Beatrice-Joanna, Isabella intends her puns, and this linguistic control equates with her perspicacity. She has internalised Calvinist doctrine and recognises the priority of spiritual worth over physical appearance. Hence, it is Isabella who admonishes Antonio's spiritual blindness and corrects his faulty vision: 'I have no beauty now,/Nor never had, but what was in my garments' (IV, iii, 137–8). Whereas Beatrice-Joanna ends the play by turning herself into a spectacle of damnation, Isabella is offered as the model of the good wife, a Protestant version of the patient Griselda, who has suffered her husband's folly and proved her moral and spiritual worth.

It is a question of the extent to which the play encourages resisting readers of its dramatic language. Does the repressive, unremitting logic of 'Calvinist psychology' finally contain the 'analytical confusion' of its word play? Whereas Ricks interprets the punning in terms of moral certainty – we, the audience, are brought to an understanding of the moral behind the pun – Annabel Patterson comes to a different conclusion. She points to the way that keywords, such as 'blood', paradoxically are 'used with absolute clarity to signify analytical confusion' (Middleton 2007: I, 1,635). The over-determined quality of the play's language is highlighted in Paul Hamlin's assessment of the encounter between Beatrice-Joanna and De Flores in Act III, scene iv: 'Within fifty brilliant lines Middleton and Rowley bring into tight proximity all the meanings of "blood" they have thus far deployed: caste, consanguinity, merit, violence, life-force, sexual drive' (2005: 229). In which cultural field do all these meanings coalesce? The various meanings of 'blood' derive from different and distinct discourses, from early modern medicine to Calvinism. One could therefore argue that such punning, which holds different cultural systems in tension, does not allow one way of seeing, as Patterson notes, 'to separate out and dominate a reading or production', resulting in an 'ethical undecidability' at the level of the play's language (Middleton, 2007: I, 1,635). Yet are there critical problems raised by privileging this 'ethical undecidability' over other systems at work in the play, such as Calvinism? While Hamlin, for example, acknowledges that the language of 'doubting, seeing, and knowing' in the play is in line with the 'sceptical currents of Jacobean thought', nonetheless it constantly 'suggests the existence of a morally responsive universe through its repeated allusions to forebounding, instinct and conscience' (2005: 220–1, 232).

PERFORMANCE: BEATRICE-JOANNA ON STAGE

The Changeling was popular on the Stuart stage from its first performances in 1622 until the first decade after the Restoration. Pepys saw a performance in 1661 at the Playhouse, and recorded that 'it takes exceedingly'. After 1668, it disappeared from the professional stage until it was revived in 1961 with Tony Richardson's production for the Royal Court Theatre in London. The next year, the RSC performed *Women Beware Women*, and four years later, Trevor Nunn staged his production of *The Revenger's Tragedy*, the first professional revival of this play since 1606. Revivals of bloody, grotesque and sexually-charged Jacobean tragedies in the 1960s were part of a wider liberalisation of the theatre that coincided with the ending of theatre censorship in England. At the same time, the new 'permissive society', said to emerge in the 1960s, created a climate receptive to their anti-romantic portrayals of sexuality and desire (McLuskie 1989: 19; see above, pp. 120–1).

Studies of *The Changeling*, since early criticism of the play in the mid-nineteenth century, have been fascinated by the misalliance between Beatrice-Joanna and De Flores, seeing this relationship as the core of the play. James Russell Lowell wrote in 1843 of Beatrice-Joanna's spoken antipathy to De Flores that the 'thought of De Flores is to Beatrice what the air-drawn dagger was to Macbeth; she foresees in her own heart the crime yet uncommitted, and trembles at the weapon even while she stretches her quivering hand to grasp it' (1990: 125). Twenty years later, Swinburne admired the subtle simplicity of skill' of the dramatists in presenting

> the fatal and foreordained affinity between the ill-favoured, rough-mannered, broken-down gentleman, and the head-strong unscrupulous unobservant girl whose very abhorrence of him serves only to fling her down from her high station of haughty beauty into the very clutch of his ravenous and pitiless passion. (1990: 129)

For Eliot, the tragic love story was not that of Beatrice-Joanna and Alsemero, but Beatrice-Joanna and De Flores. As Beatrice-Joanna becomes 'habituated' to sin, Alsemero 'disappears not only from the scene but from her own imagination': 'in the end Beatrice, having been so long the enforced conspirator of De Flores, becomes . . . more *his* partner, *his* mate, than the mate and partner of the man for the love of whom she consented to the crime' (1990: 135).

It is not surprising that, since *The Changeling*'s revival on the modern stage in the 1960s, critical attention has focused on the characterisation of Beatrice-Joanna and De Flores. Following the lead of Eliot, directors and theatre reviewers have interpreted the play as 'a warped love story' (Barker and Nicol 2004: 25); Beatrice-Joanna's early expression of revulsion towards De Flores is read in Freudian terms as a sign of repressed sexual desire. Paul Taylor's review of Donnellan's 2006 production is entirely conventional in its view that '[s]uppressed attraction quivers in the voluble revulsion of Beatrice-Joanna for the disfigured servant De Flores'; as is Donnellan's argument 'that no one apart from those two makes an issue of his ugliness', and 'that this shared, perhaps distorted perception is another mark of their fatal mutual fascination' (Taylor, *The Independent*, 23 Feb. 2006).

This Freudian reading of Beatrice-Joanna's character has placed particular demands on those performing the part. It is a role that has attracted leading actresses: Mary Ure (1961), Emma Piper (1978), Diana Quick (1978), Miranda Richardson (1988), Cheryl Campbell (1992) and Olivia Williams (2006). Reviewers, as Roberta Barker and David Nicol argue in their survey of twentieth-century productions of *The Changeling*, have enshrined a model of the ideal Beatrice-Joanna that is defined primarily in terms of the 'truth' of her performance of female sexuality on stage. The first two actresses who played Beatrice-Joanna, Ure and Piper, were criticised for their 'girlish' restraint – reviewers admired their sexual attractiveness, but often complained that it was passively rather than actively expressed, and that they failed to portray Beatrice-Joanna's perceived sexual wilfulness (Barker and Nicol 2004: 5, 7). Diana Quick in Terry Hands's 1978 production presented a very different Beatrice-Joanna to the public. 'With sequins glinting on her face', Felix Barker wrote, 'in evil scarlet robes and with a voluptuous exposure of her bosom, Miss Quick makes Beatrice a ruthless addict of her own sensual drugs'. Whereas Ure and Piper were criticised for being too cool, Quick's performance was criticised for being too hot. John Barber concluded that Quick's lascivious Beatrice-Joanna 'misconceives the role': 'Instead of the slow corruption of an innocent, we get the display of a mere wanton' (cited in Barker and Nicol 2004: 11–12). The problem may be that the beautiful, virginal, yet sexually aware young woman is a male fantasy difficult to realise even on the stage. Particular attention has focused on whether actresses can capture the 'true' perverse nature of her sexual attraction to De Flores; what drives her desire. Arguably this Freudian reading of a masochistic Beatrice-Joanna on stage and in reviews of performances correlates with Marjorie Garber's account of the male fantasy of 'what women want' (1994).

The RSC 1988 production, which starred Miranda Richardson as Beatrice-Joanna, retained the revulsion/attraction thesis that dominated earlier productions but gave it a highly politicised rereading. The play was relocated from early seventeenth-century Alicante to a nineteenth-century Spanish slave colony. De Flores was played by George Harris, a black actor, so that Beatrice-Joanna's revulsion towards his physical appearance is transposed into the vocabulary of racism. Although this production retained the reading of the play as a dark love story, it phrased this story less in Freudian terms than in terms of a postcolonial critique of racism and its forms of institutional and psychological slavery. Their transgression was not sado-masochistic sexual perversion, but rather the threat of miscegenation. By committing herself to De Flores, Beatrice-Joanna therefore undergoes a process of radical enlightenment in which she is able to see beyond race to acknowledge the desire which unites them (Barker and Nicol 2004: 17–18).

This radical revisioning of *The Changeling* ran up against limitations imposed by the play's language. In the case of De Flores, the play insists that his outer physical deformity is a manifestation of his inner corruption, and his nature is driven by lust and blood and defined by perverse appetites. Reviews of this production suggested how the producers by turning De Flores into a black man could unwittingly reproduce racist stereotypes. For Peter Kemp, Harris's De Flores was ' "a man of primitive drives which, once released, cannot be stopped" and a savage whose "alien background . . . has gouged itself into his personality" '. This production also intensified the problem of how to interpret the sexual violence of the play. Given that it encouraged, as Barker and Nicol note, 'its spectators to formulate an ideologically sympathetic reading of Beatrice's burgeoning intimacy with De Flores' (2004: 17–18), does this also leave the audience in the position of having to accept De Flores's rape of Beatrice-Joanna, and other forms of violence, as a necessary stage in the process of radical transformation?

If Eyre's 1988 production used race to reframe the play politically, the 1992 production for the RSC returned to religion. We should remember that the play opens in the church and Alsemero's discourse of love validates itself through recourse to religion: 'The place is holy, so is my intent:/I love her beauties to the holy purpose' (I, i, 5–6). The curtain opened in this production on Beatrice-Joanna kneeling before a large crucifix which dominated the stage. This image of Beatrice-Joanna at her 'devotions' is repeated throughout the production – Act II, scene i again opens with her kneeling before the crucifix; in Act IV, scene i, De Flores becomes her 'god', kneeling with arms extended at the head of the bed, in a Christ-like posture, with Beatrice-Joanna lying before him. By foregrounding the dominance of the Church over the proceedings of the play, the production emphasised its repressive attitude towards sexuality, and female sexuality in particular. Cheryl Campbell's Beatrice-Joanna relied on the allied power of religion and status in her early encounters with De Flores. Campbell suggested the extreme social and psychological pressures that the Church placed on women of her class in her impassioned, often overwrought performance, with its rapid emotional changes. Her hysterical laughter as she feigned the virginity test nicely captured the insanity not simply of the test, but of the patriarchal religious culture that produced it, embodied by Alsemero, and its fetishising of virginity. Olivia Williams took this a stage further in her performance in the 2006 Cheek by Jowl production. This Beatrice-Joanna was highly unstable – a woman on the verge of a nervous breakdown. The sparse staging and male characters dressed in suits reminiscent of the mafiosi suggested the emotional and physical repressiveness of the patriarchal honour culture that has its expression in the speeches of her father, Vermandero. That said, a number of reviewers wanted to read Williams's performance as less a response to a repressive patriarchal culture than a neurosis bred out of

Beatrice-Joanna's own repressed desire. Hence, Michael Billington concluded that the core of Williams's performance was 'a frenzied neurotic insanely attracted to the loathed De Flores' (*The Guardian*, 16 May 2006).

Both the 1992 and 2006 productions arguably allowed the audience to see the violence repressive ideologies bring to bear on women's bodies. Following in the footsteps of Hands's 1978 production, Donnellan (2006) chose to have De Flores's rape of Beatrice-Joanna played on stage – rather than occur off-stage – and as a rape and not a seduction. Whereas in the Hands production, the decision to use the line 'This fellow has undone me endlessly' meant that Beatrice-Joanna's response to her rape was greeted by the audience with 'hoots and guffaws' (cited in Barker and Nicol 2004: 14), in Donnellan's production the rape was played straight in all its brutality and made for uncomfortable viewing. Beatrice-Joanna is raped on the desk where moments before she had written the cheque with which she hoped to pay off De Flores – he takes the money *and* rapes Beatrice-Joanna. It conveys a stark picture of the powerlessness of women, whatever their wealth and status, when faced by the violence of sexually predatory men. The rape of Beatrice-Joanna draws attention to the latent misogyny of the repression/attraction thesis; if we follow the logic of this argument then when Beatrice-Joanna says no, she really means yes.

While the 1992 production did not show the rape on-stage, the staging of the final scene managed to convey the violence of the play through the man-handling of Beatrice-Joanna. The production has Beatrice-Joanna passionately embrace Alsemero as she tells him the 'story' (V, iii, 60) of the bloody deed she has committed for his love. Alsemero's response to her speech is physically violent; he throws her around the stage before pushing her into the pit that takes the place of the closet in this production, so emphasising its religious symbolism as hell. Her cries below are not orgasmic, but of pain, and give the clear impression that she is being stabbed by De Flores. He emerges from the pit with Beatrice-Joanna thrown over his shoulder. The way her body is treated on stage conveys a sense of women as the sexual property of men, to be disposed of at their will. Beatrice-Joanna ends the play in this production as a piteous spectacle. Isabella crosses herself, perhaps in protection, perhaps through pity, while the men group together on stage. The play ends with Alsemero kneeling before the crucifix, reinforcing the religious codes that structure the play's language and action. As Stachniewski says of the play's ending: 'Alsemero and Vermandero quickly perceive that their beloved Beatrice is really a piece of human refuse and take comfort in their spiritual brotherhood' (1990: 240). While this production imagines Catholicism as the principal force of repression, and Stachniewski, as we have seen, looks to the psychology of Calvinism for the mindset that drives the damnation of Beatrice-Joanna, both suggest the ways in which organised religion and patriarchy can work hand-in-glove.

The Changeling is a powerful play, and continues to be popular on stage. When assessing its psychological intensity, either on the page or in performance, we need to interrogate the assumptions behind the language that is used and the choices that are made, whether by dramatists, producers, critics or theatre reviewers.

NOTES

1. On the new private spaces in the aristocratic household, see above, pp. 60–3.
2. The Dead Sea, equated with the rivers of hell – both were believed to be 'bottomless'.
3. On Calvinism, see above, p. 18.

CHAPTER 8

Politics and Theatre: *A Game at Chess*

A Game at Chess is Middleton's last surviving play. It has been read both as a 'black and white' moral allegory and as a topical political satire. The play sets the diabolical Black House against the virtuous White House. There are two distinct, yet interlocking plots. The first plot allegorises sexual and religious corruption in the story of the attempted seduction and rape of the White Queen's Pawn by two pawns from the Black House. The second stars the Black Knight, instantly recognisable by contemporary audiences as a caricature of Gondomar, the former Spanish ambassador to the English court. The Black Knight's various plots include his efforts to lure the White Knight and his companion, the White Duke, to the Black court; a plot that rebounds and results in the defeat of the Black House, due to the superior virtue and game-playing skills of the White Knight. In 1623, Prince Charles and George Villiers, Duke of Buckingham, had travelled to Spain, on the invitation of Gondomar, to finalise negotiations for the Prince's marriage with the Spanish Infanta. Negotiations foundered, Charles returned without a Spanish bride, and the English nation rejoiced.

A Game at Chess was a popular play. It played to packed houses over nine days, to an audience drawn from across the social spectrum. Its short season ended when it came to the attention of the King, who ordered an immediate end to performances and the examination of those responsible. It is often cited as the epitome of the early modern political play and offers an opportunity to think about how theatre was political in this period and to examine the operations of censorship.

POLITICS AND THE THEATRE: MIDDLETON, THE OVERBURY SCANDAL AND SPAIN

The popularity of *A Game at Chess* testifies to the appetite for court scandal in the early seventeenth century. Early modern London was the centre of a growing news culture. Paul's Walk was a popular place for early modern Londoners to gather (see above, pp. 24–5). Here, the latest news and rumours were exchanged. Other meeting places included the Old and New Exchanges, the law courts, markets and fairs, and taverns and other drinking houses. Much of this news circulated informally, through talk. There were professional news-gatherers who compiled newsletters for patrons or employers – many of these collections survive, for example, the often-cited letters of John Chamberlain, and provide important insight into current affairs in this period. Scurrilous verses, 'railing rhymes', on courtiers or officials implicated in scandals were composed, copied by hand, and exchanged hand-to-hand, or even sung in company. Pasquils, or libellous verses, were sometimes pasted on the pillars and doors of St Paul's (Bellany 2002: 80–108).

The popular appetite for news was fed and shaped by a series of court scandals that dogged James's reign. One long-running scandal began in April 1613 when Frances Howard, daughter of the powerful Earl of Suffolk, sued her husband, Robert Devereux, the 3rd Earl of Essex, for divorce, on the grounds that the marriage had not been consummated. This would then leave her free to marry the King's favourite, Robert Carr. As part of the divorce trial, Frances Howard underwent a 'virginity test' and was physically examined by a jury of matrons – since the Countess was veiled, rumours circulated that either a virgin had been substituted or some other deception used, as one libellous verse claimed, so 'She that could reek within the sheets of lust,/And there be searched, yet pass without mistrust' (Bellany 2002: 150). In September 1613, Carr's former friend, Sir Thomas Overbury, who was a vocal opponent of his marriage to Howard, died in the Tower. In 1615, Carr and

Howard, now the Earl and Countess of Somerset, were arrested and convicted of his murder, along with their accomplices. James stepped in to save the couple from execution, and they were instead imprisoned in the Tower until their release in January 1622. The Overbury scandal gave rise to nine public murder trials, four public executions and numerous printed pamphlets, woodcuts, scandalous verses and ballads, all testifying to the intense public interest in these events (Bellany 2002: 75–80).

Middleton's own fascination with this drama is suggested by *The Witch* and *The Changeling* (Chakravorty 1996: 109–10). Heinemann suggested the links between the Overbury scandal and Middleton's *The Witch*, thought to have been composed in 1616 following the trials, and Marion O'Connor, in her introduction to the play for the Oxford *Collected Works*, argues that the 'correspondences' between the various strands of the scandal and 'all three plots of *The Witch* . . . are startling' (Heinemann 1982: 107–14; Middleton 2007: I, 1,124; see also Lancashire 1983). Just as Sebastian procures a spell from the witch to render his rival Antonio impotent in relation to his new wife, Isabella, so too at her trial Frances Howard, and her associate, Anne Turner, were accused of practising witchcraft, and it was implied they had used sorcery to render Essex impotent (Bellany 2002: 150). Francisca, the sixteen-year-old sister of Antonio, epitomises courtly sexual intrigue, 'base lust' (III, ii, 52), and conspires with her lover to cover up her pregnancy. While her name is homophonic of 'Frances Carr' and her characterisation has much in common with libels attacking Frances Carr, she is not a straightforward caricature. Rather than a simple correspondence, it is possible to argue that both *The Witch* and these libels participate in a wider cultural process in which the language of court corruption is explicitly sexualised. This means that it was possible for audiences well-versed in libellous discourse to make comparisons between Francisca and Frances Carr on the basis of misogynistic associations between female sexuality and court corruption.

The audience watching a performance of the virginity test in *The Changeling* in 1622, when Diaphanta wonders whether Beatrice-Joanna will 'search me. . ./Like the forewoman of a female jury' (IV, i, 102–3), may well have recalled this scandal, given its buoyant afterlife and the fact that the Countess had recently been released from the Tower. Yet, as Cristina Malcolmson points out, there is more to the political symbolism of the play than topical allusions. *The Changeling* is set in Alicante, Spain, and is redolent with religious imagery that in contemporary performances could easily have been given explicit Catholic associations – as we have seen, this was a feature of the set design and staging of the 1992 RSC production (see above, pp. 152–3). Given that the metaphor of the permeable body was a recurrent feature of anti-Spanish propaganda in the 1620s, then 'the vulnerable female body', represented by Beatrice-Joanna, Malcolmson argues, 'symbolizes the weaknesses of the body of the state, disturbingly open to the infiltration of foreign Catholic powers who stand ready to enter England either through "open Invaders or secret underminers"' (Malcolmson 1990: 332). Religio-political languages routinely employ sexual metaphors. Chastity, a virtue which is predicated on the intactness of the female body, was used in Protestant propaganda to denote Protestantism, while the sexually active woman was identified with Catholicism, drawing on the scriptural iconography of the Whore of Babylon. One of the key characters in *Hengist, King of Kent*, performed in 1620 at the outbreak of the Thirty Years War, when popular anti-Spanish and anti-Catholic feeling was running high, is called Castiza, or Chastity. Bohemia, governed by Frederick and Elizabeth, the daughter of James I, had been invaded by Spanish imperial forces in 1620. James's response to this crisis was to use diplomacy, by negotiating a marriage between his son, Prince Charles, and the Spanish Infanta. Castiza is contrasted in the play with Roxana, a pagan princess, who is part of a Saxon plot to invade Britain. Castiza and Roxana signify the opposing forces of English Protestantism and foreign, Spanish Catholicism. The symbolism of the play once again draws on motifs to be found in other tracts which expressed Protestant unease that James's foreign policy, which insisted on rapprochement with Spain, left Protestant states, both Bohemia and England, increasingly vulnerable to these 'foreign' Catholic forces (Hutchings and Bromham 2008: 17–18).

Middleton and Rowley were commissioned to write a masque for Prince Charles's court, *The World Tossed at Tennis*, which was meant to be performed in early 1620, as part of Charles's entertainments for his father, King James. Charles, unlike his father, advocated military support for his brother-in-law, Frederick, to defend his claim to the Bohemian crown against the Catholic Habsburgs. The masque ends with Jupiter praising Charles's military ambitions: 'where the prince of nobleness himself/Proves our Minerva's valiant'st, hopefull'st son,/And early in his spring puts armour on' (865–7). There is no evidence it was ever performed; one argument put forward is that the King put an end to the performance so that he would not be placed in the position of having 'to support the Soldier's readiness to fight in Europe' (Middleton 2007: I, 1,406). Unusually, this court masque was transferred to the public stage, and was performed by Prince Charles's Men at the Swan Theatre.

A number of Middleton's Jacobean plays, particularly those written in the troubled 1620s, addressed affairs of state that concerned their audiences and, in doing so, participated in a wider political culture. There are a variety of ways in which plays could be political. Political meaning can be conveyed through topical allusion, caricature, allegory, extended metaphor and staging. All these strategies are reliant on an audience understanding their significance, or at least grasping the general tenor. The Overbury scandal, as Bellany points out, testifies to the existence of a wide social spectrum of people, both in London and the provinces, actively interested in, and holding views on, state affairs. Just as significantly, this long-running scandal helped to educate this audience in the interpretation of political allegories and tropes.

A GAME AT CHESS, CENSORSHIP AND THE POLITICS OF IMPERSONATION

The appetite for news intensified throughout the 1620s. Proclamations restricting public discussion of domestic and foreign policy were issued in 1620 and 1621, and regulations against disorderly printing followed in September 1623. There were means available for evading restrictions. Thomas Scott, whose pamphlets Middleton drew on, wrote and published from the safety of the Dutch Republic; his pamphlets were smuggled into England, where they could then be copied by hand by commercial scribes (McRae

2004: 109). Scurrilous verses on contemporary events and individuals, such as Frances Carr or Gondomar, could also evade prosecution since they were anonymous and did not go through the channels of print but circulated surreptitiously from hand-to-hand.

Middleton, it seems, did not attempt to evade restrictions on the stage with his *A Game at Chess*. The play was licensed by the Master of the Revels, Sir Henry Herbert, on 12 June 1624. Performances began just under two months later on 5 August at the Globe. The play was an immediate success. The next day, John Woolley wrote to his friend, William Trumbull, that 'All the news I have heard since my coming to town is of a new play . . . called a game at Chess'. Woolley was amazed by the audacity of the play's anti-Spanish satire, and pointed out that 'such a thing was never before invented and assuredly had so much been done the last year, they had everyman been hanged for it'. On Saturday 7 August, George Lowe wrote to Sir Arthur Ingram with news of this 'new play . . . which describes Gondomar and all the Spanish proceedings very boldly and broadly, so that it is thought that it will be called in and the parties punished' (Middleton 1993: 193). This is just what happened. After nine days, playing to houses 'so thronged', in the words of John Holles, 'that by scores they came away for want of place', the play was closed (Middelton 1993: 198). On 18 August, the Privy Council examined the players and issued a warrant for Middleton. Middleton went into hiding, and on 30 August his son, Edward, appeared before the Privy Council – it is possible that Middleton was briefly imprisoned, although there is no record. By the end of this month, James had allowed the company to resume acting, but the ban remained on *A Game at Chess*.

There are a number of aspects of this story of censorship that have puzzled critics. Why did Sir Henry Herbert license such a controversial play in the first place? And, relatedly, why were the players and dramatist dealt with so lightly? Such leniency argues against a repressive model of censorship in which the state silences all forms of dissent. One answer proposed to the first question is that the play had powerful sponsors at court, who were able to offer protection. This was certainly the view of some contemporaries. Holles thought the play so foolhardy that 'surely these gamesters must have a good retreat' (Middleton 1993: 199). There is a famous precedent for powerful courtiers commissioning plays to further their own political agendas. The Earl of Essex commissioned a performance of Shakespeare's *Richard II* on the eve of his failed coup. Prince Charles had already employed Middleton and Rowley to provide a masque, *The World Tossed at Tennis*, which put the case for military intervention in support of Frederick and Elizabeth; an approach that put Charles at odds with his father, King James. The court was not a monolithic entity with a single political viewpoint that was consistently promoted through cultural fictions and imposed on the people. There were significant divisions at court, and within the royal family itself, over the direction of foreign policy in the 1620s. James continued to seek a resolution to the situation in Bohemia through diplomacy, by maintaining good relations with Spain. After Charles and Buckingham returned from Madrid in October 1623, and negotiations for Charles's marriage to the Spanish Infanta collapsed, they formed a loose alliance with the pro-war party at court, headed by William Herbert, Earl of Pembroke, a kinsman of the Master of the Revels. These men, Thomas Cogswell argues, sanctioned Middleton's play; he cites Woolley's belief that it could not have been licensed and performed 'without leave from the higher powers, I mean the Prince and Duke if not from the King for they were all loathe to have it forbidden and by report laughed heartly at it' (Cogswell 1984: 281). It should be pointed out that Woolley was reporting a rumour rather than a known fact, yet it is significant that contemporaries assumed that Middleton and the King's Men had powerful protectors at court.

Other critics are less convinced by the argument that this example of political theatre was necessarily reliant on powerful patrons at court. One problem with concentrating on patronage in the discussion of the play's politics is that the theatre is simply viewed as an instrument of the court, functioning in the service of the elite. The issues dramatised in *A Game at Chess* had gripped the wider populace and were discussed in the news exchanges of early modern London. Paul Yachnin claims that, in actuality, the play was not controversial in terms of its content, since events had changed considerably following the collapse of the Spanish Match in early 1624, and the mood at court and on the streets was belligerently anti-Spanish and pro-war (1987: 113–14). Woolley's comments about the timing of the play, 'assuredly had so much been done the last year, they had everyman been hanged for it', would seem to support this argument (Middleton 1993: 193). Anxieties about the vulnerability of England to papist plots were running high. At the end of 1623 and in early 1624, Chamberlain reported that the Jesuits were swarming in England. A proclamation was issued in early May 'charging all Jesuits, Seminaries, to depart the Land', and laws were passed in Parliament imposing further restrictions on English Catholics. Pamphlets claiming to discover to readers the plots and foul practices of Jesuits and priests were published in 1623 and 1624 – Middleton drew on these for his characterisations of the Jesuits and the purported debauchery of the Catholic Church in *A Game at Chess* (Howard-Hill 1995: 237–47). Buckingham strongly criticised the Spanish court in his speech to Parliament giving his account of the marriage negotiations in Madrid. In retaliation, the Spanish ambassadors, Marqués de la Hinjosa and Don Carlos de Coloma, the successor to Gondomar, made serious accusations against Buckingham – that he wanted to force James into retirement and place Prince Charles on the throne. Evidence was not forthcoming when James examined the matter, and Buckingham was restored to royal favour – Hinjosa left England in disgrace in late June 1624, but Coloma stayed on, in a very difficult diplomatic situation. Scurrilous verses quickly circulated defending Buckingham and attacking Spanish perfidy: one writer recalled England's former victories against Spain, and angrily challenged the Spanish 'Durst they insult thus then? or else demand/the head of any subject in this land' (Bellany and McRae 2005: Oi2).

This is the immediate context in which *A Game of Chess* was licensed and performed. The first person to find fault with the play and make a formal complaint to the King was the remaining Spanish ambassador, Coloma:

The Actors who are called 'the King's', today and yesterday presented a comedy so scandalous, impious, barbarous, and so offensive to my royal master . . . that this comedy has forced me to put my pen to paper and to beg in few words, and with the humility which I owe to Your Majesty, for one of two

things. Either let Your Majesty give order for the aforemen-
tioned authors and actors to be punished in a public and exemplary fashion, whereby Your Majesty will satisfy both his own
honour and the reputation and civility of the English nation;
or let Your Majesty order that I be given a ship to sail to
Flanders with the appropriate safe passage which you give to
the ambassadors of other Kings. (Middleton 1993: 193–4)

The latter option, Coloma implied, would compromise James's
honour. Richard Dutton has surmised that *A Game of Chess* was
called in because it was caught up in this difficult diplomatic situation between Spain and England. James, who had been on his
summer progress when *A Game* was being performed in London,
did not hear of the play until Coloma's letter. Angry that he had
been made to appear as if he had lost control of his kingdom, and
wanting to maintain face in the diplomatic wrangling, James acted
decisively and banned the play. Yet there were aspects of the play
itself that troubled James once it was brought to his attention. He
reminded his councillors that 'there was a commandment and
restraint given against the representing of any modern Christian
king in those Stage-plays' (Dutton 2000: 139–44). Coloma, in a
letter to the Conde-Duque Olivares, noted that 'the king of the
blacks has easily been taken for our lord the King, because of his
youth, dress, and other details' (Middleton 1993: 194). James, presumably, was also recognisable as the White King. As Dutton points
out, the King 'was only typical of his time in regarding an affront
to a fellow monarch as an affront to himself' (2000: 144). Yet there
is more to it than this, since James was concerned that any impersonation of the monarch on the public stage undermined the
perceived sanctity of his person.

The politico-religious allegory represents the Spanish Match as
the latest, and most crucial game in a long line of political game-
playing that goes back to 1588. Alongside the Black King (young
Felipe IV, King of Habsburg Spain) and the Black Knight
(Gondomar) is the Black Duke – Olivares, the Spanish ambassador
who left England in disgrace in 1624. The other characters are the
Black Queen (the Spanish Infanta), the Black Knight's Pawn (Padre
Maestro or Lafuente, Gondomar's priest), and the Fat Bishop of

Spalato (Marco Antonio de Dominis, a convert from the Catholic Church to Anglicanism). De Dominis lived in England until 1622, and was given a position in the Church of England by James in support of his efforts to unite the two Churches. The Fat Bishop is one of the White King's main spokesmen on religious matters, penning tracts in defence of the English Church, but without faith, motivated only by sophistry and ambition. In 1622, de Dominis repudiated Protestantism and left England. The Fat Bishop begins the play in the White House and is lured back to the Black House by the Black Knight Gondomar to destroy him in retaliation for his earlier betrayal. De Dominis died in 1624, a prisoner of the Spanish Inquisition.

The White House consists of the White King James, the White Knight Charles, the White Duke of Buckingham, the White Bishop, George Abbot, the staunchly Calvinist Archbishop of Canterbury, and the White Queen Elizabeth of Bohemia.[1] The castration of the White Bishop of Canterbury's Pawn by the Black Knight's Pawn signifies the censorship of Protestant preachers in the early 1620s to maintain good diplomatic relations with Spain. Contemporaries were less certain how to read the White Knight's Pawn. There is material in the play, such as the reference to his advancement from lowly beginnings through the favour of the King that points to Lionel Cranfield, Earl of Middlesex, a merchant ennobled by James, who was disgraced and impeached in 1624. But Holles thought the piece satirised John Digby, Earl of Bristol, the ambassador to Spain, who was Buckingham's scapegoat in the failed negotiations for the Spanish Match – Buckingham accused Bristol of conspiring with Spain. The White King's Pawn is a 'pastiche of topical allusion' (Howard-Hill 1991: 173). Such allusive strategies build a level of indeterminacy into the allegory that tantalisingly invites, rather than prevents further speculation.

What James found so objectionable was the play's politics of impersonation. 'Among plays presented at court or in public theatres between 1616 and 1640', as Howard-Hill points out, '*A Game at Chess* is exceptional in the extent to which contemporary figures were impersonated' (1995: 111). As Coloma's description of the actor who played the Black King indicates, considerable care was taken to caricature, relatively accurately, living individuals on stage by choosing actors physically suitable for the part, and through the choice of costume and 'other details', so that they would be recognisable to the audience. The level of detail and inventiveness that went into this process of impersonation is evident in the caricaturing of Gondomar in the Black Knight. The company either managed to acquire or made a replica of Gondomar's sedan chair, with its trademark hole cut into the seat to ease the discomfort of his anal fistula (a suppurating pipe-like growth), and also, as Chamberlain reported, the 'cast suit of his apparel' (Braunmuller 1990: 351). Gondomar had left England in 1622, but his image had been kept alive in the public memory through woodcuts, such as the 1624 title-page of Scott's *The Second Part of Vox Populi*, subtitled, *Gondomar appearing in the likeness of Matchiavel in a Spanish Parliament, wherein are discovered his treacherous and subtle practises to the ruin as well of England, as the Netherlands*. The depiction of the Machiavellian Black Knight draws heavily on the accusations made against Gondomar in the pamphlets of Scott. The Black Knight's speech in Act III, scene i, in which he boasts of triumphs in England, specifically draws on Scott's *Vox Populi* and *The Second Part of Vox Populi*, in particular: Gondomar's ability to secure the release of Catholic priests from prison; to silence his critics, especially among the Protestant clergy, 'to put a silenced muzzle/On all the barking tongue-men of the time' (III, i, 102–3); and to extract money from English gentlewomen by promising them positions in the court of the Spanish Infanta when she arrives in England (see the relevant extracts from Scott's pamphlets in Howard-Hill 1995: 247–52).

It was this daring level of impersonation that struck contemporaries, and turned *A Game* into such a sensational hit on the early modern stage. And it highlights very clearly the way that performance – the actors' strategic use of costume, stage props, voice and gesture – transforms the words of the play-script into something else, adding new levels of meaning. We should remember that the Master of the Revels only read the play-script, he did not see the performance, complete with costumes and sedan chairs, and so would not have realised just how scandalous the play's impersonations were. Impersonation is a strategy that *A Game* shares with libellous satires. Holles described the play as 'this vulgar pasquin' – the term derives from the practice of pinning anonymous libellous verses to the statue of Pasquino in sixteenth-century Rome, and was used widely to denote witty verse libels (McRae 2004: 27).

Libels are prime examples of 'embodied writing' (Bruster 2000: 50–4). Much of their scurrility derives from the liberties that they take with their subjects' bodies. Verse libels on Frances Carr, for example, mobilised a misogynist discourse in which the language of sexual corruption gained its particular charge from imagining her body corrupted by sexual diseases. Gondomar's anal fistula was a scatological gift to writers of libels. One libel on Gondomar opened by finding the origins of the nation's political ill-health in Gondomar, in particular, his fistula: 'Why? what means this? England and Spain alike/Diseased? or doth time both equal strike/ With fistulas?' The discharge which leaks from his fistula is imagined as his brood, the various plots that he has hatched, but has been able to hide, just as his anal fistula remains hidden from public view (Bellany and McRae 2005: Niii1). Fistulas loom large in the characterisation of the Black Knight in *A Game at Chess*. The Black Knight, 'the fistula of Europe' (II, ii, 41), describes his ability to plot undetected through a maritime metaphor that has obvious scatological associations:

> Of a leaking bottom,
> I have been as often tossed on Venus' seas
> As trimmer fresher barques, when sounder vessels
> Have lain at anchor (that is, kept the door). (II, i, 175–8)

The 'leaking bottom' alludes to Gondomar's suppurating fistula, yet whereas other libels confined themselves to equating his diseased body with political corruption, this passage adds a novel element of sexual corruption. The Black Knight is associated with lust in a way that Gondomar was not. Although verse libels influence strategies of impersonation in *A Game at Chess*, the play is more than an extended libel on Gondomar and other Spanish courtiers. The lustful Black Knight demonstrates Middleton's characteristic sexualising of political intrigue, also evident in the multiple seductions that drive the plot.

Woolley called *A Game at Chess* 'a Vox populi' on stage (Middleton 1993: 193). Middleton's play can be usefully compared to Scott's pamphlet in that both appealed to the 'voice of the people', to a public ready and able to make pronouncements and engage in debates on affairs of state. Yachnin places the play within a tradition of political theatre that 'continued and developed in the relative freedom of the commercial theater of the Elizabethan and Jacobean period', and provided 'a lively forum' in which 'embedded cultural values and established political and social hierarchies might be debated, tested, and analyzed' (1987: 113). That said, in moving away from repressive models of the state and its forms of censorship, we need to be wary of over-liberalising early modern culture. *A Game at Chess* was banned, and the players and its author were interrogated. Others who wrote controversial material were imprisoned and, on occasion, executed – there was a recognition of the limits of what could be said in public and the dangers faced by those who transgressed. *A Game at Chess* is a significant example of political theatre not least because of the wealth of surviving evidence that may still be able to tell us new stories about early modern culture.

POLITICAL PLAY: DRAMATIC DEVICES AND POLITICAL GAMES

A Game at Chess was admired by contemporaries as a witty, 'facetious comedy', in the words of Holles, not simply because of its strategies of impersonation but also because of its highly inventive use of the chess game to structure the allegory and the drama. Yachnin surmises the audience would have found allegory old-fashioned (1987: 121). Yet this is not what seems to have struck contemporaries, who instead focus on the play's novelty, derived in large part from the game it so self-consciously plays. *A Game at Chess* revives older forms of Reformation allegorical satire strategically rather than nostalgically. Middleton, as we have seen in *Women Beware Women*, was fascinated by chess as a dramatic device, particularly for amplifying the metaphoric range of games of intrigue (see above, pp. 126–8). With *A Game at Chess*, he took this a step further.

The play opens with a lively anti-Jesuit satire starring Ignatius Loyola, the founder of the Jesuits, who appears as a politic stage

Machiavel with Error at his feet. The monster Errour had famously appeared in the first canto of Edmund Spenser's *The Faerie Queene* – Middleton had earlier depicted this figure in his civic pageant, *The Triumphs of Truth* (1613), complete with 'all symbols of the blind ignorance and darkness, [and with] mists hanging at his eyes' (248–9; see above, pp. 92–3). Likewise, the Black Queen's Pawn and the Black Bishop's Pawn, identified as Loyola's 'children', are the key pieces within this anti-Jesuit satire. Their attempts to seduce the White Queen's Pawn signify the dangerously seductive powers of religious error and its dexterity at ensnaring the innocent. The action of the play is introduced by Error who reveals the game of chess to Loyola in the form of a dream-vision, a literary device conventionally used before an allegorical narrative. As Jane Sherman points out, Middleton is quite deliberately using 'specific dramatic idiom' and formulae recognisable to the audience to trigger particular modes of reading or viewing. This means that the audience would have been attuned at the very outset of the play that they were watching an allegorical drama and therefore were being positively encouraged to make topical connections between characters and plots on stage and actual historical figures and events (1978: 149–50).

The first appearance of the White Queen's Pawn is indicative of her allegorical function as Protestant Truth. Her opening words are 'Where should truth speak/If not is such sorrow' (I, i, 6–7); on the chess board stage she is lined up in opposition to the Black Queen's Pawn, already identified as a creature of the Jesuit. As we shall see, the play complicates this simple binary; nonetheless, it is clear that *A Game* is strategically using the allegorical idiom of Reformation polemic which pitted virtuous Protestant figures against diabolical Catholic dissemblers. The White Queen's Pawn appears before the White King in Act II, scene ii with a grievance against the Black House, only to find that she herself is denounced. This scenario was frequently played out in Reformation drama: in John Bale's *King Johan*, Lady England is denounced as 'a whore by Papistical prelates who threaten to lock her up and make her repent' (Sherman 1978: 150–2). The torture the Black Knight devises is as libertine as it is papist: he will make her kneel for twelve hours 'in a room filled all with Aretine's pictures,/More than the twice twelve labours of luxury' (II, ii, 248–9), thus sadistically aligning physical pain with pornographic scenes of sexual pleasure. In traditional estates satire, the Commonwealth, one of the estates, would receive aid from the other two – the Church and the Nobility. In *A Game at Chess*, the Protestant clergy, the White Bishop's Pawn, has been rendered impotent by the Black House, while the representative of the court, the White King's Pawn, is black at heart, secretly working in the service of the Black Knight. Even so, the White King is remarkably open to the deceptions of the Black House. The Venetian ambassador said of the play that the 'Spaniards are touched on from their tricks being discovered, but the king's reputation is affected much more deeply by representing the case [i.e. ease?] with which he was deceived' (Middleton 1993: 204). Although the play is generally positive in its portrayal of James as the White King, it does suggest that his ear was too open to Gondomar, thus leaving the commonwealth at the mercy of his plots.

The openness of the White King to foreign, black infiltration destabilises a strict binarism between black and white. It is not only the White King who is too easily swayed by the Black House. The openness of the White Queen's Pawn to the Jesuits is particularly evident in the mirror scene in Act III, scene i. The White Queen's Pawn is seduced by the vision of her future beloved in the Black Queen's Pawn's mirror. The Black Queen's Pawn here resembles an amalgam of Spenser's Duessa and Archimago, the maker of powerful false (and papist) images capable of deceiving the unwary godly. This deception appeals to the White Queen's Pawn's 'blood', as she recognises: 'What certainty is in our bloods, our states?' (III, i, 401). We know from *The Changeling* that 'blood' is a key word in Middleton's tragic and Calvinist vocabulary, and denotes the seat of the passions and sexual desire (see above, pp. 144–5). The White Queen's Pawn is aware of the dangers but nonetheless is 'caught' between her 'fear' and 'desire' (III, i, 414–15). There is a topical political reading of the White Queen's Pawn's romance that, this time, reflects critically on Prince Charles, in particular on the impetuous, foolhardy and short-sighted quest he embarked on to Spain to seek his Spanish bride, which placed not only himself, but his nation in peril (Sherman 1978: 157). Part of the reason why the

White Queen's Pawn is so open to Spanish perfidy results from her femininity – although actively chaste, her 'blood' is susceptible. To an extent, her vulnerability is corrected by the mirroring of her story in that of the White Knight, another figure for Charles. The play explicitly counsels against fears for *his* virtue. The White King assures the Fat Bishop that his 'vain hope' that the 'White Knight and his most firm assistant' are 'lost forever now' is misplaced because of his 'strong assurance/Of their fixed virtues' (IV, iv, 96–100). Yet, in order to entrap the Black House, and so win the game, the virtues of these 'Two princely pieces' (IV, iv, 98) must become momentarily unfixed in order to display their own capacity for sinfulness. Many critics have interpreted the White Duke/Buckingham's claim to 'infirmity of the blood, flesh-frailty' (V, iii, 123) as Middleton's sly satire on Buckingham's reputation for lechery. This owning of vices is, of course, a ruse to outmanoeuvre the Black House, yet mud sticks.

The redeployment of keywords from *The Changeling*, such as 'blood', extends to sight. The White Queen's Pawn has problems with her sight that are very familiar from the earlier play (see above, pp. 146–7). In the opening scene, she has already fallen into the ways of error by misapprehending the show of grief by the Black Queen's Pawn:

> Where should truth speak
> If not in such a sorrow? They're tears plainly . . .
> If I wander to loss and with broad eyes
> Yet miss the path she can run blindfold in
> (Through often exercise), which should my oversight
> (Though in the best game that e'er Christian lost)
> Raise the least spring of pity in her eye? (I, i, 6–7, 10–14)

Behind this metaphor is Matthew 7: 13: 'Enter by the narrow gate; for wide is the gate and broad is the way that leads to destruction, and there are many who go in by it.' The White Queen's Pawn is wandering in a state of moral and spiritual error and this complicates the psychological drama. It is accompanied by this figure's disturbing attraction to 'Boundless obedience' (II, i, 39). In her zeal, she greets the Black Bishop's Pawn as she would a lover:

> Holy sir,
> Too long I've missed you. O your absence starves me . . .
> Lay your commands as thick and fast upon me
> As you can speak 'em. How I thirst to hear 'em! (II, i, 32–6)

Her ardent religious zeal echoes that of Isabella in *Measure for Measure* – a play revised by Middleton – whose desire for the strictness of a chaste life is similarly excessively zealous: 'I speak not as desiring more,/But rather wishing a more strict restraint/Upon the sisterhood' (I, iv, 3–5). The characterisation of the White Queen's Pawn introduces a level of ethical indeterminacy that needs to be resolved at another level. The White Queen's Pawn is not saved by her own actions, but through the implosion of the Black House, which destroys itself through its addiction to plotting and deception. The game as a whole is won by 'checkmate by/Discovery' (V, iii, 160–1) which functions at the level of the political allegory to denote the public exposure of the Spanish and their tricks, and to praise the clear-sightedness of Charles and Buckingham. That said, the allegory insists that the White House would have won the game regardless, because they are White and the Elect, and therefore divine grace is on their side; the proper place of the unregenerate Black House will always be in the bag, in hell (on Calvinist predestination, see above pp. 18, 145–6).

We can gain a clearer sense of the 'Calvinist psychology' informing this play if we examine the use of another keyword – 'conscience'. Paradoxically, this word is most closely associated with the Black Knight's Pawn. He is incapacitated by his guilty conscience, 'so that I can follow *no* game' (IV, i, 20), because he has gelded the White Bishop's Pawn. The story of his guilty conscience is in part a running joke at the expense of Catholicism: the Black Knight's Pawn is sent to the 'Penance Chamber', the Catholic ecclesiastical office that dealt with penitents, to see if his sin is on the 'tax register' (IV, i, 30). No pardon can be bought for castration, yet the Black Knight's Pawn is able to buy 'full absolution' if he compounds the sin by killing the White Bishop's Pawn. As the Fat Bishop tells him: 'Were you to kill him, I'd pardon you./There's precedent for that, and price set down;/But none for gelding' (IV, ii, 128–30). Behind the jest is the more serious theological point maintained by

Calvinists that salvation cannot be 'bought' by works or merit since it is bestowed only by God on his Elect. Hence, there can be no reward for the Black Queen's Pawn within this Calvinist drama. It is she who effectively saves the White Queen's Pawn by double-crossing the Black Bishop's Pawn. Although her blood is corrupted, there is a poignancy to her revelation that she was motivated by the sexual abuse she suffered at the hands of Black Bishop's Pawn: 'Whose niece was she you poisoned with child, twice? / – Then gave her out "possessed with a foul spirit"?/When 'twas indeed your bastard' (V, ii, 104–6). As was the case with Beatrice-Joanna, there is no question of forgiveness, rather this 'piece of human refuse' (Stachniewski 1990: 240) must go to hell, and be turned into an edifying spectacle for the audience, the 'shame of womanhood' (V, ii, 108; see above, pp. 152–3).

A Game at Chess was Middleton's last known play for the public stage. It is possible that he was banned from writing for the stage since no plays have been credibly attributed to him after 1625. Along with his collaborator, Gerard Christmas, Middleton devised two further pageants for the City of London: a pageant for Charles I, presented some time between December 1625 and April 1626, and The Triumphs of Health and Prosperity, performed in October 1626. Middleton's own health and prosperity seem to have been at a low ebb in 1626. In January there were complaints that the devices Middleton and Christmas prepared for London's coronation pageant for Charles I were marred by 'bad workmanship'; the next month, the City threatened to withdraw Middleton's salary as chronologer; finally, the Drapers' Company, which had commissioned the Lord Mayor's Show, refused to pay Middleton and Christmas because of 'ill performance' of the devices (see above, p. 15). Middleton died a year later, and was buried on 4 July 1627. His widow petitioned the City for relief, and received a gift of twenty nobles.

Yet A Game at Chess also enshrined Middleton's dramatic reputation. The epigram published in the anthology Wits Recreations in 1640 is part of a series eulogising contemporary or near-contemporary dramatists – Jonson, Massinger, Shirley and so on. Among other early seventeenth-century dramatists, the epigrammatist distinguishes Middleton according to his particular, distinctive style:

Facetious Middleton, thy witty muse
Hath pleased all that books or men peruse.
If any thee despise, he doth but show
Antipathy to wit in daring so.
Thy fame's above his malice, and 'twill be
Dispraise enough for him to censure thee. (*Wit's Recreations*,
sig. B7v)

The countering of dispraise with praise, and the play between the two, is a conventional device of the praise poem, and is designed to magnify praise. That said, the reference to censure may recall the controversy surrounding his *A Game at Chess* fifteen years earlier when Middleton came in for censure from many quarters. *A Game at Chess* was appreciated for its politics *and* wit – Holles described it as a 'facetious comedy . . . acted with extraordinary applause' (Middleton 1993: 198). Middleton's distinctive style of wit was not decorous and safe, but bold and disruptive, with a marked tendency to rip up the times. It is this dangerous and unsettling wit that has ensured that Middleton's plays continue to be revived on stage in this century.

NOTE

1. On Calvinism, see above, pp. 18, 145–6.

Bibliography

Altieri, Joanne (1988), 'Against Moralizing Jacobean Comedy: Middleton's *Chaste Maid*', *Criticism* 30, 171–87.

Archer, Ian W. (1991), *The Pursuit of Stability: Social Relations in Elizabethan London*, Cambridge: Cambridge University Press.

Archer, William (1990), '[*The Revenger's Tragedy*] (1923)', in R. V. Holdsworth (ed.), *Three Jacobean Revenge Tragedies: A Casebook*, Basingstoke and London: Macmillan, pp. 32–3.

Barbour, Richmond (2003), *Before Orientalism: London's Theatre of the East, 1576–1726*, Cambridge: Cambridge University Press.

Barker, Richard Hindry (1958), *Thomas Middleton*, New York: Columbia University Press; London: Oxford University Press.

Barker, Roberta and David Nicol (2004), 'Does Beatrice Joanna have a Subtext?: *The Changeling* on the London Stage', *Early Modern Literary Studies* 10:1, 3.1–43.

Batchelor, J. B. (1990), 'The Pattern of *Women Beware Women*', in R.V. Holdsworth (ed.), *Three Jacobean Revenge Tragedies: A Casebook*, Basingstoke and London: Macmillan, pp. 207–21.

Bawcutt, N. W. (1990), 'The Double Plot of *The Changeling*', in R. V. Holdsworth (ed.), *Three Jacobean Revenge Tragedies: A Casebook*, Basingstoke and London: Macmillan, pp. 151–7.

Bellany, Alastair (2002), *The Politics of Court Scandal in Early Modern England: News Culture and the Overbury Affair, 1603–1660*, Cambridge: Cambridge University Press.

— and Andrew McRae (eds) (2005), *Early Stuart Libels: An Edition of Poetry from Manuscript Sources*, EMLS Text Series I: http://purl.oclc.org/emls/texts/libels/

Belsey, Catherine (2001), 'Tarquin Dispossessed: Expropriation and Consent in *The Rape of Lucrece*', *Shakespeare Quarterly* 52, 315–35.

Berger, Thomas L. (1969), 'The Petrarchan Fortress of *The Changeling*', *Renaissance Papers*, 37–46.

Bergeron, David (1985), 'Middleton's *No Wit, No Help* and Civic Pageantry', in D. Bergeron (ed.), *Pageantry in the Shakespearean Theater*, Athens: University of Georgia Press, pp. 65–80.

— (2003), *English Civic Pageantry, 1558–1642*, rev. edn, Medieval and Renaissance Texts and Studies, vol. 267, Tempe: Arizona Center for Medieval and Renaissance Studies.

Biester, James (1997), *Lyric Wonder: Rhetoric and Wit in Renaissance English Poetry*, Ithaca and London: Cornell University Press.

Bly, Mary (2000), *Queer Virgins and Virgin Queans on the Early Modern Stage*, Oxford: Oxford University Press.

Bowers, Rick (2003), 'Comedy, Carnival, and Class: *A Chaste Maid in Cheapside*', *EMLS* 8: 3, 1.1–22.

Bowers, Roger (2000), 'The Playhouse of the Choristers of Paul's, c. 1575–1608', *Theatre Notebook* 54: 70–85.

Brathwaite, Richard (1617), *A Solemn Jovial Disputation, Theoretick and Practick; briefly shadowing the Law of Drinking*, London.

Braunmuller, A. R. (1990), ' "To the Globe I Rowed": John Holles Sees *A Game at Chess*', *English Literary Renaissance* 20, 340–56.

Bromham, A. A. (1995), 'Thomas Middleton's *The Triumphs of Truth*: City Politics in 1613', *The Seventeenth Century* 10, 1–25.

Brooke, Nicholas (1979), *Horrid Laughter in Jacobean Tragedy*, New York: Barnes and Noble.

Brooks, Douglas A. (2000), *From Playhouse to Printing House: Drama and Authorship in Early Modern England*, Cambridge: Cambridge University Press.

Bruster, Douglas (2000), 'The Structural Transformation of Print in Late Elizabethan England', in Arthur Marotti and Michael Bristol (eds), *Print, Manuscript and Performance*, Columbus: Ohio State University Press, pp. 49–89.

Bushnell, Rebecca (1990), *Tragedies of Tyrants: Political Thought and Theater in the English Renaissance*, Ithaca and London: Cornell University Press.

Cathcart, Charles (2000), 'Plural Authorship, Attribution, and the Children of the King's Revels', *Renaissance Forum* 4: n.p.

Certeau, Michel de (1988), *The Practice of Everyday Life*, trans. Steven Rendall, Berkeley, Los Angeles and London: University of California Press.

Chakravorty, Swapan (1996), *Society and Politics in the Plays of Thomas Middleton*, Oxford: Clarendon Press.

Chatterji, Ruby (1965), 'Theme, Imagery, and Unity in *A Chaste Maid in Cheapside*', *Renaissance Drama* 8, 105–26.

Clark, Ira (2003), *Comedy, Youth, Manhood in Early Modern England*, Newark, DE: University of Delaware Press; London: Associated University Presses.

Clare, Janet (2006), *Revenge Tragedies of the Renaissance*, Tavistock: Northcote House.

Clegg, Susan Cyndia (1997), *Press Censorship in Elizabethan England*, Cambridge: Cambridge University Press.

Cogswell, Thomas (1984), 'Thomas Middleton and the Court, 1624: *A Game at Chess* in Context', *Huntington Library Quarterly* 47, 273–88.

Comensoli, Viviana (1987), 'Play-Making, Domestic Conduct, and the Multiple Plot in *The Roaring Girl*', *Studies in English Literature, 1500–1900* 27, 249–66.

Davies, Steven Paul (2002), film notes to *The Revenger's Tragedy* dir. Alex Cox, screenplay Frank Cottrell, London: Tartan Video Ltd.

Day, Angel (1586), *The English Secretary*, London.

Dollimore, Jonathan (1984), *Radical Tragedy: Religion, Ideology and Power in the Drama of Shakespeare and his Contemporaries*, Brighton: Harvester Press.

Dutton, Richard (2000), *Licensing, Censorship and Authorship in Early Modern England: Buggeswords*, Basingstoke and New York: Macmillan.

Eccles, Mark (1931), 'Middleton's Birth and Education', *Review of English Studies* 7, 431–41.

— (1957), 'Thomas Middleton a Poett', *Studies in Philology*, 54, 516–36.

Eliot, T. S. (1990), 'Thomas Middleton', in R. V. Holdsworth (ed.), *Three Jacobean Revenge Tragedies: A Casebook*, Basingstoke and London: Macmillan, pp. 133–7.

Elliot, John (1984–97), 'Drama', in T. H. Aston (ed.), *The History of the University of Oxford*, 8 vols, Oxford: Clarendon Press, IV, pp. 641–58.

Engelberg, Edward (1990), 'Tragic Blindness in *The Changeling* and *Women Beware Women*', in R. V. Holdsworth (ed.), *Three Jacobean Revenge Tragedies: A Casebook*, Basingstoke and London: Macmillan, pp. 186–95.

Ewbank, Inga-Stina (1991), 'The Middle of Middleton', in Murray Biggs, Philip Edwards, Inga-Stina Ewbank and Eugene M. Waith (eds), *The Arts of Performance in Elizabethan and Early Stuart Drama: Essays for G. K. Hunter*, Edinburgh: Edinburgh University Press, pp. 156–72.

Forman, Valerie (2001), 'Marked Angels: Counterfeits, Commodities and *The Roaring Girl*', *Renaissance Quarterly* 54, 1,531–60.

Foucault, Michel (1979), 'What is an Author?', in Josué V. Harari (ed.), *Textual Strategies: Perspectives in Post-Structuralist Criticism*, London: Methuen, pp. 141–60.

Frost, David L. (1990), 'Notes on *Women Beware Women* and *The Changeling* (1978)', in R. V. Holdsworth (ed.), *Three Jacobean Revenge Tragedies: A Casebook*, Basingstoke and London: Macmillan, pp. 221–6.

Gair, Reavley (1982), *The Children of Paul's: The Story of a Theatre Company, 1553–1608*, Cambridge: Cambridge University Press.

Garber, Marjorie (1991), 'The Logic of the Transvestite', in David Scott Kastan and Peter Stallybrass (eds), *Staging the Renaissance: Reinterpretations of Elizabethan and Jacobean Drama*, London: Routledge, pp. 221–34.

— (1994), 'The Insincerity of Women', in Valeria Finucci and Regina Schwartz (eds), *Desire in the Renaissance: Psychoanalysis and Literature*, Princeton: Princeton University Press, pp. 19–38.

Gill, Roma (1983), 'The World of Thomas Middleton', in Kenneth Friedenreich (ed.), *'Accompaninge the Players': Essays celebrating Thomas Middleton, 1580–1980*, New York: AMS Press, pp. 15–38.

Gordon, D. J. (1941), 'Middleton's *No Wit, No Help Like a Woman's* and della Porta's *La Sorella*', *Review of English Studies* 17, 400–14.

Gurr, Andrew (1987), *Playgoing in Shakespeare's London*, Cambridge: Cambridge University Press.

— (1992), *The Shakespearean Stage, 1574–1642*, Cambridge: Cambridge University Press.

Hamlin, William (2005), *Tragedy and Scepticism in Shakespeare's England*, London: Palgrave.

Happé, Peter (1999), *English Drama before Shakespeare*, London and New York: Longmans.

Heinemann, Margot (1982), *Puritanism and Theatre: Thomas Middleton and Opposition Drama under the Early Stuarts*, 2nd edn, Cambridge: Cambridge University Press.

Hirschfeld, Heather Anne (2004), *Joint Enterprises: Collaborative Drama and the Institutionalization of the English Renaissance Theater*, Amherst and Boston: University of Massachusetts Press.

Hopkins, Lisa (1996), 'Art and Nature in *Women Beware Women*', *Renaissance Forum* 1: 2, n.p.

Howard, Jean E. (1992), 'Sex and Social Conflict: The Erotics of *The Roaring Girl*', in Susan Zimmerman (ed.), *Erotic Politics: Desire on the Renaissance Stage*, New York: Routledge, pp. 170–90.

— (2007). *Theater of a City: The Places of London City Comedy, 1598–1642*, Philadelphia: University of Pennsylvania Press.

Howard-Hill, T. H. (1991), 'The Unique Eye-Witness Report of Middleton's *A Game at Chess*', *Review of English Studies* 42, 168–78.

— (1995), *Middleton's 'Vulgar Pasquin': Essays on A Game at Chess*, London and Toronto: Associated University Presses.

Hutchings, Mark and Bromham, A.A. (2008), *Middleton and his Collaborators*, Tavistock: Northcote House.

James, Mervyn (1974), *Family Lineage and Civil Society: A Study of Society, Politics, and Mentality in the Durham Region*, Oxford: Clarendon Press.

Jardine, Lisa (1983), *Still Harping on Daughters: Women and Drama in the Age of Shakespeare*, Brighton: Harvester Press.

Jeanneret, Michel (1991), *A Feast of Words: Banquets and Table Talk in the Renaissance*, trans. Jeremy Whiteley and Emma Hughes, Cambridge: Polity Press.

Jenstad, Janelle Day (2002), ' "The City Cannot Hold You": Social Conversion in the Goldsmith's Shop', *EMLS* 8: 2, 5.1–26.

Jones, Ann Rosalind (1991), 'Italians and Others: *The White Devil* (1612)', in David Scott Kastan and Peter Stallybrass (eds), *Staging the Renaissance: Reinterpretations of Elizabethan and Jacobean Drama*, New York and London: Routledge, pp. 251–62.

Jonson, Ben (1985), *Ben Jonson*, ed. Ian Donaldson, Oxford: Oxford University Press.

King, John (1990), *Spenser's Poetry and the Reformation Tradition*, Princeton: Princeton University Press.

Knutson, Roslyn L. (2006), 'Theatre Companies and Stages', in Garrett A. Sullivan, Patrick Cheney, Andrew Hadfield (eds), *Early Modern English Drama: A Critical Companion*, New York and Oxford: Oxford University Press, pp. 12–22.

Lancashire, Anne (1983), '*The Witch:* Stage Flop or Political Mistake?', in Kenneth Friedenreich (ed.), *'Accompaninge the Players': Essays Celebrating Thomas Middleton, 1580–1980*, New York: AMS Press, pp. 161–81.

Leinwand, Theodore (1986), *The City Staged: Jacobean City Comedy, 1603–1613*, Madison: University of Wisconsin Press.

— (1994), 'Redeeming Beggary/Buggery in *Michaelmas Term*', *ELH* 61, 53–70.

Leonidas, Eric (2007), 'The School of Wit: Trading on Wit in Middleton's *Trick to Catch the Old One*', *EMLS* 12:3, 3.1–27.

Levin, Richard (1971), *The Multiple Plot in English Renaissance Drama*, Chicago and London: University of Chicago Press.

Loewenstein, Joseph (2003), *Ben Jonson and Possessive Authorship*, Cambridge: Cambridge University Press.

Lomax, Marion (1987), *Stage Images and Traditions: Shakespeare to Ford*, Cambridge: Cambridge University Press.

McElroy, John F. (1972), *Parody and Burlesque in the Tragicomedies of Thomas Middleton*, Salzburg Studies in English Literature, Salzburg: University of Salzburg.

McLuskie, Kathleen (1989), *Renaissance Dramatists*, Hemel Hempstead: Harvester Wheatsheaf.

McManus, Clare (2006), '*The Roaring Girl* and the London Underworld', in Garrett A. Sullivan, Patrick Cheney and Andrew Hadfield (eds), *Early Modern English Drama: A Critical Companion*, Oxford: Oxford University Press, pp. 213–24.

McMullan, Gordon (1994), *The Politics of Unease in the Plays of John Fletcher*, Amherst, MA: University of Massachusetts Press.

McRae, Andrew (2004), *Literature, Satire and the Early Stuart State*, Cambridge: Cambridge University Press.

Malcolmson, Cristina (1990), ' "As Tame as the Ladies": Politics and Gender in *The Changeling*', *English Literary Renaissance* 20, 320–39.

Marotti, Arthur F. (1969), 'Fertility and Comic Form in *A Chaste Maid in Cheapside*', *Comparative Drama* 3, 65–74.

Masten, Jeffrey (1997), *Textual Intercourse: Collaboration, Authorship, and Sexualities in Renaissance Drama*, Cambridge: Cambridge University Press.

Maus, Katharine Eisaman (ed.) (1995), *Four Revenge Tragedies: The Spanish Tragedy, The Revenger's Tragedy, The Revenge of Bussy D'Ambois, The Atheist's Tragedy*, Oxford and New York: Oxford University Press.

Menzer, Paul (2007), 'Theatre Review: *The Changeling* and *Twelfth Night*', *Shakespeare Bulletin* 25, 94–100.

Middleton, Thomas (1993), *A Game at Chess*, ed. T. H. Howard-Hill, The Revels Plays, Manchester and New York: Manchester University Press.

— (2000), *Michaelmas Term*, ed. Gail Kern Paster, The Revels Plays, Manchester and New York: Manchester University Press.

— (2002), *A Chaste Maid in Cheapside*, ed. Alan Brissenden, 2nd edn, London: A. & C. Black; New York: Norton.

— (2007), *Thomas Middleton: The Collected Works and Companion*, ed. Gary Taylor and John Lavagnino, 2 vols, Oxford: Clarendon Press.

Middleton, Thomas and Dekker, Thomas (1997), *The Roaring Girl*, ed. Elizabeth Cook, 2nd edn, London: A. & C. Black; New York: Norton.

Middleton, Thomas and Rowley, William (1990), *The Changeling*, ed. Joost Daalder, 2nd edn, New Mermaids, London: A. and C. Black; New York: Norton.

— (2005), *A New Way to Please You (or The Old Law)*, London: Nick Hern Books.

Mooney, Michael (1979), ' "Framing" as Collaborative Technique: Two Middleton–Rowley Plays', *Comparative Drama* 13, 127–41.

Muir, Kenneth (1983), 'Two Plays Reconsidered: *More Dissemblers besides Women* and *No Wit, No Help Like a Woman's*', in Kenneth Friedenreich (ed.), *'Accompaninge the Players': Essays Celebrating Thomas Middleton, 1580–1980*, New York: AMS Press, pp. 147–59.

Muldrew, Craig (1998), *The Economy of Obligation: The Culture of Credit and Social Relations in Early Modern England*, London: Palgrave Macmillan.

Mulryne, J. R. (1975), 'Manuscript Source-Material for the Main Plot of Thomas Middleton's *Women Beware Women*', *Yearbook of English Studies* 5, 70–4.

— (2005), Programme notes, *Women Beware Women*, RSC.

— and Margaret Shewring (1989), *This Golden Round: The Royal Shakespeare Company at the Swan*, Rugby: Jolly and Barber.

Munro, Lucy (2005), *Children of the Queen's Revels: A Jacobean Theatre Repertory*, Cambridge: Cambridge University Press.

Nashe, Thomas (1985), *The Unfortunate Traveller and Other Works*, ed. J. B. Steane, Harmondsworth: Penguin.

Neill, Michael (1997), *Issues of Death: Morality and Identity in English Renaissance Tragedy*, Oxford: Clarendon Press.

Newman, Karen (2006), '*A Chaste Maid in Cheapside* and London', in Garrett A. Sullivan, Patrick Cheney and Andrew Hadfield (eds), *Early Modern English Drama: A Critical Companion*, Oxford: Oxford University Press, pp. 237–47.

Nochimson, Richard L. (2001), ' "Sharing" *The Changeling* by Playwrights and Professors: The Certainty of Uncertain Knowledge about Collaborations', *Early Theatre* 5: 37–55.

O'Callaghan, Michelle (2007), *The English Wits: Literature and Sociability in Early Modern England*, Cambridge: Cambridge University Press.

Orgel, Stephen (1992), 'The Subtexts of *The Roaring Girl*', in Susan Zimmerman (ed.), *Erotic Politics: Desire on the Renaissance Stage*, New York: Routledge, pp. 12–25.

Paster, Gail Kern (1993), *The Body Embarrassed: Drama and the Disciplines of Shame in Early Modern England*, Ithaca, NY: Cornell University Press.

Peltonen, Markku (1995), *Classical Humanism and Republicanism in English Political Thought, 1570–1640*, Cambridge: Cambridge University Press.

Phialas, P. G. (1955), 'Middleton's Early Contact with the Law', *Studies in Philology* 52, 186–94.

Ribner, Irving (1962), *Jacobean Tragedy: The Quest for Moral Order*, London: Methuen.

Ricks, Christopher (1990), 'The Moral and Poetic Structure of *The Changeling*', in R. V. Holdsworth (ed.), *Three Jacobean Revenge Tragedies: A Casebook*, Basingstoke and London: Macmillan, pp. 157–71.

Rose, Mark (1993), *Authors and Owners: The Invention of Copyright*, Cambridge, MA: Harvard University Press.

Rowe, George E. (1979), *Thomas Middleton and the New Comedy Tradition*, Lincoln and London: University of Nebraska Press.

Russell Lowell, James (1990), '[*The Changeling*] (1843)', in R. V. Holdsworth (ed.), *Three Jacobean Revenge Tragedies: A casebook*, Basingstoke and London: Macmillan, pp. 125–7.

Sanders, Julie (1999), *Caroline Drama: The Plays of Massinger, Ford, Shirley and Brome*, Plymouth: Northcote House.

Shapiro, Michael (1977), *Children of the Revels: The Boy Companies of Shakespeare's Time and their Plays*, New York: Columbia University Press.

Shepard, Alexandra (2003), *Meanings of Manhood in Early Modern England*, Oxford: Oxford University Press.

Sherman, Jane (1978), 'The Pawn's Allegory in Middleton's *A Game at Chesse*', *Review of English Studies* 29, 147–59.

Shrank, Cathy (2004), 'Foreign Bodies: Politics, Polemic and the Continental Landscape', in Mike Pincombe (ed.), *Travels and Translations in the Sixteenth Century*, Aldershot: Ashgate, pp. 31–44.

Slater, Ann Pasternak (1983), 'Hypallage, Barley-Break and *The Changeling*', *Review of English Studies* 34, 429–40.

Spiller, Ben (2003), ' "Today, Vindici Returns": Alex Cox's *Revengers Tragedy*', *EMLS* 8: 3, 3.1–14.

Stachniewski, John (1990), 'Calvinist Psychology in Middleton's Tragedies', in R. V. Holdsworth (ed.), *Three Jacobean Revenge Tragedies: A Casebook*, Basingstoke and London: Macmillan, pp. 226–47.

Stallybrass, Peter (1991), 'Reading the Body and the Jacobean Theater of Consumption: *The Revenger's Tragedy* (1606)', in David Scott Kastan and Peter Stallybrass (eds), *Staging the Renaissance: Reinterpretations of Elizabethan and Jacobean Drama*, New York and London: Routledge, pp. 210–20.

Steggle, Matthew (1998), *Wars of the Theatres: The Poetics of Personation in the Age of Jonson*, Victoria, BC: University of Victoria.

Stern, Tiffany (2007), 'Watching as Reading: The Audience and Written Text in Shakespeare's Playhouse', in Laurie Maguire (ed.), *How to Do Things with Shakespeare: New Approaches, New Essays*, Oxford: Blackwell, pp. 136–59.

Stone, Lawrence (1964), 'The Educational Revolution in England, 1560–1640', *Past and Present* 42: 69–139.

Sullivan, Ceri (2002), *The Rhetoric of Credit: Merchants in Early Modern Writing*, London: Associated University Presses.

— (2007), 'Thomas Middleton's View of Public Utility', *Review of English Studies* 58, 162–74.

Swinburne, A. C. (1990), 'On *The Changeling* (1886)', in R. V. Holdsworth (ed.), *Three Jacobean Revenge Tragedies: A Casebook*, Basingstoke and London: Macmillan, pp. 128–30.

Taylor, Neil and Loughrey, Brian (1984), 'Middleton's Chess Strategies in *Women Beware Women*', *Studies in English Literature* 24, 341–55.

Thomson, Lesley (1986), ' "*Enter Above*": The Staging of *Women Beware Women*', *Studies in English Literature* 26, 331–43.

Todd, Janet and Spearing, Elizabeth (eds) (1994), *Counterfeit Ladies: The Life and Death of Mal Cutpurse, The Case of Mary Carleton*, London: William Pickering.

Twyning, John (1998), *London Dispossessed: Literature and Social Space in the Early Modern City*, Basingstoke: Macmillan.

Wells, Susan (1981), 'Jacobean City Comedy and the Ideology of the City', *ELH* 48, 37–60.

Wit's Recreations (1640), London.

Womack, Peter (2006), *English Renaissance Drama*, Oxford: Blackwell.

Yachnin, Paul (1987), '*A Game at Chess*: Thomas Middleton's "Praise of Folly"', *Modern Language Quarterly* 48, 107–23.

Zimmerman, Susan (2002), 'Animating Matter: The Corpse as Idol in *The Second Maiden's Tragedy*', *Renaissance Drama* 31, 215–43.

Index

Renaissance Dramatists
Series Editor: Sean McEvoy

An invaluable resource for all students of Elizabethan and
Jacobean theatre, each volume in this series provides an
authoritative and up-to-date survey of a major dramatist's work
with a focus on the plays in performance.

Also available in the Renaissance Dramatists series:

Christopher Marlowe, Renaissance Dramatist
Lisa Hopkins

192pp
Paperback, 978 0 7486 2473 7
Hardback, 978 0 7486 2472 0

Ben Jonson, Renaissance Dramatist
Sean McEvoy

192pp, 5 black & white illustrations
Paperback, 978 0 7486 2302 0
Hardback, 978 0 7486 2301 3

For more information please visit:
http://www.euppublishing.com/series/rend